Overcoming
ADVERSITY

CONQUERING
LIFE'S CHALLENGES

A practical guide to surviving emotional suffering and loss

EILEEN S. LENSON

MSW, ACSW, BCC

FOREWORD BY VICE ADMIRAL DAVID H. BUSS, UNITED STATES NAVY, RETIRED.

AUSTRALIANACADEMICPRESS

First published 2018 by:
Australian Academic Press Group Pty. Ltd.
18 Victor Russell Drive
Samford Valley QLD 4520, Australia
www.australianacademicpress.com.au

Overcoming Adversity:Conquering Life's Challenges

ISBN   9781925644067 (paperback)
ISBN   9781925644074 (ebook)

Publisher: Stephen May

Copy editing: Rhonda McPherson

Cover design: Luke Harris, Working Type Studio

Typesetting: Australian Academic Press

Printing: Lightning Source

'Adversity Is good. Overcoming it is even better. Trees grow stronger in high winds and people grow stronger with adversity and resistance. If I hadn't gone bankrupt forty plus years ago, I would not have discovered that my problems were my transportation to my destiny i.e. becoming world's bestselling non-fiction author and a high paid professional speaker. We all go through adversity and this book will inspire you to overcome it with excellence, elegance, and a decision to win bigger than ever.'

Mark Victor Hansen, Co-Creator of the *Chicken Soup for the Soul* series and Co-Chairman/Founder of Metamorphosis Energy LLC.

'Everyone will face adversity at some time. Lenson provides a wealth of information that can change the way we look at life's challenges. Research driven and written in a clear and insightful manner, this book is a must-read for discovering how to successfully thrive in the face of complicated life situations.'

Marshall Goldsmith, New York Times #1 bestselling author of *Triggers and What Got You Here Won't Get You There.*

'Eileen Lenson has created an essential crutch read. A lifetime psychotherapist and life and business coach, she provides a detailed and elevating map to follow when we are slammed by unexpected and enervating adversity. And we shall be slammed. Long lives assure it and we are longer lived. Lenson identifies the reset button, and creates a practical guide to hold us up and to let us move forward. Hers is a lifetime read.'

Frank Keating, Former Governor of Oklahoma who oversaw the tragedies of the 1995 Oklahoma City bombing and the 72 devastating tornadoes of 1999.

'Surviving was only part of my journey. The toughest part was continuing on. This insightful book will give you the tools to thrive in life to the fullest no matter what adversities you encounter.'

George Lamson, sole survivor of Galaxy Airlines Flight #203 in Reno, Nevada Featured in CNN 2014 documentary 'Sole Survivor.'

'Through ample clinical experience and cut-edge medical theory, Eileen Lenson shows us how our past traps us, and how to move forward by redefining our lives; for our own well-being, so as not to suffer secondary victimization by the offender. A long awaited guide book that promises to go beyond the individual and well into international relations.'

Akira Chiba, Consul General of Japan in Los Angeles

'I know Eileen Lenson to be a committed and compassionate individual who has put much research and applied practice into this study. This book will assist its readers by offering practical means to apply in order to overcome hurt and adversity in their lives.'

Jeffrey D. Armstrong, President, California Polytechnic State University, San Luis Obispo CA

'For anyone who is struggling with a conflict, Eileen's book can help you overcome whatever obstacles are holding you back from living the life you truly want. Highly recommended.'

Hal Elrod, #1 bestselling author, *The Miracle Morning*

'This is a warm, wonderful, inspiring book that will give you the practical tools you need to live a wonderful life.'

Brian Tracy, Author, *Maximum Achievement, Earn What You're Really Worth, Eat That Frog!* and *The Psychology of Achievement.*

Dedication

To Rachel and Michael

Together may you triumph and find resilience over any challenge that crosses your path.

To Lloyd, my husband of almost 32 years

Without your tolerance for leftovers and a messy house, this book could not have been written. You have influenced every aspect of this book, from introducing me to remarkable people, to cover design to providing critical analysis of chapters on long cross-country and transatlantic flights to and from work. You have supported me in everything I have done or gone through, including tolerating the three of us being in bed together; you, me, and my computer. I don't deserve you, yet would never want to think about being without you. I realize how incredibly fortunate I am to have you by my side. I married very, very well.

Foreword

'Our service puts us in harm's way far from our families, often for long periods of time. What we do is hard and dangerous, but it is bigger than any one of us. So we do it as a team. Hardships are shared.'

From *Who We Are*, the Creed of the U.S. Navy's Aviation fleet

Harm's way. Shared hardships. Dangerous undertakings. Sounds thrilling … and difficult … and edgy, doesn't it? This is the world in which I spent the majority of my adult life. Naval Aviation. Flying high performance jet aircraft from the flight deck of the United States Navy's aircraft carriers. Day and night. The night flights are harrowing. Trying to find, and then land, on a thousand foot long piece of steel that's bobbing like a cork in the middle of the ocean in the middle of the night will get one's hear rate and blood pressure up … every time. Flying missions in combat. Shooting and being shot at. Often. Long overseas deployment, normally to turbulent 'hot spots' around the globe. And sometimes not everyone comes home.

I have not had the honor and privilege of meeting Eileen Lenson. Yet. I know Eileen's husband, though. We sat next to each on a flight from Washington, DC, to Los Angeles last year. As we got to know each, naturally the conversation turned to families. Spouses, children, grandchildren. When Eileen's husband told me that she was life coach and helped those in need work their way step-by-step through adversity and return to hope in life, something resonated with me. Given my military career and background, coping with adversity had kinda come with the job description. When Eileen reached out and asked me to share a few thoughts from my own experiences, particularly surrounding loss and recovery, I thought it important to do so. Stories of recovery and resilience should be shared and celebrated. To me, at least, these stories represent a triumph of sorts of the human soul. The journey through Forgiveness, Courage, Perspective, and Perseverance to arrive again at Hope is to take the journey of Eileen's wonderful book. It is a read filled with stories. What follows is mine.

I felt good about working in service to others, but sometimes making sense of the personal losses endured was emotionally draining. I've seen probably more than my fair share of adversity over the four plus decades I spent in uniform in service to the United States. I've buried close friends, too many close friends. Squadron mates lost along the way, some in training and some in combat operations. All unique individuals with stories of their own being crafted with their lives, and then suddenly cut short. Ended seemingly before they had begun; unexpectedly and unpredictably. Left behind were families — mothers, fathers, sisters, brothers, spouses, children — and friends, buddies, and squadron mates.

I was the Operations Officer in an aircraft carrier-based jet squadron that had just deployed to the Middle East in December 1990 in the run-up to the Operation Desert Storm, the First Gulf War. One of my best friends had joined my squadron within weeks before we deployed. He and I had been flight instructors together several years prior. We had trained together. Our wives had become friends over the years because, frankly, that's how military life is. Hardships are shared, and one of the greatest hardships is in saying goodbye to one's family and heading overseas ... into harm's way ... for six, seven, eight months at a time. Sometimes longer.

My friend and I, like the entire squadron, were excited, nervous and apprehensive about the looming combat operations in mid-January 1991 as we arrived on station in the Persian Gulf. We were well-trained and mentally prepared, but you never know how you will do until you are actually 'in the moment ' as they say. The first two weeks of combat went exceedingly well. While there were some losses of US forces, by and large, the air campaign in Iraq and Kuwait was what the media called 'clean' and 'antiseptic.' Our squadron had performed brilliantly from the first night of combat onward. And then it happened.

I was about to launch from the aircraft carrier on a mission about two weeks into Desert Storm and received word that one of our squadron aircraft had been shot down in the northern Persian Gulf near the Kuwaiti coastline. It didn't take long for me to figure out that it was my friend and his young copilot who were down and missing. We launched from the ship and were sent to their last known location, tasked with performing a combat search-and-rescue mission in the event that either pilot had successfully ejected from their crippled aircraft.

Compartmentalization. It's the ability to take something really bad that has happened in your life and mentally put it away for the time being so that you can deal with the crisis at hand. We learn this skill early on in flight school and it comes in handy in a profession like combat aviation that is hard, dangerous and unforgiving. The only way I could perform the search-and-rescue mission we needed to execute for my missing friend and his copilot was to compartmentalize. I would deal with the emotions and impact of this potential loss later. For now, there was work to be done to find him if he was still alive and help get him out of harm's way.

It was a brutally long mission. Almost five hours of low altitude searching, avoiding enemy fire in the area, and coordinating assistance from other US and allied aircraft in the vicinity. In the end, though, it was fruitless. He was gone, along with his young copilot. Nothing left in the area where they were shot down but a few pieces of aircraft wreckage and an oil slick on the water's surface. Now began the long flight back to the aircraft carrier and the realization setting in that my friend was gone. He would not be coming home. His wife and three young children would never see him again. Stark realizations.

We landed back on the aircraft carrier and the squadron commander called a meeting of all the pilots to talk about our loss. We only had a few hours to process what had happened as we were scheduled to begin flying combat sorties again that night. We had to be ready to go. My friend would have insisted on it!

We were reminded of the 'rubber ball' analogy. You see, before we left the States in December 1990 on what we knew would be a difficult combat deployment, we had several Vietnam era Navy pilots who had been shot down, captured by the North Vietnamese, and held as Prisoners of War (POWs) for up to seven years come speak with our squadron. Each reinforced something else every pilot learns in flight school as we go through Survival, Evasion, Resistance and Escape (SERE) training. They talked about being a rubber ball when something really bad happens in your life. For them, it was the torture sessions they experienced at the hands of their captors. As they explained to us, everyone has a breaking point. That really doesn't matter. But what DOES matter, what defines us a professionals and human beings, is how you recover once you've broken. They told us there are really just two options: "You can be an egg or you can be a rubber ball. When you are dropped and hit the ground hard, how will you react? Will you bounce back or not?"

Resilience and perseverance are traits of rubber balls. That night we all got into our jets and went right back into combat. My friend would have kicked all of our butts had we not. And my friend's image is still with me to this day.

While his body was never recovered, his copilot's body was found on Easter Sunday 1991.

My two squadron mates have grave sites at Arlington National Cemetery in the section set aside for those from the First Gulf War who gave what Abraham Lincoln called "the last full measure of devotion." I visit my buddies each time I go to Arlington and I'm not alone. Most pilots from my squadron that experienced that combat deployment do the same. We are, after all, still squadron mates. Talking with our lost mates, telling them what is going on in our close-knit naval aviation community (because they would want to know) and reliving their time with us, with me, helps us not only survive, but thrive. And we have stayed connected with the families of our departed buddies. We lean on each other. We allow them to lean on us. We tell stories (which get better and better … and probably less true each time we tell them). We have persevered and have hope once again.

Eileen's book isn't just another one of many on the topic of overcoming adversity. Instead, she shows readers how to become that rubber ball I mentioned. How to use challenging times as a catalyst for personal growth and discovery in finding new meaning and deeper purpose in one's life. In devoting a chapter to each of five specific factors that can be barriers to overcoming adversity — forgiveness, courage, perspective, perseverance, and hope — Eileen demonstrates the recipe for moving beyond adversity and loss, using the three often overlooked areas of support — Self, Society and Spirituality.

I have flown this flight plan and landed safely.

Vice Admiral David H. Buss, United States Navy, Retired
Coronado, California

Contents

Acknowledgements

My deep appreciation and gratitude goes to each of the following individuals who, without hesitation or condition, agreed to be interviewed for this book. I am indebted to their generosity in sharing their stories, and humbled by their courageous struggles and insights gained in overcoming adversity: Jerry Bame, Edgar Allen Basto, Ron Lum Shue Chan, Melissa Coleman, Lanny Cordola, Max Desfor, Sarah Gilchriese, Taletha Guinn, Vann Henderson, Bert Klein, David 'Candyman' Klein, Alan Levy, Stephen Madelon, Stephanie Parker, Maxwell Peters, Major Ed Pulido, Laura Ratschave, Erin Runnion, Silvio Scaglia, Ronnie Steen, Dwight Stones, Joyce Stromberg, Azadeh Tabazadeh, Misty Wilson, and Jill Yanke.

My deepest appreciation to Vice Admiral David H. Buss, United States Navy, Retired, for providing the foreword and sharing heartfelt professional challenges experienced while honorably serving our country.

Thank you to those who provided kind words for my book:

Dr. Jeffrey Armstrong, who as President of California Polytechnic State University, San Luis Obispo, CA, helps bolster student success. He accomplishes this by encouraging relationships with the larger community, and helping when coping with unforeseen setbacks, including academic, family and peer conflicts occur.

Akira Chiba, Consul General of Japan in Los Angeles, who cares deeply about reducing world suffering. While keenly aware of concerns following the 2011 earthquake/tsunami tragedy, he also looks at healing relationships following the toll wars take on individuals and countries.

Hal Elrod, who discovered the value of focus and purpose in adversity. At age 20, following an automobile accident, he was dead for 6 minutes before resuscitated, had 11 broken bones, suffered permanent brain damage and was told he would not walk again. He found the resilience to became a marathon runner, recording artist, husband, father and author.

Marshall Goldsmith, author of several best-selling books, who helps business leaders worldwide achieve lasting change. Rated as one of the world's most influential leadership thinkers and executive coaches, he helps people be successful and their lives a little better by identifying how to create change for themselves.

Mark Victor Hansen, Co-Creator of the Chicken Soup for the Soul series, who personally experienced the gifts one can find in adversity. As he says, "If I hadn't gone bankrupt forty plus years ago, I would not have discovered that my problems were my transportation to my destiny i.e. becoming world's bestselling non-fiction author and a high paid professional speaker."

Former Governor of Oklahoma Frank Keating, who in his two terms as governor, helped thousands of people overcome both man-made and natural disasters. He oversaw the recovery from the 1995 domestic terrorist bombing of the Alfred P. Murrah Federal Building in Oklahoma City that killed 168 people and injured over 800, and in 1999, 72 devastating tornadoes that claimed more than 40 lives, injured hundreds, and destroyed over 1,500 buildings.

George Lamson Jr., who, as a teenager, was thrust into learning about emotionally surviving a profound personal tragedy. As the sole survivor of the Galaxy Airlines crash in Reno, Nevada, he learned how to grapple with this challenge while treasuring life's gifts.

Brian Tracy, international trainer and developer of individuals and organizations and author of over 70 books, who has devoted his career to helping people move forward toward their goals while showing the courage and strength in turning to others for assistance.

I am particularly grateful for the assistance given by: Rabbi Richard Steinberg, for reading portions of the manuscript, introductions and resources, and most importantly your continuous friendship; my father Dr. Robert R. Stromberg, for reviewing early chapters, sending me relevant articles (they're still coming in the mail even as we approach publication) and connecting me with an interviewee; Jodi Greenbaum, for saving me from the 'death-by-endnote' style of writing; Rachel Lenson for random but helpful facts and comments; Michele Gold, Rachel Lenson, Michael Rogers, DVM and Hope Sherwood-White for lending me their eyes on my cover design, Donald Altman, Pastor Michael Clark, Dr. Masi Hashemian, Shelley Jones, Steve Kinney, Bob Updegrove for their helpful input.

My special thanks are extended to my many clients, whose experiences and courageous efforts to move forward at difficult times in their lives provided me with the inspiration to write this book.

I am also particularly grateful to my publisher, Stephen May, at Australian Academic Publishing, for showing confidence in my work and guidance. You helped make the publishing part of writing this book an unexpectedly pleasurable experience.

An Introduction
to Overcoming Adversity

No one searches for adversity. Bad experiences are simply part of life. The likelihood that you will encounter adversity at some point in your lifetime comes with a 100 percent guarantee. Unfortunately, the chances that you will cope well when a terrible situation occurs are not guaranteed. The lack of an automatic successful coping strategy though isn't our fault! If we have not been provided with the tools and understanding for dealing successfully with traumatic events that threaten our safety, careers, emotions, health, or relationships, we won't be prepared when painful events occur. That's why this book is for anyone who finds themselves wanting to improve their life in times of hardship.

The seeds of this book were planted several years ago, when I was working with a client who had only known adversity in his childhood. As a psychotherapist, I was leading a therapy group, and had asked each member to draw a horizontal line across a sheet of paper. This line reflected the group member's lives, with the date of their birth being the starting point, and continuing up to present day. Each member was asked to write positive life experiences with corresponding dates that they recalled above the drawn line, and painful experiences and dates below the line.

One member, Jay, told the group that his first negative experience occurred on the day he was born. Jay went on to say that his earliest recollection was his parents telling him that he was an unwanted child. Growing up, his parents blamed most of their unhappiness and failures on him, and not infrequently, physically abused him. This experience impacted negatively on his sense of self-worth. Jay fought with others, spent time in juvenile hall, and dropped out of high school at 16 years old. While other teens were going to proms and learning to drive, Jay was living on the streets, often high on drugs. A young man with little to hope for, he was on the path for a lifetime of suffering; poor physical and psychological health, and facing a premature, if not violent, death.

This sad scenario plays itself out in every city, often with tragic endings. But by the time Jay was in my therapy group, he was living a life that reflected success at overcoming his childhood adversity. Jay had managed to get not only a bachelor's degree, but also a master's degree in his chosen field. He owned a modest home, and he and his wife showered their affection on their mix Labrador–Pit Bull puppy. Others in the group shook their heads in disbelief when they heard his painful life story, and referred to Jay as 'one of the lucky ones.'

Yet luck should be associated with winning the lottery, not with overcoming adversity. Surviving, even thriving after adversity is never based on luck. Nor is it based on genetics, culture, or race. Fortunately, like Jay, we all have the ability to successfully move through adversity if we have the knowledge and skills to do so.

It made sense to me then, to create a practical guide to help remove the mystery from what is required to survive emotional suffering and unbearable losses. Answering the question of how to overcome adversity is at the core of my professional life. I have spent the past 30 years in private practice as a psychotherapist and life and business coach, working with individuals, couples, families and groups. I have spoken internationally, been an invited guest on radio stations, written many newspaper and magazine articles and columns, and a book chapter on adversity. My experiences have provided me with a front row seat to observe and learn from people suffering from medical, physical, spiritual, material, and emotional crises.

In the pages that follow I will share with you a pragmatic 'can-do' approach that can help anyone who finds themselves in a painful place, regardless of socioeconomic status, culture, religion or intellect. It provides tools on how to turn suffering into hope and develop personal resourcefulness by bringing together new information extracted from scientific research with an understanding of the emotional and spiritual lives that we experience when coping with adversity. Whereas science may sometimes conflict with religion, this book explains how the measurable world of science and the intuitive world of spirituality come together and influence how we experience adversity and recovery. Each chapter describes from a scientific, psychological and spiritual perspective, why we do the things we do, guiding us how to manage our feelings and respond to devastating events, and how to use this knowledge to seek healthy coping options. Its purpose is to help readers not just learn how to survive, but how to thrive. This means helping people discover how to find personal growth by making changes, and living life with value, meaning and purpose. These changes can help people cope better with not just current, but also future emotionally challenging situations.

Throughout this book you will read personal interviews from people who have experienced and overcome their own adversities and found resilience. These shared stories and insights are proof that resilience is a process rather than a fixed innate characteristic, offering us hope for a better future. The combination of experiencing positive emotions from reading about others, and learning scientific or psychologically based factual information is a powerful tool in dealing with challenges during times of significant emotional upset. We can gain insight into our thoughts, feelings and behavior, and respond in a way that best helps us.

Yet we learn not simply by listening. It is important to not just be told specifically what behavior to change to overcome a life hurdle. While instructions have appeal and value, the problem is that we are not all the same, and the adjustments we have to make when facing adversity is uniquely different for each of us. This book explains the deeper issue of why we react the way we do, and what we need to do to grow. To not take this 'deep dive' is to fail to fully understand our underlying motivations. If we do not explore the possibility of changing our thoughts and feelings, we will fail to develop the insights necessary for overcoming adversity, and still be burdened by repeating our familiar — and unproductive — coping styles. It is important also to bridge the gap between theory and application.

We must learn more than valuable new information; it is necessary that we *know how to apply it to our lives.* Multiple exercises provided at the conclusion of each of the following chapters will enable readers to practice and anchor their new skills. Increased resilience is likely experienced when we try a suggested exercise and discover a sense of achievement.

The Five Personal Components to Overcoming Adversity

There are five specific components, sometimes called virtues, that can be identified as vital to overcoming adversity — *forgiveness, courage, perspective, perseverance,* and *hope.* Each of these components is addressed in detail in separate chapters of this book. How you understand and integrate these components into your life affects whether they become barriers or resources on your journey toward overcoming adversity. The structure of the five chapters is designed to provide a learning style that makes the information simple to read, easy to apply to personal situations, and readily accessible for future reference.

For each component, you will learn what it is (and what it isn't), why it is important, the barriers you may face, and how to overcome them. At the conclusion of each chapter are a series of suggested practical exercises you might like to try to enhance your mastery of each component.

Chapter 1 addresses the subject of forgiveness of others and self-forgiveness. Forgiveness helps us find the resilience to survive periods of conflict. When feeling angry or vengeful towards others, we become chronic victims. Our pain is unresolved and we remain emotionally bound to the offender. When we are able to forgive others we take back our power, are able to experience a change in our feelings or attitude, and can begin the healing process.

Chapter 2 addresses the importance of courage in overcoming adversity. Courage helps strengthen our determination, gives us the confidence to conquer obstacles, and counteracts the inhibiting impact of fear and uncertainty. When courageous we are able to step outside our comfort zone of predictability and familiarity. We can take in new information and ideas and broaden our understanding of the world, an important tool in overcoming adversity.

Chapter 3 helps us understand the role of perspective in developing resilience. Perspective-taking is the process of looking at an issue from more than one point of view, attaching a meaning to these facts, and developing feelings about them. This process can influence the difference in making a good or bad adjustment following adversity. When our perspective is broader, we are able to entertain a shift in thinking, resolve problems, and experience self-empowerment.

Chapter 4 emphasizes the critical role of perseverance during times of adversity. When we are faced with numerous decisions, problems, and challenges, the refusal to give up, and instead, to persist even when facing continued discouragement and ongoing problems, helps us achieve the goals we want.

Chapter 5 is about finding hope. Hope is, hands down, one of the most powerful components for overcoming adversity. It is wonderful to know that hope is available to every living person on this planet. Hope is what makes the difference between feeling overrun with negative emotions and wanting to give up, and feeling motivated to persevere towards a brighter future. Without hope, we would be discouraged and unable to develop clarity on how to reach our goals.

The Three Spheres of Support in Overcoming Adversity

Support is the secret sauce that helps us find forgiveness, courage, perspective, perseverance, and hope. Support helps us make changes in our thoughts, feelings, and behaviors, and increases the sense of control over our lives. The three spheres of support that play a significant role in helping us work successfully through the five components of adversity are *Self* (self-awareness), *Society* (being a part of a greater social network), and *Spirituality* (receiving support from a powerful spiritual energy.) It is these three spheres that help us not just to return to a former level of functioning but instead move through the most challenging aspects of adversity and find personal growth, new insights, and new meanings. These spheres of support provide structure across the five chapters introduced above to both the discussion about how to achieve forgiveness, courage, perspective, perseverance, and hope as well as to the suggested exercises. In this way readers learn how to weave together this combination of information and emotional support so as to empower themselves and increase control over their lives.

This book is written to help you, wherever you find yourself struggling with adversity. It can be read either in its entirety, or out of sequence, however I recommend that you read it in the traditional manner because of the interconnection between the sections. Give yourself permission to move through the book at your own pace. This will allow you to grasp a deeper level of understanding of the specific task you must work through. You will then more likely experience those 'aha' moments, which are the catalysts for the insight and change we all seek.

I want to thank you for choosing to read this book. I wish you my very best, and hope your reading experience is positive.

Chapter 1

Forgiveness

"While revenge weakens society, forgiveness gives it strength."
— Dalai Lama (20th century)

As these words of the Dalai Lama's reflect, throughout the centuries people have been exposed to the universal notion of forgiveness. Examples range from the bullied child being told by their parents to "turn the other cheek," to the husband telling his angry wife to "just let it go," to the Bible, which in various forms mentions 'forgive' over 100 times.

And yet, from the beginning of time, history provides examples of people who view themselves to be the injured parties, unable to forgive and reciprocating with revenge. According to many accounts, the infamous Appalachian American story of the Hatfields and McCoys started as a small, two-family dispute in 1857 when Randolph McCoy accused Floyd Hatfield of stealing his hog. In the absence of apologies and forgiveness the feud intensified, resulting in a quarter century cycle of intense anger and retaliatory vengeance between the families. It spiraled out of control to the point where offenders became victims and victims became offenders. Like the proverbial snowball rolling downhill, the dispute grew in size, affecting everything and everyone in its path. The economy and politics of the area were affected; the Governor of West Virginia threatened to have his militia invade Kentucky,1 and the U.S. Supreme Court had to step in. Tragically, the generations-long cycle of violence and revenge resulted in the biggest family rivalry in the history of the country. Twelve family members died as a result of unforgiveness following the theft of a single hog.

This escalating sort of grudge-match occurs, according to research, because when someone is hurt, the victim becomes angry with the offender and wants to retaliate. A phenomenon little known outside of the world of psychology, "fundamental attribution error," is likely stirring the pot. What this means, in plain English, is that it is human nature to overestimate the pain when another person hurts us, while underestimating any harm we cause others.

Think back to the time you were a young child. Remember the infinite number of physical conflicts you had with a sibling or friend? If the other child hit you, you likely viewed the child as being mean, or unfair. In other words, you considered the hurt to be a result of their personality. If you retaliated and swung a fist back at the offender, you wouldn't see yourself as being mean or unfair. You wouldn't see it as a reflection of your personality. Rather, you'd view your behavior as being a response to the situation you were in.

The motivations for the altercation were straightforward and justifiable to you. However, on the flip side, the other child was viewing the situation in exactly the opposite way. In their mind, their initial swing at you was based on something you said or did. They believed you deserved to be hit because of how they were interpreting and explaining your behavior to themselves. When you responded to their swing with one of your own, they were viewing you as being mean. We can see that each child has received injuries. But each see themselves as victims rather than offenders. Both attribute their punches as having to respond to the situation in which they find themselves.

This is how a Hatfield and McCoy cycle of retaliatory reactions is born. The Hatfields and McCoys likely continued their epic conflict, which escalated from theft of a hog to political friction, to multiple murders, because each act of revenge was perceived as justified in settling the score. In their case, the lack of forgiveness went down in folklore as an infamous story of vengeance that affected not only two individuals but also multiple families and society.

Like the revenge exhibited by the Hatfields and McCoys, these wounded feelings and continual angry attacks can take place long after the injury is sustained. The pain and suffering continues to grow, fueling an already existing adversarial situation, if forgiveness is not offered.

We all make mistakes and hurt others because we are human and therefore imperfect. Unfortunately, we tend to find it easier to make mistakes than to apologize and ask for forgiveness. In past generations, many people did not have the knowledge or the skills required to move through the process of forgiveness. Like the Hatfields and McCoys, too many people pay dearly by not letting go of resentment and thoughts of revenge. They instead get stuck, mired in adversity.

Forgiveness helps us find the resilience to survive periods of conflict and personal distress. Forgiveness helps us develop a deeper understanding of both others and ourselves. This chapter explores how to find forgiveness when dealing with adversity, even when forgiveness appears unlikely or undeserving. It addresses the significant and fundamental roles our relationship with our Self, Society, and Spirituality plays in lessening the impact of adversity, and how these relationships can boost our well-being when going through this process of forgiveness.

What is Forgiveness?

On August 17, 2004, in his 19th year in the U.S. Army, Major Ed Pulido, U.S. Army (Ret.) was serving a combat tour in Baqubah, Iraq. Driving an unarmored vehicle, he inadvertently ran over an improvised explosive device (IED). Major Pulido had little protection from the impact of the IED and sustained extensive bodily injury. At that moment, his military career was suddenly cut short, and his life forever changed.

Following the amputation of his left leg, he faced a year-long recovery. During this recovery period, he struggled with loss of faith, depression, suicidal ideation and post-traumatic stress disorder. However, Major Pulido quickly realized he had no choice but not to be resentful towards the Iraqis who placed the bombs that nearly took his life. Instead, he decided that he had to accept what had happened rather than develop a self-identity of 'victim.' Major Pulido states that, "if I allowed myself self-pity or anger, it would have overtaken and overwhelmed me."

Forgiveness was a gradual process, but today, Major Pulido reports that losing his leg was the best thing that ever happened to him. Before being injured by the roadside bomb, Major Pulido felt that he had 'shallow' moments in his life. Now, he believes his attitude is healthier, and that every moment in his life counts. Before the traumatic event Major Pulido rarely cried, but now states he has found emotions that he might not have discovered for years.

Currently a sought after speaker for veteran affairs, he jokingly tells audiences, "I think some of the blood transfusions I received were female blood. I've got more emotion, caring, and insight. I feel more like a man of hope and integrity, more humble and understanding, less rigid, and more collaborative in my decision-making process."[2]

Major Pulido chose not to be consumed by bitter feelings of resentment and revenge for the war injury that resulted in the loss of his limb and career. Instead, he has turned this tragedy, combined with his clearer vision of how he wishes to think, feel, and live his life, into a tool to help others. He serves as Vice President of the Folds of Honor Foundation, Senior Advisor for Pros 4 Vets, and founder and spokesperson of Warriors for Freedom, all charities focused on the recovery of U.S. military veterans. Even portions of the proceeds from his memoir, *Warrior for Freedom: Challenge, Triumph and Change, The Major Ed Pulido Story*, goes towards helping wounded veterans.

Major Pulido's resilience is due in large part to his ability to experience forgiveness. He decided not to allow his life to be defined by his hurt and losses. His choice to let go of his negative feelings of anger towards the Iraqis was done voluntarily and for himself. Insights developed from his traumatic event provided Major Pulido with the ability to replace former feelings of resentment with a greater appreciation for life and the belief that he had grown and was a better person.

Appreciation of the value of forgiveness has moved from the realm of theologians to being of interest to physicians, neuroscientists, and psychologists. Extensive research performed in the past two decades provides us with an understanding of how different components of forgiveness help us heal following adversity. Frederic Luskin, author of *Forgive for Good*, along with other researchers, has identified the essential elements of forgiveness, described below.[3]

Forgiveness is Done Voluntarily for the Victim, by the Victim

It is not done because we are taught by parents or religious sermons that it is the right thing to do. It is not done because we are told it will help the offender. Rather, forgiveness is done exclusively for ourselves. We choose to forgive for the simple reason that we want to let go of the toxic feelings of hurt, anger, fear and revenge, and be able to rediscover our peace of mind and happiness. It is our choice to forgive, and we do so even though the offender does not deserve our forgiveness.

Forgiveness is a Personal Healing Process

Forgiveness will look different for each of us in each situation. Sometimes we cannot restore a relationship with the offender, such as in cases when the offender has died or is incarcerated. Sometimes we may choose not to maintain a relationship with our offender, because it would be dangerous to us to do so. In other times, we may hope to repair the damaged relationship, such as with a marital partner who strayed, and will be motivated to work on making this happen. At all times, however, forgiveness is exclusively about our own healing and not about those that hurt us, other's timelines or other's expectations of us. Everyone heals differently. Forgiveness may come more slowly to some than to others. It is a process that cannot be rushed.

Forgiveness is About Taking Back Your Power

Much like a wound heals on our body, progressing from injury to scab, forgiving can be a slow healing process. Yes, we bleed at first, and we may be consumed with valid feelings of hurt, rage, resentment and vindication. But if those feelings are left unresolved, we will be handing our personal power over to the person who inflicted the pain on us. We will suffer, becoming chronic victims facing indefinite suffering. It will feel like being stuck in quicksand. We can flail around with blame, tears, prayer or self-pity, but none of these behaviors will likely get us unstuck. On the contrary, the struggle may cause us to sink deeper and deeper into despair.

There is a high risk in holding onto anger, and the decision to let go of negative feelings that bind us to our offender is the first and most important step in taking back our power and moving to a place of peace. Painful as it may be, acknowledging our anger rather than prematurely squashing our feelings and pretending the hurtful event never happened helps us avoid getting trapped in living our lives smothered by these negative emotions. Recognizing these feelings helps us let go of the power they have on us. We will then be able to remove any destructive emotional baggage keeping us stuck in the past, and experience the space to move forward in the healing process.

Forgiveness is a Shift in Thinking Towards Someone Who has Injured You

When we are able to change our perspective about the offender we stop taking the hurtful action personally. We start to find our internal emotional feelings change and discover it is possible to rid ourselves of the debilitating energy that disempowers us. For instance, we may be able to consider that the offender's DNA, so to speak, does not contain a need to hurt others. Something happened to the offender to make him able to cause someone else so much pain, and to have the inability to view life in a wiser, more consciously aware manner. This is not an easy path for us to tread, but when we are able to shift our thinking in this way, we can begin to realize that given the offender's history, he was behaving exactly as we would expect him to.

Another shift in our thinking can occur if, despite our pain, we know that the offender did not intentionally mean to hurt us. Even though the impact of the wrongdoing is the same to us whether it was committed on purpose or by accident, it is how we interpret the event that causes the greatest amount of pain. It can make it easier for us to resolve our resentment and move towards forgiveness.

This realization can help our feelings move from anger, blame and resentment to feelings of pity towards the offender. Sonja Lyubomirsky, professor of psychology at the University of California, finds that this change allows us to begin to be less emotionally connected with the offender (4) and frees us from choosing the path of victimhood.

Offender Self-Forgiveness

Typically, forgiveness is focused more on the well-being of the victim rather than the offender. In fact, for the most part, we do not view the offender as being deserving of our concern. Our legal system allows us a retribution style "eye-for-an-eye" of punishing offenders. It enables us to "even the score," feel safer in our community, and possibly discourage offenders from recidivism.

And yet, we need to pay attention to the often-overlooked matter of the offender's self-forgiveness, which has been referred to as "the step-child of forgiveness research."[5] Psychologists do not consider self-forgiveness to include condoning the wrongdoing. In no way does self-forgiveness enable the offender to get off scot-free. It can be a lengthy and emotionally painful process. The offender has to do the hard work of fully and honestly admitting responsibility for any hurt he has caused without minimizing or rationalizing his behavior, or blaming the victim. He has to believe that not only was his past behavior wrong, but with his new insights into causes and conditions that led him to commit the hurtful act, he knows he will act differently in the future. He also has to examine his feelings of shame and guilt, and learn how to remove them. This new awareness helps the offender make amends, either in the form of apology or compensation, to the victim. Doing so will reduce the likelihood for recidivism by the offender in the future.

Researchers has shown that a lack of self-forgiveness can have an adverse impact on an offender's physical, mental, social, and spiritual health. It can imprison the offender in a place in which he emotionally beats up on himself, resulting in a downward spiral of emotions, including depression, shame, remorse, guilt, and anger, all capable of contributing to a lowered self-esteem. Low self-esteem is a gateway to harmful, self-destructive behaviors such as excessive drinking. Used as "self-medication," alcohol abuse can negatively impact on all aspects of one's life. Careers can stall, marriages collapse, parent-child relationships splinter, spirituality fray, and medical problems develop, even resulting in premature deaths. So in essence, self-forgiveness can serve all: the victim, offender, and society.

Self-forgiveness is required in cases where reconciliation is desired by both the offender and victim. A desire to resolve the wrongdoing and rebuild their damaged relationship is commonly seen when there has been a history of a valued and healthy relationship between the two individuals. Examples range from feuding neighbors, to colleagues with escalating hostility, to marriages threatened by infidelity and betrayal. To repair these relationships, the victim must work on forgiveness of the offender, and the offender must work on self-forgiveness. This is a challenging task, because the offender must make sufficient changes to earn the victim's trust once again.

Self-Forgiveness of Others

Sometimes self-forgiveness also needs to take place in people close to the victim, who, while they did not have direct involvement, blame themselves for not protecting the victim from being hurt. For example, Melissa Coleman spent most of her life blaming herself for her younger sister Heidi's tragic death. When Ms. Coleman was seven years old, her mother shooed the two girls outside to play so she could clean the house and prepare for their grandmother's visit without young children under foot.

Ms. Coleman went to the woodshed and climbed the ladder to play in the loft by herself, ignoring her younger sister's pleas for help up the ladder.

Dejected, Heidi eventually walked away. When her grandmother arrived, her mother came looking for the two girls. Three-year-old Heidi was nowhere to be found. To the family's horror, Heidi was soon discovered lifeless, along with her toy boat, floating face down in the nearby pond.

The family was overwhelmed with grief. Ms. Coleman recalls, "For so long I felt guilt about her death; that it was my fault that my sister had died. We didn't have a spiritual connection to go to when bad things happened. We didn't have a community that had any spiritual foundation. Each member of the family suffered alone with their pain." Shame, fear, grief, and lack of a support system created isolation and alienation. "My parents separated not long after my sister's death, and I never got to see that this is how you grieve, or this is how you move forward after tragedy. It was like everything just falls apart, and everything goes terribly wrong," she recalls.

When she, herself, became a parent, Ms. Coleman felt the weight on her shoulders and the need to better understand her sister's drowning. "I didn't know how to parent that stuff because I hadn't had the role model." As a professional writer wanting to work through her painful early life experience, Ms. Coleman approached the healing process in the manner she knew best, by writing a book about her sister.

For the first time, she talked with her parents about that disastrous day when Heidi died. "In the process of asking them lots of questions," recalls Ms. Coleman, "they were able to share things and open up. I always had this memory that I pushed her in the pond and that she died." Gathering information from her parents helped her learn that "it wasn't even my fault. It turned out that [pushing Heidi in the pond] had happened the day before."

Ms. Coleman was not alone in her misperceptions, shame, and self-blame. After disclosing her own misguided sense of responsibility in Heidi's death, her mother readily talked about her hidden feelings of guilt. "My mother would open up and say, 'Oh my God. It wasn't your fault. I was the last person to see her that day.'" Her mother felt responsible because she had been cleaning rather than supervising Heidi. Blaming herself, and worried that her husband would fault her as well, she grieved alone and without emotional support.

Later, while on a hike with her father, she told him about how she and her mother had each felt responsible for her sister's drowning. He, too, opened up that he had felt at fault. "My dad was the last one to see Heidi as she walked by him with her little red boat in hand. So he always thought she [her mother] would blame him whereas he was blaming himself. He blamed himself for Heidi's death because he had not put down his work and gone with her to the pond," Ms. Coleman sadly recalls.

After years of struggling with feelings of self-condemnation and shame, each family member was able to examine and correct their assumptions and begin the emotional journey of healing. "Everyone got to see that there was no one to blame. There's just a tragedy that happened, and we have to do the best that we can. Now that we understand that, I see it in my parents. There is a yoke that has dropped off of them," she observes.

In her book, *This Life Is In Your Hands*, Ms. Coleman identifies the importance of discovering self-forgiveness. Her experience conveys that it is our interpretation of an event that affects how we think and feel about the adversity. She helps readers understand the value of turning to others for understanding and support as a way to heal wounds rather than remaining behind isolating barriers of self-recrimination. Reaching out to others allows the pain from our thoughts and hearts to be released.

Finding self-forgiveness meant Ms. Coleman was able to move her focus from struggling with the past to becoming more self-compassionate and connecting to the future in a positive way. "I think spirituality or religion is the most important way to overcome tragedy and to overcome any struggle in life. This wasn't a part of my upbringing, and it wasn't anything I learned from my parents. This is what I learned from coming to terms with my own pain and struggle."

For Ms. Coleman, spirituality came in the form of meditation. Meditation "really helped me to move forward and to have renewed faith in my life, the world and (awareness) of the bigger plan … to be able to see that there is someone outside of you, watching. It is so liberating to have that perspective. If you trust it, it will lead you to the greatest things. It just makes you stronger and better able to help other people when they're dealing with something. If you don't know how to help yourself through pain and tragedy, you won't be able to help anybody else. And so it is a gift," observes Ms. Coleman.

Spirituality has helped Ms. Coleman learn how to find meaning in her suffering. While her past catastrophe cannot be undone, and she still struggles with the pain, she now has a connection with something bigger than herself, which gives her comfort, perspective, and hope. She reflects that, "There are a lot of things happening to me, some good, some bad, but when I can be grateful for the good things, and grieve and learn from the bad, I can be okay with it all. This is the perspective that ideally can be found when something tragic happens. It is the gift behind the tragedy."[6]

Forgiveness is a Process

Going down the rocky path of discovering both forgiveness and self-forgiveness, and being able to move from merely surviving to finding resiliency, is an intensely personal journey that can take an indefinite amount of time. Tapping into the fundamental relationship influences of Self, Society and Spirituality, makes this process possible, and will be discussed later on in this chapter.

Why is Forgiveness so Important?

The process of working towards forgiveness of oneself and others is tremendously challenging. It is complicated because we are experiencing considerable pain. Nevertheless, we forge forward through the forgiveness process because we realize that, as Herbert Benson, M.D., a pioneer in mind body medicine observed, "Hatred is a banquet until you realize that you are the main course." Following are some of the benefits for pursuing forgiveness.

Forgiveness is a Pathway for Positive Emotions

Forgiveness releases us from the never-ending sentence of suffering caused by an offender. It enables us to instead experience life with a greater sense of peace and contentment. Without forgiveness, we are connected tightly to our unresolved pain. The typical emotional impact of not granting forgiveness is so expansive it has been linked to a whole boatload of emotional, physical and spiritual problems. We can feel helpless, angry, isolated, lonely and fearful. These painful wounds wreak havoc in our lives. When we are angry, our emotions dominate our thinking, which in turn diminishes our judgment, and can result in making poor decisions. Think about the times you have retaliated against someone who hurt you. Was it an angry, reactive decision, with you feeling victimized by the other person?

The emotional energy we use to maintain grudges is exhausting. Continually being hurt by unresolved pain stresses us and weakens our ability to cope with normal activities of daily living. Our bitterness and focus on the offender cause us to fill our thoughts and heart with negativity instead of enjoying the positive influences in our lives. Sometimes without noticing the changes, we slowly wear down, start to feel disconnected from who we really are, and bit by bit, lose our authenticity. Perhaps even worse, we may come to resemble the source of all our pain — the offender.

Imagine yourself surrounded with five pieces of luggage. Now, fill one with anger, another with hurt, and the remaining ones each with vulnerability, sadness, and fear. This is the emotional baggage you will carry from being unable to forgive your offender. If unresolved, you will have no choice but to drag this baggage with you to other existing and even future relationships and experiences. I guarantee that this will result in your personal happiness being diminished. This is because your daily perspective will become one of focusing on how you have been wronged, and being defensive and guarded because of your fear about it happening again. Your attempt to protect yourself from further emotional hurt means you will put up a protective barrier between yourself and others, much like the Plexiglas barrier installed between bank tellers and customers. The barrier does not differentiate between the well-meaning bank customers and the potential bank robbers. Each can see and communicate with the other, but closeness between everyone is obstructed. Your baggage causes you to increasingly isolate yourself emotionally from supportive and meaningful relationships.

Forgiveness Prevents Ruminating

What happens if we stay angry and don't forgive? We ruminate.

Ruminating is what we do when we repetitively focus on, mull over, and analyze our upset feelings resulting from a past experience. Those bad, unresolved feelings are invisible, but they tug at us, demand our attention, create a lot of noise and chaos in our head, and prevent us from moving forward. Rumination keeps our bitterness, resentment and blame alive, often for years and decades, keeping us victimized.

Rumination is a carcinogen to our entire being, putting us at risk for depression, medical ailments, spiritual alienation and social isolation. Just like when we do not self-forgive, when we ruminate, we are more likely to engage in self-destructive behaviors such as compulsive eating, smoking, or drinking. Many studies have found that holding onto anger and unforgiveness can create hormonal imbalances and a weakened immune system, increasing our susceptibility to illness and disorders. It even has a lethal implication for us. Anger has been connected not only to increased cardiovascular and coronary disease but also a higher risk for dying from these diseases.

When ruminating, our perspective becomes pessimistic, which zaps our energy and puts us on a downward spiral. We become more critical of others and ourselves. Because we are so focused on our anger, we talk a lot about it, which puts a strain on our social relationships. We are held hostage in resentment and wanting/plotting/executing revenge. Increasingly, the horrific results of retribution have been occurring in places where people should be most safe — our public schools. In the years between 2000 and 2016, acts of revenge were a factor in approximately 230 school-related injuries and 164 deaths in the United States.[7]

Curiously, revenge is not only embedded in the human culture and psychological makeup but is also found in animal cultures. When rhesus macaques, a species of monkeys, do not give food calls announcing they have found desirable food, they are "more likely to be the target of aggression than individuals that do alert, and share with the others, their discovery."[8] Baboons are capable of revenge, having been observed searching for and chasing another baboon that attacked their 'friend.' Elephants in Africa, apparently grieving when a passing train accidentally killed one of their own, were witnessed retaliating by attacking a neighboring human village.[9]

We needn't respond like the animals, because as humans, we have the capacity for abstract thought and a broad field of knowledge. We are able to understand that taking the passive path of harboring negative emotions causes us to engage in self-defeating attitudes and behaviors. Instead, we can let go of the cycle of hurtful thoughts and engage in the alternative path of forgiveness, which leads us to an increase in positive feelings and better outcomes.

Forgiveness Builds Empathy

Connectedness with others is the bridge over the toxic waters of revenge that can lead us to forgiveness. As the Dalai Lama, the spiritual leader of Tibet, comments, "We humans are social beings. We come into the world as the result of others' actions. We survive here in dependence on others. Whether we like it or not, there is hardly a moment of our lives when we do not benefit from others' activities."[10]

Amy Banks, M.D., instructor of Psychiatry at Harvard Medical School, reports, "Neuroscience is confirming that our nervous systems want us to connect with other human beings ... that we are literally hardwired to connect."[11] She goes on to say that when two people are in a conversation, they stimulate each other's mirror neurons in the brain. Mirror neurons are cells that are activated when we observe another's actions. These neurons "mirror" the behavior of the other person, as though the behavior belonged to us, and not the other person. This identification with the observed behavior helps us understand other people's feelings and actions, and may be the underpinnings of empathy. Little wonder that mirror neurons are referred to as "empathy neurons" or "Dalai Lama neurons."

Empathy is a significant component in the work of finding forgiveness. It helps us walk in the offender's shoes, so to speak, allowing us to understand how the offender thinks and feels. Our mirror neurons pick up on the offender's feelings, allowing us to learn why the offender chose the adversarial behavior. We can see that the person is more than, and separate from, his offensive behavior. We better understand that other human beings have flaws, which can cause us to reflect on past events when we, too, have been flawed and injured someone else. When we start to understand why the other person acted in the hurtful manner we start to have a shift in our thinking. We experience an increase in compassion and empathy and a reduction of our own anger. Letting go of anger is an important part of forgiveness, because anger serves as a psychological shield against fully feeling our own pain, and fuels our need to be vindictive or resentful. Sometimes this forgiving may lead to reconciliation between the offender and victim. But even in situations where reconciliation is not appropriate or doable, empathy can help dislodge us from our grudge holding and revenge seeking feelings. It helps move us from an unforgiving, unhappy, and unhealthy place of blame, and propels us into a more peaceful place of understanding and acceptance.

Forgiveness Promotes Prosocial Behavior

Forgiveness is the gift that keeps on giving. Studies show that people who forgive are more likely to volunteer for charity work and donate money to charity organizations than those who remembered unforgiven offenses.[12] This demonstrates the positive impact forgiveness has not only on the victim but also on relationships individuals have with their community and the larger society as well.

What Forgiveness is Not

Forgiveness is not discussed very much in our society, so if we attempt to practice it, we often get it wrong. Fortunately, considerable scholarly research has gone into removing confusion and traps that can impede our efforts to experience the personal growth and personal harmony that accompanies forgiveness.

Conditional

Forgiveness is only experienced when we make the decision to release our bitterness toward the other person, independent of their behaviors.

Denial That Harm was Done

Denial is a defense mechanism we may use to avoid facing our upsetting thoughts and hurt feelings. But there are consequences for indulging in denial. Offenders who deny their hurtful behavior are at risk for recidivism, because they have not taken accountability for their behavior. Victims also must give up their defenses, and not minimize or pretend they don't feel the pain. As in forgetting, if the impact of the adverse event is minimized or denied, victims may put themselves at risk of being hurt again.

Learning to own responsibility for the choices we made and for which we now regret, is to accept that we are human. It is important to take comfort in the realization that all people err at some point in their lives. When we acknowledge true remorse and accept that we need to make a change, we have the inner serenity of knowing we will not likely repeat that event, and that going forward, will make better choices. The stage is then set for true self-forgiveness, better psychological adjustment and improved interpersonal relationships.

Dependent on Offender's Actions

Forgiveness needn't include an apology from the offender. In many cases, the offender never changes, and never owns responsibility for the hurt. Remembering that forgiveness is about our attitude, not the offender's attitude or action, will help us reduce our bitterness and gain back our power.

Excusing or Pardoning

We are at risk of minimizing the wrong doing when we make excuses for the behavior. Many of us have heard the phrase, "let bygones be bygones." To do so is to accept and even condone the painful act. We can, however, find forgiveness for the person and move forward with our lives, while still not forgiving the behavior. Letting go of the resentment towards the offender need not cancel out wanting the person punished for their wrongdoing.

Forgetting

There is no delete button in our hearts and minds regarding memory of an offense. The experience stays in our memory, but we can choose to look at it differently. In doing so we may still feel emotionally upset, but are able to avoid the intense anger, vengeance and fear. Allowing it to remain in our memory is probably a good thing. To "forgive and forget" is to put ourselves at risk of getting hurt again. Remembering helps us learn from our past and protects us going forward.

Justice, Punishment, Revenge or Restitution

Seeking justice or punishment is likely to result in a downward spiral for someone who has been victimized by another person. The offender may not ever acknowledge the wrongdoing, resulting in the victim's vengeance growing rather than receding. The judicial system can help remove a victim's desire for retaliation by obtaining restitution for the wrongdoing.

Obligation

Forgiveness is a choice, not an obligation. It is very personal, and cannot be done simply because it is expected or requested by others. There is no correct time frame for it to be achieved, even if others moved through a similar process in a shorter amount of time. Forgiveness is a choice exclusively exercised by the victim for the purpose of letting go of toxic feelings of anger, fear, and retaliation. It is done so as to be able to move forward with one's life rather than remain burdened by the pain caused by another person.

Pseudo-Forgiveness

Forgiveness is also not to be confused with 'pseudo-forgiveness,' which is a term coined for when we say we forgive but in reality, have not. For the offender pseudo-forgiveness means he hasn't admitted the wrongdoing and responsibility. For the victim, it indicates he is still holding onto pain and resentment.

Pseudo-forgiveness can be appealing as it is the quick and easy, albeit disingenuous, way to move forward. People gravitate toward pseudo-forgiveness for different reasons. It may be that the victim is intimidated by the offender's possible reaction. It may be what the victim perceives forgiveness to be the right thing to do or an obligation. It can be a way of avoiding one's pain and instead trying to repress it and make it go away. After all, who can blame someone for wanting to skip the long string of complicated and painful emotions that must be experienced in achieving true forgiveness? For the victim, pseudo-forgiveness can be a way of publically humiliating an offender, which is a manipulation to make the offender feel guilty. In other situations pseudo-forgiveness occurs because the victim over empathizes with the offender, is struggling to feel in control, or wants to look better to others.[13]

Like most shortcuts in life, pseudo-forgiveness skips the hard work that has to be done in achieving forgiveness. But emotions cannot be outsmarted, and what we are putting off — or ignoring — will catch up with us eventually. Without remorse and an attempt to make amends to the victim, offenders will fail to understand the consequences of their hurtful behavior, fail to empathize with the victim, and may hurt the victim again. The victim who engages in pseudo-forgiveness may develop future difficulties with poor boundaries, re-victimization, and greater psychological distress.

Reconciliation

Forgiveness is a solo experience, whereas reconciliation is a joint process. Forgiveness need not require interacting with the offender and returning to the old relationship. This is especially the case when the offender is not motivated to change, is not present, (i.e., psychiatric disorder, in prison, in another country) is deceased, or continues to be a threat to the well-being of the victim.[14] Author Lewis Smedes expresses the conviction that we can successfully increase our sense of personal power and decrease our toxic feelings of anger without reconciliation. His quote, "It takes one person to forgive, it takes two people to be reunited," reminds us that we can let go of the grudge towards the offender without needing to reconcile.

Simple

There is no shortcut for forgiveness. Forgiving is harder work than remaining unforgiving. It is a process that requires a lot of time, energy, and the working through of many raw emotions.

Forgiveness can't be created just because the offender utters the words, "I'm sorry," or the victim says, "I forgive you." Forgiveness is an often lengthy and arduous process. We may feel we have worked through our painful feelings only to have them re-emerge when we experience deep emotional pain from a subsequent adversity. This does not mean that we did not successfully work through our forgiveness relating to a previous event. Rather, it means we are human, and the new hurt has triggered the old hurt residing deep within our memory, making us feel vulnerable.

The amount of hurt that we received, along with how we have dealt with hurt in the past, will influence our ability to move through the forgiveness process. We need to be patient, acknowledge our feelings, and give ourselves permission to move toward the goal of forgiveness at the pace that feels right for ourselves.

Trust

It is not about trust, either. We may wish to forgive because we want to maintain a relationship with the offender. Yet the person may still not be trustworthy. We can set boundaries so that it is not easy for them to hurt us again. If for example, someone has hurt us by failing to keep a commitment, such as returning money, helping out, or keeping confidential information secret, it may be wise to protect ourselves. We can modify how we relate towards this person so as to prevent future pain. Trust needs to be earned, and only consistent behavior over time will indicate if the offender can earn back the trust.

Turning It Over to God

Forgiveness is not exclusively about 'turning it over to God'. Trusting that God will take care of punishment can reduce our anger and need for revenge, but is only unforgiveness reduction, not forgiveness.

Barriers to Forgiveness

There is a saying, 'To resent someone is to take the poison and expect the other person to die.' Yet barriers to forgiveness can be so challenging and complex that some people do not know how to overcome these obstacles. As a result, they never successfully resolve the burden of painful emotions and instead remain stuck in a place of unforgiveness that continues to do them emotional and physical harm.

History and religion have at times condoned this attitude of unforgiveness. A commonly repeated verse from Exodus 21:25, refers to seeking 'burn for burn, wound for wound, bruise for bruise.' This biblical excerpt conveys the sanctioning societies place on retribution and punishment for wrong doings, as opposed to encouraging self-reflection, emotional growth, and forgiveness. Unfortunately, if we get stuck with feelings of resentment, we cannot do anything to become happier. We remain stuck ruminating, reliving the offense, and being chronically bitter.

Anger

Negative emotions, especially anger, can be difficult for us to relinquish because they bring us a sense of personal power; for a little while, that is. We feel less vulnerable when we are angry with the person who caused us harm. We hold onto anger because it offers protection; much like that from a coat providing defense against a bitter wind. Our support system, frequently consisting of family and friends, validates our right to hold onto our pain.

But research conclusively reveals anger to offer a false sense of safety because it distorts our judgment. We become self-righteous when angry, and instead of examining and tending to our pain we fixate on the wrong doings of the other person. By keeping the spotlight off of us we avoid painful feelings that may go deeper than the current hurt. Sometimes it is a deep-rooted hurt that occurred before the current event, which has convinced us that we are worthless or unlovable. It is human nature to want to avoid the awful truth behind the hurt, and blaming and resenting the offender provides such protection.

Being angry creates the desire to 'even the score.' These feelings create more problems — in our social network, our emotional well-being, and our spiritual connection. As anguish builds, chances of forgiveness diminish. Anger turns into rumination. We find ourselves in a rut, obsessively playing our negative thoughts over and over in our minds. This creates problems, as we are focused on the past hurtful behaviors instead of looking forward.

Even worse is the fact that we're changing our brain, and not in a good way. We have a processing center in our brain that regulates emotions, emotional behavior and motivation, called the amygdala. When activated by emotion the amygdala increases in activity, making us either fearful (and more avoidant) or angry (and more vengeful) toward the offender. Our negative feelings toward the offender not only continue but also are at risk of escalation.

If anger is the greatest poisonous threat to forgiveness, then apology appears to be the antivenin. When an offender can apologize, the victim is able to change his or her perspective on both the offender and the offense, reducing the intensity of the anger, and better able to move toward the path of forgiveness.

Secondary Gains

On the surface, remaining stuck in a blaming and resentful place doesn't seem like a very desirable place in which any of us would choose to exist. But we all do things for a reason, and in this case, being unforgiving can provide what psychologists identify as 'secondary gains.' Secondary gains are the hidden reasons or benefits a person receives for not overcoming a problem. For example, if we have interpersonal conflicts at work, and are sick, staying home from work enables us to not only recuperate from the illness but also provides us with the secondary gain of not having to interact in an unpleasant work-place situation that we would prefer to avoid.

Most people are not consciously aware of the secondary gain being obtained. But once it is addressed with them, the insight into their behavior is like flipping on the car's windshield wipers in the midst of a rainstorm. Very rapidly the person can clearly see how the secondary gain was being used to avoid the original cause of the painful or stressful situation, how it was negatively impacting on his life, and what he can do to correct and start healing the situation.

Past Experiences (or Frame of Reference)

Memories of how we felt following past experiences with adversity can inhibit our ability to forgive present and future incidences. If we felt our attempt to resolve the previous matter was unsuccessful, then we will likely remember our negative thoughts, feelings, and behaviors, and not be willing to risk forgiving another hurtful event.

Injustice Against Another Person

Another barrier to forgiveness is when one's loved one has suffered horribly at the hands of others. Examples include a loved one killed by a drunk driver, abusive spouse, or terrorist. Nowhere has it been more discussed than with survivors of genocidal regimes such as the Nazis in Germany, who exterminated six million Jews, or the 1.7 million killed by the Khmer Rouge in Cambodia. It is common for survivors to find the concept of forgiving the perpetrator to be problematic, and even inappropriate. They may feel that as a nonvictim it is impossible to provide forgiveness for a crime committed to someone other than themselves. When visiting the Holocaust concentration camp, Bergen-Belsen, in Germany, then Israeli president, Chaim Herzog, said, "I do not bring forgiveness with me, nor forgetfulness. The only ones who can forgive are dead."[15]

Modeling Unhealthy Family Lessons

Barriers to forgiveness can occur unwittingly in our own living rooms. Young children view parents as the experts. Children learn about how to cope with forgiveness and unforgiveness by observing how their family deals with resolving adversity.

When reminiscing about the past, parents and grandparents share their impressions about conflicts they encounter, and how they managed their feelings. They share stories of how they coped with and resolved conflicts.

Sometimes, rather than helping children learn healthy ways to handle their feelings, children are taught to repress them. Parents may admonish siblings to be 'mature' and 'rise above it' when engaged in a conflict, rather than being helped in processing their feelings. Discussions among adults regarding past family conflicts offer the opportunity for children to either learn valuable or unhelpful life lessons on coping with adversity.

Education

We know that self-forgiveness is good for both our physical and mental health. Research now tells us that education plays a role, and can be either a benefit or a barrier, in achieving self-forgiveness.

Studies show that people with less than a high school education are less likely to report being self-forgiving than those with more than a high school education. This is likely due to the sense of control we feel we have over our lives. Typically, a higher level of education provides people with more access to both income and other supportive resources. When we have more resources at our disposal we have a softer landing when adversity strikes, and our bounce back ability is faster.

Those with a higher education are more likely to have a strong support system. This social network contributes to a person's sense of self-worth, belief that they can have control over their destiny and can successfully endure the emotional energy required in overcoming adversity.

How to Use the Three Spheres of Support to Achieve Forgiveness

Forgiving is hard work. Moving beyond crippling anger and vengeance requires changes in our thoughts, feelings and behaviors. There is no shortcut, but the end result is well worth the effort. As stated by Frederic Luskin, Ph.D., former director of the Stanford Forgiveness Project, "Letting go of a grudge is a way to return to the peaceful center inside you." We all deserve that inner peace that comes with forgiveness. Our three spheres of support — Self, Society, and Spirituality — help us not just to return to a former level of functioning but instead move through the most challenging aspects of forgiveness associated with a crisis or tragedy and find personal growth, new insights, and new meanings.

Self

Anger following an adversity is understandable. When we feel we have been treated wrong, or the injury was severe and caused suffering, wanting to blame and punish the offender is a natural reaction. But anger can be one of the most maladaptive emotions that surfaces.

We're all familiar with the saying, 'revenge is sweet.' In actuality it is sour, even toxic. If not attended to, our anger can grow into rumination, blame, and intensify to the point where we are plotting or engaging in revenge for the wrongdoing. Research with adolescents has found that allowing the negative emotions of anger and revenge to fester was the motivating influence in half of their crimes against other people.[16] And its not just the adolescents who are influenced by anger. It has been found that a reduction in anger correlates with an overall decrease in acts of infidelity, shoplifting, rape, arson and homicide. Increasing our self-awareness, self-compassion, and self-acceptance helps us in the journey of working through our anger.

Personality Traits

Forgiveness, which helps us transform our lives, comes easier to some of us than others. Psychologists have discovered that interestingly enough, there are differences between people who are more likely to be forgiving and those less likely to be less forgiving. Our likelihood of being a forgiving person can be determined in large part on what researcher Dr. Lewis Goldberg identified to be the five primary factors of the personality. Termed the Big Five personality theory, these personality traits include openness, conscientiousness, extraversion, agreeableness and neuroticism. While the term 'personality' encompasses a huge category, we can look at these as being the quirks and characteristics we all come to be known for, such as being funny or dower, pensive or impulsive. Researchers have found consistency for these five attributes in all cultures, so it appears that there is a biological predisposition to forgiveness. Most of us don't fall into exactly one of the five traits, and on different days we may exhibit one trait more than another. Yet overall, we most likely actively connect with one of the following five personality traits:[17]

Openness

People who have a high level of openness exhibit curiosity and a willingness to venture outside their comfort zone. This flexibility exposes them to new experiences, which in turn influences how they view matters. The result is that they are more likely to consider non-traditional views and values of others. This perspective-taking helps them develop creative and fresh insight into problem solving, which aides in reducing negative feelings, and helps in the transition from anger to a more neutral acceptance of the offender's wrongdoing.

Conscientiousness

Of the Big Five personality traits, people high in conscientiousness tend to avoid conflict, are more likely to say things that will enable them to get along with others, and be more willing to forgive someone who wronged them. Conscientious individuals are thoughtful, goal-oriented, and have good impulse control. They consider the long-term consequences of their words and actions, are organized and mindful of details. These are the people who are less likely to experience vengefulness towards those who have wronged them and are generally more satisfied with life than those who rank high on neuroticism and are easily upset.

Many studies have been conducted on the connection between conscientiousness and forgiveness and the findings appear to not be as strong as openness and forgiveness. Yet conscientiousness plays a vital role in being able to willfully control one's emotions, develop empathy towards others, and not exact revenge on the offender, all traits that contribute towards making forgiveness more possible.

Extraversion

Extraverts are sociable, emotionally expressive, have high reserves of energy and genuinely like being around others. Some research does not identify the strong relationship between extraversion and forgiveness that one might readily expect. Yet their natural positive emotions reduce the tendency to harbor negative feelings of vengeance. They are less likely to avoid situations and more likely to be straightforward about asserting their concerns, thus less likely to harbor resentment and ruminate over transgressions from another person.

Agreeableness

People who are agreeable tend to be trusting and friendly. They tend to want to understand and even accept another person's perspective. Being able to consider issues from the offender's perspective, and having a tendency to be motivated to resolve conflicts, people who score high in agreeableness have traits that are consistent with the ability to move toward forgiveness.

Neuroticism

While some personality types find it relatively easy to develop and maintain relationships, those who are high in neuroticism experience more struggles. People with strong neuroticism traits tend to be less emotionally stabile. They are sensitive, more easily stressed, irritable, or anxious. They negatively focus on their anxiety, fear, sadness and what could go wrong rather than optimistically focusing on problem resolution. For this reason, they are inclined to ruminate about a wrongdoing. They are the 'eye-for-an-eye' personalities. Their reaction will more likely be vengeance than forgiveness and therefore their ability to experience forgiveness more challenging.[18]

Our personality type influences our feelings, but feelings are not fixed in concrete. Learning to not be afraid of our feelings, and to understand and befriend them, is an important part of the forgiveness process. Sometimes, time away from the offender offers us the space necessary to address our negative feelings associated with the offense and begin to forgive. Instead of directing all of our feelings towards the offender in the form of anger, we need to allow ourselves time to feel the hurt feelings we were avoiding.

Our personality type may influence the amount of time and support to work through this process, as these feelings may touch core fears, such as questions we have about our worthiness, lovability, intelligence, etc. Instead of using defense mechanisms to avoid this painful feeling, giving ourselves permission to intentionally feel this hurt enables us to successfully work through it. This work is not for the faint of heart. It is emotionally challenging. But being surrounded by caring people provides a buffer against emotional hurt because of the trust and respect received. As a result, we will feel safe and empowered, the negative feelings we have been avoiding will lose power and the positive feelings will help drive us forward. Sometimes, simply being able to face the feelings we have been avoiding lessens, or even removes the resentment. By taking care of our feelings that surround the event, we end up changing our view of ourselves, our relationship with others, and our approach to life.

Neuroplasticity

While a portion of how we respond to forgiveness is biologically determined, there is no reason to believe that we have to be constrained by personality traits bestowed upon us by our mother and father. Unlike what scientists previously believed, our brains are now considered to be more 'plastic' and pliable, than fixed. We have continual control over how we think, feel and behave. Just because we didn't do so well in the forgiveness department in the past does not mean that we cannot retrain our brains and do better in the future.

Neuroplasticity, the process of retraining our brains and creating new pathways, is beneficial in helping us find forgiveness. Neuroplasticity helps us change our well-worn pathways of unforgiving anger and grudge holding that we developed years ago into more positive feelings and thoughts. One doesn't have to be an Einstein to create new pathways, but it does require conscious effort on our part to retrain our brains. If practiced over and over again, with time, our brain circuitry will be rewired. Focusing on positive emotions will result in the development of new circuits in our brain. Like exercise is to going to the gym, regularly practicing the experience of positive emotions will strengthen the muscle of the new and healthier neural pathways. With time, the underused negative neural pathways associated with unforgiveness will atrophy and fade away and be replaced with more desirable pathways that contribute to our resiliency.

This ability to develop new neural pathways is reflected in the research of Carol Dweck, author of *Mindset*. She believes that while biology influences the way we tend to approach forgiveness, changing our thinking will change our reactions as well. To do so, Dweck suggests we have to understand whether we tend to have either a 'fixed' or a 'growth' mindset.[19] Those with a fixed mindset have less success at overcoming adversity, and are more likely to get stuck at hurt and revenge, because they believe they don't want to take risks. They get discouraged by failure and are likely to give up. They don't like to be challenged at things they are not good at, so they don't learn and grow from their mistakes. Their motto is, "You can't teach an old dog new tricks." Growth mindset individuals, on the other hand, find more success with overcoming adversity because they are comfortable with uncertainty, and know that with effort, focus, and repeated tries, they will be able to bring about a desired change. Their motto is, "As long as the dog is breathing, he can learn tricks."

Neuroplasticity helps fixed mindset individuals strengthen positive emotions important in helping us find forgiveness. This can be done by writing down things one is grateful for, writing down a positive experience that occurred recently, or sitting and visualizing a positive occurrence happening. In time, neuroplasticity will enable them to feel released from the emotional pain, less connected to the offender, and possibly more empathic or understanding of their offender. They will find the negative forces that inhibit forgiveness, such as anger and rumination, dissipating, and in its place develop a growth mindset, allowing the creation of new pathways in their brain.

This means that even when we are struggling with adversity we can still sit at the helm of our own ship, and steer ourselves towards forgiveness and healing. Our ability to be forgiving is not set in stone. Nor is it determined by our seemingly flawed DNA, old response habits, or a rigid, unchangeable brain. We can cultivate new habits, attitudes and behaviors through neuroplasticity, which allows for the rewiring of our brain. New pathways are developed in the process, which help us work better at finding forgiveness amidst pain and adversity.

Society

Societal relationships are influenced by factors such as gender, age, culture, race, socioeconomic status, interpersonal relationships and the legal system, all of which, in turn, influence our forgiveness patterns. Just about all of our societal relationships, from business to friendships, to intimate love, require that we get along with others.

When we are emotionally connected with someone, and we find value in that relationship, we are more inclined to work toward forgiveness of his or her wrongdoing. Betrayal by others when growing up can have a negative impact on how we relate to others in society today. If we have been victimized emotionally, physically or sexually as a child, and the hurt was not attended to, we are likely to develop a tendency to not forgive, and instead, hold onto our feelings of distrust, hurt and anger. We may face future adversity with defensive responses from the past, such as avoidance, denial, and anxiety. This protective coping style has been previously imprinted on our brains as an attempt to safeguard us from being hurt again by others. But it puts us at risk of being cynical and losing connectedness with others. Without trust, we will keep others at arms length and we will see little value in forgiveness. Our relationships will be hollow and the task of overcoming adversity more challenging.

However, if when growing up, our extended family and others in our community successfully modeled forgiveness, our view of how to respond to adversity will be very different. We will have the experience and awareness of the usefulness of forgiveness. We will feel valued by others, which increases our self-esteem.

A strong self-esteem can give us the courage to try things, accept challenges, and to persevere in overcoming fears that could otherwise prevent us from surviving adversity. The positive relationships found throughout society are powerful in the emotional strength they offer us from helping shift from a life of resentment and immobilized victim to a life of strength, understanding, greater possibilities, and happiness.

Despite our age, religion or geographical origins, we all find that positive relationships in society help us overcome adversity by enabling us to "take risks that we'd never take on our own ... give us meaning and purpose, help us to take risks and leaps that we could easily rationalize away if left alone ... become both more honest ... when our defenses aren't fooling people ... expand our minds and worlds because we can't read everything or be informed about everything...give us emotional depth when we share an emotional experience with others ... strengthen our empathic connection ... stimulate endorphins by helping us laugh, and give us a sense of structure and belonging."[20] Little surprise then, that researchers from various fields find that good social networks are the crown jewel to achieving happiness.

Gender

Many people find that men and women tend to view offenses differently, and also that they deal with forgiveness differently. These gender differences are likely due to a combination of different biology and socialization styles.

New research using functional magnetic resonance imaging (fMRI) technology that measures brain activity has found differences in the brain patterns between men and women with regard to grudge holding. Men are more likely to respond to offenses with vengefulness than women. However, when men are encouraged to reflect on their own former wrongdoings, empathy towards the offender rises along with their level of forgiveness.[21] Interestingly, a study found that the same was not true for women; that unlike men, women's grudge holding did not decrease after reflection on their own past offenses.

This may be where nature crosses paths with nurture. Since the time of the predatory saber-toothed tigers, society has needed men to be strong. This may lead men to view forgiveness as weakness, and vengeance as their 'go-to' reaction when faced with adversity. Be it through the movies, video games, literature, playground or toys, throughout their lives males will view their gender as being tough, detached from emotions, and ready to respond to adversity with a revengeful attack or be attacked, and win or lose attitude.

Very likely, women have been socialized as a counterbalance to men. Women customarily are encouraged to consider different perspectives, and to have empathy for others. Women, seen as nurturers, are more inclined to try to maintain relationships and promote harmony in times of adversity. These traits reduce the probability of wanting to seek revenge. Women also tend to be more religious then men, and as most religions include teachings on the value of forgiveness, women may be more exposed to the importance of forgiving.[22]

Yet if provided with guidance, men can develop and catch up with women in their feelings of empathy. Empathy can lead to compassion, which in turn can facilitate forgiveness, an essential element in overcoming adversity.

Age
Interestingly, the older we are, the more likely we are to forgive; older adults are likely to be more forgiving than younger adults, who in turn are more likely to be forgiving than teenagers. This may partly be because having decades of life experiences under our belt provides us with a perspective on the importance of forgiving.[23] With age, we learn to let go of minor offenses and place less value on revenge. Also, studies find that our personalities change with age. We tend to be more agreeable and less neurotic, which, as the Big Five personality traits reflect, makes us more capable of forgiveness.

Language
We all have the capacity, following an adversity, to forgive or seek revenge. Language influences the path we choose. Language is inseparable from culture, and conveys the speaker's values and beliefs. If we do not understand the importance of understanding cultural differences, we are at risk of projecting our biases and stereotypes onto the other person, making communication more complicated and forgiveness more challenging.

In other words, it's not just what we say that will facilitate or sabotage forgiveness, but how it's said. Language includes nonverbal behaviors such as facial expression, gesture, body posture, and use of timing and space, all typically learned early and subconsciously within the context of our childhood culture. Some cultures, such as Latin and Middle Eastern cultures, are expressive, with often-used dramatic gestures and gesticulation. This might be misinterpreted to be an indication of distress or excitement to someone from an

East Asian culture, who is more accustomed to nominal gesturing and softer voices.

Americans view eye contact as a sign of respect. Other, more reserved, cultures, may view direct eye contact as aggressive, while their own style of looking away or down is interpreted as an indication of guilt, insincerity or deceptiveness by other cultures. It is easy to appreciate, from these few examples, how challenging the process of forgiveness is when factoring in awareness and sensitivity of different cultural and social variables in verbal and nonverbal body language.

Race

Much like age and gender, race has variances in forgiveness as well. But identifying racial differences in forgiveness is complicated because forgiveness is also connected to cultural, social and economic influences in our lives.

While differences exist among races, one example of forgiveness and race can be found in the African American community. Research has shown that generations of negative forces including discrimination, racism, economic disadvantage and oppression have influenced many African Americans in their perspective on forgiveness. They have learned from personal family stories, as well as the history of slavery, that adversity happens and is an unavoidable fact of life.

Extended family, tight social networks and religious involvement are valued resources in the African American community. They provide tangible and spiritual support, and help in the management of feelings and stress reduction resulting from past and present adversity. Churches value forgiveness, and meaningful relationships are established when following the ways of the church. Being able to rely on these social support systems is important to an individual's sense of self-worth and dignity, and may increase positive emotions while decreasing negative reactions to conflicts, helping to focus on the possibility of forgiveness.

Socioeconomic Class

Forgiveness helps improve our emotional and physical health. Yet as mentioned previously, forgiveness is not granted equally. The socioeconomic class in which we live can create a barrier or a benefit to our ability to forgive others and ourselves. Members of the middle or higher income groups are more likely to be more forgiving about minor offenses than are those in a low socioeconomic group. It all tends to boil down to the availability of social support, resources, and survival.

Resources are scarce for those in lower socioeconomic groups. The poor tend to live in crowded, deteriorated, polluted neighborhoods. Forgiveness may not be viewed as an option where support from others in the community is weak and conflict is high. Individuals will not want to risk being vulnerable by turning to their community for help because such actions could be viewed as weakness. Weakness may open oneself up to the risk of being preyed upon by others. Victims may also fear revenge from the offender, the police or the courts. As such, the economically disadvantaged are more likely to have less social support and committed community relationships and experience lasting emotional distress in times of adversity.

At the other end of the continuum of feeling in control of one's life are members of the middle and upper class. They have more options, both economically and socially, than do those in the lower class. When they encounter a crisis they are more likely to be employed in salaried positions that provide disability and other benefits if medical crises arise. They are more connected with others in the community who can offer encouragement, advice, or material support. Their community is more likely to include supportive resources including hospitals, social service agencies, and places of worship. This support and options can mitigate any potential vengeance felt towards an offender, enabling them to regain control over their lives more readily, and provide a more expedient path towards forgiveness.

Feelings of being forgiven by a higher power are also associated with income. Those in the middle-income report feeling forgiven more than those in the lowest and highest income brackets. Higher income individuals may be less likely to feel the necessity to turn to a higher power for forgiveness. They have other resources in society — a strong social network, stable relationships, and income — providing them with a greater sense of personal control over their lives.[24] Persons in the lower income brackets without the tangible and social support system may feel more isolated, struggle more following an offense, and thereby feel unforgiven by God.

Interpersonal Relationships
Since forgiveness assumes a significant role in maintaining relationships, and unforgiveness hurts relationships, it is important to identify community members who are in a position to empower individuals struggling with adver-

sity. Listed below are several components of our interpersonal relationships that are instrumental in helping us find forgiveness:

- *Family.* Parents, along with teachers, mental health professionals, clergy and the legal system, are in a position to help people struggling to overcome obstacles. They can provide meaning, vision and direction when an awful injustice has taken place. Family can understand the importance of forgiveness as a path to emotional healing and personal growth and contribute to this goal.

  Parents can model how to ask for, receive, and give forgiveness. Parents can go beyond admonishing children who fight with their siblings by providing them with the steps to take, such as compassion, in the process of forgiveness. Children can learn to own responsibility when they have harmed another, to express heartfelt remorse, and to attempt in the restoration of the relationship.

- *Schools.* Schools can help students learn new skills that may not be available at home. Teachers may assist students in learning communication skills essential for forgiveness, ranging from playground to classroom conflicts.

- *Clergy.* Clergy can help their congregants move towards forgiveness through sermons, Bible study, classes, seminars, study groups and fellowship, which offers encouragement.

- *Mental Health Professionals.* In individual psychotherapy as well as in support and therapy groups, mental health professionals can help individuals develop the courage to try new communication styles that will benefit them in moving beyond adversity in their lives. Such help keeps people going when discouraged, provides novel viewpoints, and helps prevent them from isolating themselves and ruminating about problems.

- *Community Support Groups.* A societal organization that has helped countless people discover the healing power of forgiveness is the twelve-step program for people with addictions (such as Alcoholics Anonymous, Narcotics Anonymous, Gamblers Anonymous, Sex Addicts Anonymous, etc.), which help people go through the process of stopping and recovering from their addictions. The 12-step philosophy perceives forgiveness to be central to the healing process. Six of the 12 steps members are expected to work through in the program's recovery process focus on forgiving themselves and others.

The programs help members reconnect with the three components of support identified in this book as being essential for overcoming adversity; Self, Society and Spirituality. Individuals going through the 12-step programs increase awareness of their dysfunctional behavior by taking ownership of their actions and working through feelings of anger, shame and sadness that may impede this process.

Holding onto the painful feelings of resentment, anger, shame and fear associated with past offenses is to relive them, over and over and over again. It can hijack one's thinking and judgment and does not change the past. Instead, people going through a 12-step program can learn to forgive themselves because while they are imperfect, they are worthy of forgiveness. The offender is released from his wrongdoing and granted another chance, much as a judge would release an offender from prison for a fresh start in life.

Legal System

The legal system is another critical component of societal support that helps the victim progress along the path of forgiveness. It is the judicial system's responsibility to protect society by imposing punishment in the form of fines, restitution and incarceration against offenders.

Knowing that society, through laws and the court system, can find the offender guilty of an injustice can provide victims with a sense of relief, the opportunity to have their voices heard and feelings validated. It provides clarity as to who was the victim and who was the offender. For example, children who are sexually victimized by an adult may have been manipulated and told that they were acting provocatively, or that they were bad and deserved punishment. The perpetrator may deny the abuse to others in the community and blame the victim for lying. In these cases, punishment of the offender by the courts, and recognizing that the offender will be suffering in some manner can reduce the victim's motivation for vengefulness. This can be helpful in the victim's self-forgiveness and recovery.

Despite the effort of the court to seek fairness, justice is not always served. Punishment may not be assigned, the offender may never acknowledge any wrongdoing, apologize, or try to correct his wrong behavior. As it is not the court's responsibility to address the role of forgiveness, the emotional well-being of the victims may be impacted, and their ability to progress towards forgiveness impaired. Regardless of what takes place in the legal system, we can still choose to forgive our offender because forgiveness occurs independent of the legal findings. However, forgiveness does not in any manner imply that we should not follow through with legal action against the offender.

Spirituality

The magnificence of spirituality is that it is found in all cultures, throughout history, and in all geographical nooks and crannies of the world. Spirituality provides us with the inner strength in life to move through adversity, offering us a place to go to when we are lost, and direction so that we can move forward in our lives. When feeling isolated, it helps us reconnect with a presence that is greater than us, providing us with unconditional support, and guiding us in self-compassion. When feeling disconnected, it can help us reframe our perspective so that we can begin the process of forgiving others and ourselves. When we are lost, it offers us direction.

Hope

Spirituality provides the foundation for being able to take on the difficult task of forgiveness. This relationship between spirituality and forgiveness has been in existence for a long, long time, as reflected in the 18th century English poet Alexander Pope's adage, "To err is human, to forgive divine."

Spirituality helps us transcend our suffering, release our hold on anger toward ourselves or someone else, and provide us with hope. Hope is powerful. In his research on hopefulness, Jerome Groopman, M.D. of Harvard Medical School has found that hope can alter our neurochemistry and block pain by releasing endorphins and enkephalin, which serve as the body's natural painkillers. Endorphins, our so-called happiness hormones, are released when we are upset, elevating our mood, and strengthening our ability to move towards forgiveness.

Hope is future oriented. It gives us the belief that despite the pain, fear and uncertainty of today, that tomorrow may be better. Spirituality not only helps us find hope by believing tomorrow may be better, but it also helps us let go of the hope that the past could have been anything different. Accepting this, we can begin the task of finding forgiveness for others and ourselves. When we surrender to the difficult notion that what happened in the past cannot be changed, and we need to move forward, we begin to find the power in ourselves to travel in the direction we want; and to which we have always wanted to head.

Psychological Benefits

Spiritual and emotional healing has included forgiveness since the Stone Age when shamanic priest-doctors performed spiritual healings. Modern day physicians, psychologists, philosophers and theologians studying the science of forgiveness are in agreement that forgiveness of others and self-forgiveness brings about positive emotions, such as greater feelings of happiness and confidence, and decreases feelings of anger. They have also found that when people are able to forgive God for a particular negative life event, they experience a healing effect on depression and anxiety. Research studies show that people who find spiritual meaning to be "less susceptible to mortality than do those who are not connected in any meaningful way to a spiritual belief system."[25]

Religion

Spirituality is intangible and not necessarily connected to religious viewpoints. When found inside a formal religion, spirituality becomes attached to a particular set of beliefs and practices, ritual observances, teachings, prayers, texts and organized manner of worship.

All major religions value social support, encourage relationships with others and view forgiveness as a way to ensure the ongoing personal bonds of connectedness. Connectedness with others and the use of forgiveness to sustain relationships can be traced back to the beginning of time. According to the Bible, when creating both Adam and Eve, God said, 'It is not good that man is alone. I will make a helpmate opposite him." (Genesis 2:18) God undoubtedly understood the importance of being a part of a community with meaningful relationships. God demonstrated the importance of forgiveness by forgiving Adam and Eve for eating fruit from the forbidden tree of knowledge of good and evil even though they did not ask God for his forgiveness, or apologize for their wrongdoing.

When we are unforgiving, we develop a dark mindset of distrust, which can result in a feeling of estrangement from a spiritual connection. Most people don't want to experience this isolation, and for this reason, many people turn to religion, in search of forgiveness.

Forgiveness is learnable, and if we believe that God can forgive others and us, then we can begin to think that we can learn to do the same. Being in a place of worship helps us experience a connection with God, but merely walking into a place of prayer and attending a service is not enough to feel forgiveness of God or to stimulate our own feelings of forgiveness. Forgiveness most likely occurs because we go beyond the cognitive aspect, and truly experience the importance of forgiveness. Fellowship groups provide emotional support and help us feel safe to share our unexpressed feelings. The common bond felt through rituals, tradition, and confessions, along with feeling closeness with God, discourages grudge holding. Realizing we are not alone in our journey, and that God and others are with us, helps us find compassion for others and ourselves. Compassion improves our sense of well-being; our happiness increases while our stress decreases. Even our immune systems get stronger, enabling us to be better able to cope with our adversity.

Most of the world's religions emphasize that forgiveness is highly valued. Religious expectations for forgiveness differ among the religions. Yet it appears that a benefit of belonging to religion — any religion — is the help it affords us finding compassion and forgiveness in times of adversity.

Following are some of the variations that exist among the faiths, ranging from some teaching that God unconditionally forgives human offenses, to other religions that believe God will forgive after the offender is brought to justice.

Judaism

Judaism believes that God forgives follower's sins, but Judaism does not teach unconditional forgiveness. Maimonides' Rules of Forgiveness states that forgiveness can only come from the offended person, and that victims should offer forgiveness when the offender has expressed remorse and, if appropriate, offered compensation.

Judaism values significant relationships, and forgiveness is viewed as a pathway to this goal. In fact, one of the most significant Jewish religious holidays is Yom Kippur, the Day of Atonement. Jews devote 24 hours to fasting and asking for forgiveness from God and those they have harmed in the past year.

Followers may seek forgiveness from God for their wrongdoings. But if they have wronged another person they are to ask forgiveness from that person. If this apology is genuine, the victim is expected to grant forgiveness to the offender. The *Torah* reads, "When asked by an offender for forgiveness, one should forgive with a sincere mind and a willing spirit ... forgiveness is natural to the seed of Israel." (Hilkhot Teshuva 2:10) God's assistance is available for those seeking help with self-forgiveness.

While forgiveness may have qualifications, vengeance is shunned in Judaism. "He who takes vengeance or bears a grudge acts like one who, having cut one hand while handling a knife, avenges himself by stabbing the other hand," (Jerusalem Talmud, Nedarim 9:4).

Christianity

While there are variations within the denominations, followers of Christianity are taught that they should forgive others.

Christianity embraces the belief that when Jesus was crucified, he took the punishment for the sins of others so that others could be both spared and forgiven. Followers believe that only through faith in Jesus as their Savior can they can find true forgiveness from God (Ephesians 1:7) and have eternal life.

Unlike Judaism, the expectation is that forgiveness should be unconditional and without requiring remorse from the offender, even if the adversarial behavior has not stopped. When asked by Peter if he should forgive a person who has committed seven offenses against him, Jesus, trusting in his belief that offenders can change, instructed his disciples to forgive again and again, "until seventy times seven." (Matthew 18:21–22)

Hinduism

Hindus see forgiveness as one of the greatest, most significant powers one can possess. This is because forgiveness is seen as being filled with compassion, which in turn controls hatred and intolerance, thereby providing peace and happiness.

Followers of Hinduism believe that through prayer and devotion, God may forgive their wrongdoings. However, forgiveness of others, letting go of anger or retribution, without judgment or apology, is most highly praised. Their ability to forgive is made possible through their belief in the Law of Karma, that choices we make will impact on us in a future life. Offenders are accountable for their adversarial behavior, and will receive consequences for their actions through the Law of Karma, making it unnecessary for the victim to spend the emotional energy plotting revenge. Meanwhile, victims will find it difficult to blame the offender, feel angry or vengeful, or even engage in forgiveness, because they will view the offense to be the wrongdoing be a result of their past actions in this or a previous life.

Buddhism

Buddhism is similar to Hinduism as it focuses more on forgiveness from the perspective of the individual than from a higher power. These Eastern religions focus on insight; learning skills to avoid unhealthy emotions and actions like anger and hatred that would cause us to suffer. To live a spiritual life it is important to have compassion and kindness, because if a life is lived with anger and internal conflict, the consequences (bad karma) may appear in the next life. Siddhartha Gautama Buddha, the sage on whose teachings Buddhism was founded, emphasized the importance of sweeping clear the path of inner pain and negative emotions. "You will not be punished for your anger, you will be punished by your anger."[26]

Resentment that does occur is to be redirected into meditation. People are to release their negative emotions rather than to hope for an apology from the offender. Buddha is quoted as saying, "'He insulted me, he struck me, he cheated me, he robbed me': those caught in resentful thoughts never find peace … those who give up resentful thoughts surely find peace. For hatred does not cease by hatred at any time: hatred ceases by love. This is an unalterable law."[27]

Islam

A final religion to look at with regard to spirituality and forgiveness is Islam. Disciples of Islam believe that God is compassionate and forgiving of those who own responsibility for their wrongdoing, repent their sins, and make a commitment to not repeat the offense. If another person is involved, in addition to these three requirements, the believer must also ask for pardon from the offended person and make amends. The Qur'an reads: "… the recompense for an injury is an injury equal thereto (in degree): but if a person forgives and makes reconciliation, his reward is due from Allah: for Allah loves not those who do wrong." (Qur'an 42:40)

Conclusion

Forgiveness is the penicillin that cures the ails caused by rumination. It heals and strengthens the part of us that anger threatens to injure by altering our perspective of ourselves and other people. When we forgive, we think, feel and act differently about ourselves as well as the offender. It empowers us, saving us from a downward spiral in self-destructive behaviors and poor mental health. Self-forgiveness can prevent declining physical health. Some studies have found that self-forgiveness can even improve treatment outcomes for medical problems ranging from spinal-cord injuries to cancer, whereas the inability to forgive oneself has been associated with a higher risk of dying. When finding forgiveness we are more open to others and our social support system improves, providing us with emotional and material resources. We are more inclined to turn to, instead of shut out, our spirituality.

It is in the interest of all humanity to forgive others and ourselves. The world is filled with diversity in race, religion, politics and basic needs. Conflict between different groups has occurred throughout history, and sometimes the piling up of resentment creates horrific adversarial events. Forgiveness of these grudges does not change the past but it can help us shed the role of victim while also give us the opportunity to let go of destructive feelings connected to the past and move on. The often generations long, never-ending cycle of resentment can be replaced with hope for a future with greater harmony, well-being and life satisfaction.

Unlike the infamous and multigenerational story of unforgiveness from the Hatfields and McCoys, an obscure yet extraordinary societal effort to forgive was once made in a small dairy town located less than a dozen miles away from Randolph Hearst's castle in San Simeon, California. In the late 19th century a feud developed between rival ranchers. The conflict escalated and resulted in one rancher killing another. Local legend has it that the townsmen didn't want to live in a vengeance-fueled community trapped in a never-ending cycle of Wild West shoot-out style retaliations. So, following the death of their neighbor, the community came together and collectively decided to call a truce. To prevent ever repeating the painful tragedy that nearly ruined their community, and to remind themselves of the importance of keeping forgiveness in their lives, they renamed the town Harmony.

Suggested Exercises for Using the Three Spheres of Support to Enhance Your Forgiveness

South African Archbishop Desmond Tutu is quoted as having said that there can be "no future without forgiveness." Forgiveness requires effort. Below is an assortment of techniques to help achieve your goal of forgiveness. Whichever method you choose, it is important to purposefully and steadily set about creating the outcome you want to achieve. Respecting that everyone comes to the issue of forgiveness with different biology, experiences, coping skills and style is important in understanding how to seek forgiveness of our self and others.

Self

1. *Visualize Success*

    You have to be able to see where you are going to get there. Imagine, in your mind's eye, how you would feel if the person who wronged you apologized. Or how you would feel if you apologized to the person you hurt? What would that do for your sense of self-worth, your feelings of worry and anger? How might you react to the person? Practice mentally envisioning a feeling or event you want to have happen. Five minutes each day is all the time you need to commit to this exercise.

2. *Journaling*

    The act of getting in touch with the thoughts and feelings in your head, and transferring them onto paper is powerful with regard to finding forgiveness. It can help clarify what you are thinking and how you are feeling. This is not a graded essay exam, and grammar is not being judged. Write down whatever comes to your mind that is related to the adversarial event. To be effective, however, it helps to set aside about 20 minutes of quiet time each day for this activity. Use pen and paper rather than the computer for this exercise, as it will connect you more closely with the emotions deep inside.

3. *Gratitude*

    Keep the positive side of your life going and growing so as to prevent ruminating about the adversarial event. Recognize and honor the positive interactions you have with others. Support from others helps you experience positive feelings of gratitude, helps nurture your social relationships with others and helps you rebuild your trust. It is good to know that at a time when you have been hurt, you can begin to build trust with others and develop deeper relationships.

    It is natural, when receiving kindness, and feeling appreciative, to want to reciprocate. Doing so helps in achieving forgiveness.

    Make a list of things/events/people for which you have gratitude, and what you are going to do to make them reoccur. Keeping a daily log will help keep your positive emotions flowing.

4. *Letter Writing*

Putting your thoughts down in writing carries more meaning and impact than if you only mull it over and over in your mind. Hand writing a letter is more effective than doing so on the computer. It will connect you more with your heart and genuine feelings, making the exercise more meaningful to you. Use attractive stationary, as this is an important process.

Letter of Forgiveness to Offender

As the victim, write a letter of forgiveness to the offender; not to send, but to document what happened and how the offender's behavior affected you. Write in detail about your feelings towards the offender. Share with the offender what you imagine he or she must have been going through. Include what you imagine it must be it is like having to live with having committed that act. Tell the offender what you wish he or she had done at the time, what you wish he will do now, and end with a statement of understanding and forgiveness. Reassure yourself that you will never allow the offender or anyone else to hurt you in this manner. Reading aloud what you wrote makes this experience even more meaningful.

Offender's Apology Letter

Here, the victim writes an imaginary letter from the offender. Try to envision what the offender would say as an explanation for his behavior, and the hurtful impact on you. The goal of this exercise is for you is to replace feelings of revenge by broadening your perspective. You have the opportunity to understand that the offender made the bad decisions because of information of which you were unaware. Possibilities include the offender not knowing you would be so burdened with pain, or that he or she has a distorted view of the world because of his or her upbringing.

Offender Asking for Forgiveness

This is an acknowledgement of accountability. As the offender, write a letter (never to be mailed) to the person you victimized. Pay a considerable amount of attention to the words you select. Share your feelings about the event, and why you are asking to be forgiven. Do not use this as an opportunity to justify, explain or defend your position. What is important is for you to demonstrate an understanding of how your actions harmed the victim. Acknowledge and validate the victim's feelings. Own responsibility for your actions by offering to make restitution to the person you hurt. Explain how you would respond differently today, if you knew back then what you now know. Finally, share with the victim what you have learned from this event, and what you are doing to change your behavior so that you do not do this again. Do not expect any response in return.

As you describe the hurtful event, think about the feelings you were having and when, in the past, you have had similar feelings. Write them down in detail. What were they in response to? Allow yourself to feel the pain because that is ground zero for the real hurt that caused you to do the hurtful act to someone else.

Write that you forgive yourself because given the opportunity, you know that today you would act differently. You are wiser, have more information, and are more aware of your feelings than you were back then. Decide that while you are not absolving yourself for what you did, that you do not want to burden yourself by having to deal with it all the time. To continue to punish yourself puts you at risk for repeating this behavior.

When the letter is completed to your satisfaction, select a meaningful manner in which to discard it (burning, burying, throwing in ocean, etc.)

5. *Revisit Your Story*

    If you view yourself as a victim of another person, revisit and rewrite the end of your story. Instead, in your mind's eye, make the decision to see yourself as courageous by choosing forgiveness of the person who hurt you.

6. *Meditation*

    Meditation can help transform your perspective and develop a feeling of well-being and compassionate spirituality and tolerance toward all, including yourself. Attend a class in your community, or select a quiet place to sit and clear out your mind. An alternative is to listen to a relaxation recording. Use this technique whenever you begin to feel troubled over the adversity.

7. *Focus On Your Own Shortcomings*

    By examining our own limitations, we can become more tolerant of other's imperfections. Empathy towards others helps with forgiveness.

8. *Honor Your Feelings*

    Suppression of feelings can result in preventing us from being able to identify what feelings are still affected, and understanding why that is so. Get in touch with the feelings you have, and be curious as to why the adversity is upsetting. To not honor your feelings is to risk revisiting those hurt feelings again and again.

Society

1. *Talk As a Couple*

    For a couple sharing the goal of reconciliation, develop ground rules: select a time to talk when you will not have interruptions. Turn off electronics. Agree to not 'kitchen sink' fight by bringing up multiple past resentments. Rather, only discuss one topic at a time. Agree to listen fully to the other person without building up your defense. Listen to the feelings behind the facts, as they tend to typically be more important than the subject. The victim should ask for an apology. The offending partner should acknowledge that this request was made and express an apology as specifically as possible. The victim should offer the partner an acceptance of the apology. Discuss how you will avoid this hurt in the future. Accept the fact that time may be needed after the exercise to allow for healing.

2. *Cultivate Friends*

    Being too busy with work or other commitments interferes with your ability to develop friendships. The more friends you have the more coping skills you will observe for dealing with hurt and angry feelings and approaches to forgiveness. Establish conversations with people about their views.

3. *Establish Boundaries*

    If you are attempting to re-establish a relationship and trust with someone who hurt you, an important step can be your decision to develop better boundaries. Identify what this person did to hurt you, and express clearly to this person why it was unacceptable. Explain what will happen if the person repeats this behavior again, as well as what the positives will be for your relationship if your need is respected.

4. *Protect Family Relationships*

    Your family is your history. Because they know everything about your past, they have a bond with you. Deciding to move beyond the event and remove your bitterness can be the start of a new beginning. Replaying the past in your mind keeps the hurt alive. Modeling empathy, kindness and a commitment to working through emotional pain for your children is important. You will be providing them with tools for forgiving others in their lifetime and showing them how to stop being a victim and take responsibility for their lives.

5. *Do Community Service*

    When you are distressed, your world narrows because you tend to withdraw into yourself. Providing community service can help broaden your view of the world. You will have the opportunity to be exposed to others who also have experienced hardships. Your empathy for others can grow as you imagine what it is like to be in someone else's shoes, you will see how others have coped with the concept of forgiveness, and be able to see different choices you can make for yourself.

Spirituality

1. *Walk in the Woods*

    Getting out of your home and into nature is a way to experience spirituality. You can feel connected with the greater world and get an appreciation of your purpose in this world. It can give you a sense of why you may want to let go of hurt or angry feelings and find forgiveness.

2. *Remember You are Not Alone*

    Regardless of the wrong you committed, or that was committed against you, remember that you are not alone. God will never abandon you. Use this support to resolve pain, find forgiveness and a new purpose in life. Start making a list of what you can do to move forward with your life.

3. *Give Power Back to God*

    It might seem that it is your responsibility to seek justice for the wrong that was done to you. The problem is that this responsibility requires you to hold onto destructive anger and thoughts of retribution. Consider that it may not be you who has to hold onto this anger. Trust that God will take care of justice. Visualize yourself letting go of this anger. As it departs, you can feel your emotional hurt begin to heal.

4. *Join a Religious Community*

    Being able to share your beliefs with others, via prayer and worship, helps provide support and encouragement in difficult times. Studies have found that closeness to God and religion can bring out the best in people, and correlates highly with forgiveness.

Chapter 2

Courage

"Fear and courage are brothers."

— Proverb

Courage. We want it for ourselves. We admire and respect it in others. We lionize courageous individuals into our history books and commemorate their actions by erecting statues. Many religious, as well as secular holidays, are established so that we will remember and teach future generations the stories about courageous behaviors exhibited in past generations.

We often secretly wonder if facing adversity, would we act courageously like our heroes, or be disabled by intense fears?

Adversity impacts on us in every aspect of our lives — spiritually, emotionally, mentally, financially, relationally, and professionally. Courage is an important quality to have, because the greater our courage, the less impact adversity has on our lives. Courage strengthens our determination, gives us the confidence to conquer obstacles, and counteracts the inhibiting impact of fear and uncertainty.

We are surrounded by people who have responded well when faced with adversity. Few people know that Bill Gates' first business, Traf-O-Data, failed. Nonetheless, we all know he went on to become the richest man in the world by launching his software company, Microsoft. Andrew Jackson's father had died before he was born, was orphaned at age 14, grew up without money or much education. When only 13 years old he was captured by the British and held as a prisoner. But he went on to become a lawyer, obtained the rank of Major General in the military, and became the seventh President of the United States.

However, not everyone demonstrates courage when faced with adversity, and there are those who have dealt with it poorly. Most are familiar with one of the most disastrous maritime catastrophes, the sinking of the RMS Titanic. Although Captain Edward J. Smith was officially found to be innocent of any wrongdoing when the ill-fated luxury liner collided with an iceberg, some reports indicated that Captain Smith might have become overwhelmed with fear, resulting in indecisiveness instead of courageously making life-saving decisions. He appeared to have not organized his crew quickly and allowed partially empty lifeboats to leave the sinking ship, knowing there were not enough lifeboats for all passengers and crew. Tragically, over 1,500 people died as a result of the lack of courageous decision-making from the captain. History has viewed Captain Smith's actions poorly, as we tend to scorn leaders who fail to demonstrate courage.

What is Courage?

Courage is often a word associated with facing one's enemy on the battlefield. However, it is "not the act per se that is courage but the inner character of the person expressed through the physical act."[1] Components of courage include the head (thinking about the desired goal), the heart (subjective psychobiological reactions such as fear, doubt, and uncertainty),[2] and feet (not running away in spite of the fear and uncertain probability of success).

Courage is also a relative concept, as what is courageous for one might be ordinary for another. For example, jumping out of an airplane would be a courageous undertaking for this author, who has never engaged in a comparable skydiving experience. However, for thrill seekers or professional jumpers, it may not require courage to execute the jump.

Often, people incorrectly think that to be courageous means to be fearless. That more accurately would be the description of rashness or recklessness. Fear is an unequivocal, inseparable part of courage. In fact, for us to experience courage, we have to have first experienced fear. But when we believe that the goal is worth the risk, we courageously make the decision to push back against our fear and take action.

Different Types of Courage

While we typically associate courage as physical bravery, courage also comes in many other forms. Moral courage involves disregarding our gut instinct to keep our head down and mouth shut, and instead listen to that quiet voice inside, our conscience. Our ethics and integrity compel us to match our words with our behaviors, be it in speaking out, questioning, challenging, or taking a public stand. Social courage involves leadership, as seen in the passengers aboard United Airlines Flight 93 who fought back against their hijackers. They knowingly caused their airplane to crash, killing everyone aboard, in an effort to prevent an attack on the United States Capitol building in Washington D.C. on September 11, 2001. Courage can come in the form of ethical integrity as was repeatedly exhibited by Dr. Martin Luther King when speaking out against racism while receiving recurring death threats and being investigated by the FBI. Several other forms of courage include existential, psychological and political courage.

Courage looks different in different arenas. One of America's earliest courageous moments, and which changed history, was a dramatic decision of political courage by President Abraham Lincoln. In the summer of 1864, Lincoln's campaign managers came to him and said, "Mr. President, you're going to lose re-election this fall, and the reason is that you insist on this Emancipation Proclamation of yours. Many northern voters were willing to fight the Civil War to bring the South back, but not to free the slaves. If you want to be re-elected, get rid of that thing."[3] President Lincoln didn't allow fear to sway him, and our history started righting the wrongs of discrimination and inequality from that decision forward.

Courage may be brash, dramatic and attention grabbing. Who could forget the unknown student protester who faced down and blocked a column of Chinese tanks and the People's Liberation Army during the 1989 student protests in Tiananmen Square? Turning the pages of history back further in time is the example of the lesser-known Rev. Dietrich Bonhoeffer, a Lutheran pastor in Germany during the Nazi regime. Despite personal risk, he publicly criticized the genocidal persecution of the Jews and other minority groups and plotted to assassinate Adolf Hitler. His brave actions were discovered, resulting in his arrest and execution by hanging in 1945.

Courage may also be quiet and only scarcely acknowledged by the individual. Max Desfor, an Associated Press photographer, best known for his heartrending 1951 Pulitzer Prize winning photograph, 'Flight of Refugees Across Wrecked Bridge In Korea,' spent decades traveling the world photographing history being made. His photograph of India's Mahatma Gandhi and Jawaharlal Nehru became a United States postage stamp, and he photographed well-known personalities including the Kennedys, Beatles, Mickey Mantle, Marilyn Monroe, and Queen Elizabeth II when still Princess Elizabeth.

However, his professional exploits were not always glamorous. Often his photography would take him into unsafe, even life threatening situations. On multiple occasions, Mr. Desfor encountered adversity because he was on the front lines during periods of political unrest and war. He was chased with brooms by Japanese envoys after the bombing of Pearl Harbor. He was caught up with the troops when the North Koreans were pursuing the South Koreans. He parachuted from Seoul to Pyongyang, covered the war and war crime trials, and was abruptly hustled out of Tinian because the secret atomic bomb was being readied for Hiroshima. When asked about how he felt when encountering such dangerous obstacles, he gently responds that despite his fear, "I did what I thought was necessary, what I thought was the right thing. It's taking an attitude or defining an attitude. It's part of my life, part of my living, and part of my existence."[4] In other words, despite the dangers, Mr. Desfor followed his inner convictions and ideals that the "deed must be done." In order to satisfy his moral values, he bravely, in a quiet and unceremonious manner, endured life-threatening perils. Mr. Desfor's courage was hinged to his beliefs about civic honor and responsibility, and he pushed through fear so that he could act accordingly.

As you can see, courage evolves for different reasons and is executed differently in different situations. It is a subjective experience, in which each person needs to evaluate his or her commitment to an internal set of principles. Each person must engage in careful moral reasoning and thought as to whether they interpret the situation to be an issue in which they place value. Then they have to ask themselves if it is worth allowing oneself to risk being vulnerable, and if so, what action will be selected to address the issue. Be it bold or quiet, physical or moral, many would agree with psychologist Rollo May's conclusion that the common denominator of "courage is not the absence of despair; it is, rather the capacity to move ahead in spite of despair."[5]

Why is Courage so Important?

The Greek philosopher, Aristotle, believed courage to be the most important quality in a man. "Courage is the first of human virtues because it makes all others possible."[6] When we are courageous, we step outside our comfort zone of predictability and familiarity and are exposed to new ideas. We can take in new information and broaden our understanding of the world, an important tool in overcoming adversity.

Build's Psychological Muscle

Having courage enables us to stay our course when external circumstances threaten to challenge our well-being. It empowers us to confront problems head on, even if having doubts, rather than risk experiencing fear, resignation and victimization. Through courage, we are better able to control our destiny and honor who we are and in what we believe. We have a chance to avoid even greater problems that might have resulted had we not been courageous.

We develop a psychological muscle when we push through fear. This muscle helps us when we need the strength and resilience to overcome or avoid adversity. The more we exercise this muscle, the more our self-confidence and faith will grow. We will feel empowered to confront problems head on and courageous in challenging times that fill us with pain and fear.

Generates Positive Behavior

Courage is good, and courage begets more courage. It is socially contagious because we like what we see in the courageous actions of others and naturally model those behaviors. We learn how courageous people persevere and continue to move towards their goal, even if experiencing fear. We admire their confidence in dealing with adversity and take lessons on how to perform our own acts of courage.

What Courage is Not

We are not born with courage. There are no courageous people because courage is not a fixed trait. It is not in our DNA, and despite how it might appear individuals are not genetically predisposed to either fear or courage. Rather, courage is an attribute that can be developed, and everyone has the equal potential to be courageous.

Instinctive

If courage were an instinctive response, like breathing, swallowing or blinking, we would respond to all events fearlessly. Our reactions would be consistent and our feelings predictable. There would be no emotional meaning to our response, just as there is none to our blinking while reading this text. Instead, courage is reactive and differs for each event. Our ability to respond courageously will depend on many factors, including the amount of fear we are experiencing, our self-confidence in being able to respond, and the meaning the event holds for us.

Fearlessness

As the proverb aptly states, "Fear and courage are brothers." Courage exists because fear exists. Courage is about recognizing our fear, yet finding the strength to push through it. Fear of the situation will be felt psychologically or physiologically — as in anxiety, perspiration, or increased pulse or blood pressure — when we are courageous.

Thrill Seeking

Courage must be done for a meaningful purpose. To act in a way for the purpose of demonstrating bravado is to miss an important component of courage, which is fear. If the motivation is personal enjoyment, such as engaging in high-sensation, adrenaline rush inducing behaviors, the act is not courageous.

Reckless

When engaging in reckless behavior, there is a probability that unnecessary risks are being taken in the absence of deliberately considering one's level of preparedness. Engaging in these endeavors is foolhardy or rash, rather than courageous behavior.

Impulsive

Courage involves an evaluation of what is required in this risky situation. Impulsiveness could lead to overconfidence, resulting in failure to accurately judge the safety of the situation. Tragically struck in 2016, when two BASE jumpers leaped off a 290-foot bridge in Monterey County, California. BASE is an acronym that stands for the four objects from which one can jump: buildings, antennas, span, and Earth. It is considered an extreme and dangerous sport. Jumping off most bridges is illegal and authorities routinely monitor bridges known to attract BASE jumpers to prevent the activity. The jumpers' intent was to leap off the concrete guardrail in the center of the bridge and parachute onto a nearby beach. The GoPro video footage recovered from the helmet of the second jumper shows the woman, who jumped first, missing landing on the beach, being pulled under water by her parachute, and disappearing. The video indicates that when the second jumper landed, he removed his helmet and parachute, and tried to save her, also drowning in his futile attempt. While courage requires risk taking, too much confidence without proper consideration for taking unnecessary risks makes such tragic actions thrill seeking as opposed to courageous acts.

Mandatory
Courage cannot be forced because of pressure from others. Courage is an individual decision to devote ourselves to something bigger than what we currently encounter. When we exhibit courage, it is about opening ourselves more fully to our personal potential in a thoughtful way.

Lack of Emotions
If we do not experience emotions, and are apathetic, we won't be interested in changing our situation or motivated to consider options for moving beyond our adversity. Fear is the primary component of courage. Other emotions, such as anger, excitement, confusion, hurt and joy are also often associated with courageous acts.

Always an Action
Sometimes, not engaging in an activity can be an act of courage. Choosing to not join others in bullying, or an illegal behavior, can involve risks of retribution from those who choose to engage in these behaviors. Taking a position on our values and ethics, and going against the group, can be a courageous decision.

Barriers to Courage

Irrational Fear

John Wayne once said, "Courage is being scared to death — and saddling up anyway."[7] Everyone, even the most courageous among us, experiences fear. Yet the ability to push through fear is the most significant challenge to courage.

Our brains are developed in layers, much like an onion. Scientists have concluded that two of these layers play a very active role with how we respond to adversity, the amygdala and the subgenual anterior cingulate cortex (sgACC).

The amygdala, which is two tiny almond-shaped masses of cells located deep in the primal portion of the brain, stores our memories, including emotions, thoughts, and experiences, of fearful events in our past.

Responsible for our survival, the amygdala, often considered to be the fear center of the brain, is hard wired to react instinctually to protect us from threats of danger. When we sense danger, our amygdala hijacks our normally calm emotions, and fear is only a nanosecond behind. If we respond to one incident with fear, the amygdala will do so again and again and again, every time a similar situation arises. The amygdala does not have time to waste by factoring in reality. It just wants you to hightail it out of there and will respond behaviorally or physiologically with knee-jerk, lightning fast speed.

For example, take the case of a friend startling you by coming up from behind and shouting, "Boo!" The primal part of your brain, the protective amygdala, thrusts into action and unconsciously triggers physical responses of increased heart rate and blood pressure, dry mouth, perspiration, the release of stress hormones, and a general feeling of upset. Your reaction may be fear, and instinctively move away from the perceived threat. These are the physical and behavioral protective responses triggered by your amygdala. This has all happened before you can logically assess what occurred, recognize you are not in danger, and send an "all clear" signal to the amygdala.

The control button for thinking and decision-making is located in an outer layer of the brain called the subgenual anterior cingulate cortex (sgACC). This is the second layer of the brain that plays an active role in our response to adversity, but it plays second fiddle to the amygdala. By the time a thought has passed through the amygdala and reached the sgACC, which is our reasoning portion, our body is already reacting. We are faced with trying to use reason and logic from an outer part of the onion, when the inner amygdala, which responds speedily, already has a jump-start on mounting a protective and often fearful reaction to the perceived danger.

An Israeli study of snakes showed how our brains work to overcome fear and be courageous. Nonpoisonous snakes were placed on a conveyor belt and brought closer and closer to participants. Scientists found that courage exists by managing, not removing, fear.

Participants in the study showed more brain activity in the amygdala when they experienced fear and more brain activity in the sgACC when they intentionally decided to overcome fear and be courageous. The scientists discovered that the two regions in the brain, the amygdala, and the sgACC, are actually in competition with each other for deciding whether we choose to be fearful or courageous.

If participants in the snake study allowed themselves to be fearful, the amygdala would rapidly become more active, and their emotional reaction to the event being a threat would increase. This instinctual reaction can create problems for us as was experienced by one participant's fear, which escalated to the point he had to withdraw from the study. This is understandable, because avoidance makes us feel more comfortable, and therefore is self-reinforcing.

If, however, the participants consciously stepped outside their comfort zone, did not surrender to fear, and allowed the snakes to approach closer, the other region of their brain, the sgACC, would become more active. The sgACC, the thinking part of our brain, is associated with courageous behavior. The more active the sgACC became in the snake experiment participants, the less active their amygdala became. The participants' fear level was decreased, they sweated less, their heart rates slowed down, and their breathing became more normal.[8]

What this means for everyday life situations is that if we push through and show courage we can keep our sgACC activated and cope with fear-related circumstances. Our amygdala is trying to help us, but memories that are triggered can bring up a feeling that a situation may be more unmanageable than it really ought to be, causing unfounded feelings of intense fear. We can find ourselves giving in to our irrational fear before we can even figure out why we are fearsome. It's neurobiology 101: the more we panic the more we will panic. This can create obstacles to overcoming adversity in our lives. Our ability to be courageous is thwarted, and we will more likely trigger a reaction of being overwhelmed and freezing or fleeing. Giving in to avoidance of that which we feared will then make it harder to activate the sgACC and we will be stuck, having conditioned ourselves to be fearful and not believe that we can change our lives.

Age

Young children conceptualize courage differently than older children and adults, and cannot be expected to understand or demonstrate courage in the same manner. Toddlers have limited comprehension of language. Their understanding of emotions is quite basic, and they will be restricted in grasping the meaning of courage. Children under five years of age have short attention spans. This will inhibit their ability to think of anything that is not right at the moment and directly in front of them. It is also possible that if young children do attempt to be courageous, it is because of expectations from an adult caregiver.

But as age increases, so does the understanding of the concept of courage. A German study of 90 children found that children five to six years old perceive courage as being solely comprised of taking physical risks, not viewing fear as a part of courage. Around the age of eight or nine, children are less egocentric and are capable of considering viewpoints of others. They will develop an understanding of and include moral criteria as a motivator for courage. Children nine to eleven years old are at a higher developmental level and are more likely to view it to be more courageous to take a social or emotional risk than a physical risk.

The elderly may conceptualize courage differently than younger adults. The decline of faculties and loss of control and resources in old age may impact on their ability to embrace courage; not wanting to take the same risks they may have when younger. On the other hand, years of experience with varied life events will prepare them to have a realistic level of awareness of costs and benefits to exercising courageous behavior. Their experience with both positive and negative life events has established tried and true chains of behavioral reactions to adversity. The choices they make in a new situation are likely largely determined by past experiences.

How to Use the Three Spheres of Support To Achieve Courage

In the famous movie, *The Wizard of Oz*, the lion needed a heart to find courage. The heart is our inner source of strength. It is the organ that keeps our blood flowing, sustains life and is associated with emotions. It is at our core, and if our core is strong, we will have the courage not to shrink from challenges. We will have the courage to stand by what our heart wants. While courage comes from within, our spheres of support can help us find the courage we didn't know existed. They help us to keep going, to push through crippling fear and despair and to live by our truth. Our supports prevent us from falling and pick us up when we do. It is in our three spheres of support — Self, Society, and Spirituality — that we find the heart to act courageously.

Self

Our thinking can both define our actions, and help provide us with the courage to progress from adversity to resilience. If we perceive ourselves in a healthy manner, we will be able to confront our anxieties and believe that we have the skills necessary to accomplish our goals. We will find ourselves empowered and more resilient, capable of moving forward in life.

Mindset

As addressed in chapter one, researcher Dweck, describes individuals as having either a fixed or growth mindset. People with a fixed mindset believe that success comes without effort; that their primary qualities of intelligence or talent will determine their success. A fixed mindset can stifle their ability to adapt in times of adversity because they are avoiding risk and do not know how to manage challenges.

Those with a growth mindset, on the other hand, focus on their abilities and how they should develop their talents. They take ownership of the need to work hard to make success happen. These are the cornerstones for establishing resilience. A growth mindset requires courage because it hinges on a willingness to learn, unlearn, and relearn, even when there are setbacks and no guarantee of success. In other words, courage is a mindset.

Maxwell Peters, an octogenarian residing in Canada, has exhibited a growth mindset repeatedly throughout his life. World War II intersected with the life of Mr. Peters when he was six years old. Living with his parents and younger sister in Ukraine, he was functionally orphaned when the Nazis executed his mother and exiled his father to Siberia. To survive the hostile environment in which Nazis were exterminating Jews and other minorities, before being exiled, his father handed Mr. Peters and his younger sister to a Polish family. This family concealed the children's real identities and raised them as Catholic cousins. Mr. Peters recalls the World War II period as difficult, austere years. "There was little to eat and a lot of hardship. I didn't own a pair of shoes for three to four years. I would wrap a cloth around my feet. At times, to break away the hunger, I found that to chew up and eat charcoal filled my tummy."

Attempts for personal growth did not come without repeated failures. When the war concluded, Mr. Peters was ten years old. He discovered he was not Catholic, as he had believed, but was Jewish, and most likely an orphan. He decided to leave everything familiar and seek a better existence, even though there was no guarantee or promise of success. Exhibiting a growth mindset at a young age, Mr. Peters states, "I always search out how I can better myself or how I can move on."

Government authorities sent him to live in an orphanage with other Jewish children. Following a narrow escape from a pogrom, Mr. Peters was forced to move again, this time to a converted hotel in France, to live with 300 other orphans. But rather than view the obstacles and repeated failures as barriers, he demonstrated courage time and again by facing the challenges head-on. In doing so, Mr. Peter's courageous approach to his existence helped him develop skills and mastery over an otherwise uncertain future riddled with obstacles.

Aristotle observed that courageous people "are able to assess the danger, their own resources, and then take the proper action."[9] Mr. Peters did exactly that. Dominance ensured survival in the loosely run, poorly supervised facility. He learned that despite being small in stature, he could exert command through agility, wit, and speed. He learned how to develop the courage to resist conformity and instead to rely on his inner beliefs; to develop his view of, and trust in himself. Mr. Peters went to study at the Yeshiva, an institution where Jewish texts are studied. He learned to not fear being different in thought, feelings or behaviors, and to respect differences in others. "At the Yeshiva we could argue over one sentence for an hour, trying to interpret the way you see it and the way they see it. That Yeshiva taught me how to listen to everybody else. Going through this gave me an understanding of how to deal with myself and the world. Nothing is black or white," recalls Mr. Peters. "This gave me my primary education because I never had formal education whatsoever."[10]

His growth mindset, as opposed to fixed mindset, was being honed. This foundation of embracing change, being open-minded and flexible, opened up his willingness to learn new ways to relate to society and life. Rather than cowering and retreating when granted asylum to Canada at age 16, Mr. Peters fervently studied his Canadian peers, eager to learn new perspectives. He embraced his new reality rather than retreating from it by listening to what his friends divulged of their parents' views and behaviors, as he had no similar role models. Over the years, as he entered the work force, he didn't get discouraged by what he didn't know or by occasional failures, but instead continued to learn. By talking with others he learned how to seek better wages, to not allow his heavy accent be a deterrent from successfully selling men's clothing, and how persistence could help him get a loan from an acquaintance when the banks refused.

Mr. Peters was not given many gifts early in life. But with each risk he undertook, he increased his self-mastery, self-confidence, and reduced his possibility of failing. Continually confronting his fears when struggling and making mistakes, he persevered, believing that the skills he needed could be learned. This growth mindset provided Mr. Peters with the courage to overcome what many would view as overwhelming obstacles. Staying motivated to adapt over the years to challenging political, social and economic situations enabled Mr. Peters to move successfully through decades of adversity, eventually have a family, and establish a thriving real estate development, management and consulting company.

Self-Efficacy

When we have the belief that we have the ability to face our fears, we are more likely to act courageously. This feeling of competence helps us choose action and growth over staying stuck with the safe and familiar.

If we have had success dealing with similar crises in the past, then we will have the realistic conviction that we can successfully cope with today's challenge. We will believe that we can make tough decisions and face unknown risks. On the other hand, if we run into a problem when experiencing a situation outside our comfort zone we may become uncertain, stressed and forget the skill set we used in the past. We will then develop self-limiting beliefs and lose the ability to look past our immediate circumstances. As a result, our conviction about being able to make decisions drops, our anxiety intensifies, and we find ourselves stuck.

Holding on to our feelings of self-efficacy is vital when dealing with difficult times, but sometimes it feels impossible; like sand sifting through our fingers. Some people find that sitting down and writing a list of past experiences and detailing what they did to overcome these situations will help remind them of their inner source of strength and sustenance, rather than focusing solely on their perceived weaknesses. Others prevent themselves from becoming overwhelmed by the enormity of what needs to be done by taking small steps to improve their confidence before moving on to bigger tasks. These feelings of success give them the confidence to take risks outside of their comfort zone again and again, in a graduated manner.

Another way to increase confidence when we are facing an obstacle we fear is to participate in behaviors that reduce our anxiety and give us a sense of control. Athletes are notorious for engaging in ritualistic behaviors that allow them the illusion of being in control of a stressful situation. Ice hockey's Anaheim Ducks has Corey Perry, who performs an eight-step ritual before every game that includes tapping the ice and doorframes. Former major league baseball player Turk Wendell would leap over the baseline when leaving the field, crouch when the pitcher stood, chew four pieces of black licorice (because he didn't like chewing tobacco) when pitching, spit them out and brush his teeth at the end of each inning. Two-time world champion bull rider Julio Moreno keeps the same four coins, one dime and three pennies, in his pocket, with Abraham Lincoln and Franklin Roosevelt's heads facing up. The champion bull rider is now a stock contractor, but still carries the same 13 cents in his pocket.

Little has changed for these athletes by engaging in ritualistic behaviors. But they have discovered ways to feel more confident and in control rather than having to white knuckle the situations. Research finds that believing in the value of these repetitive or rigid behaviors has a positive effect by improving confidence and may actually increase the athlete's success. Instead of focusing on their fear of failure and their limitations, they are able to change their attitudes, increase their confidence, and break down psychological barriers that would otherwise distract them from their ability to perform. Their use of superstitions and rituals enables them to build their courage and use the skill set they already have within themselves.

Actions such as list writing, taking incremental steps and engaging in rituals can serve to strengthen everyone's muscles of courage. In turn, we will be able to face challenges head-on, develop the resilience needed when faced with adversity, and get to "keep on keepin' on."

Learning Through Exposure

Be the stimulus a spider, a bully, or fear of drowning, scientists and psychotherapists are in agreement that one of the best ways to learn to overcome whatever we fear is through repeated exposure.

Exposing ourselves involves pushing through the eye of the storm of fear; to decide not to listen to the scripts in our head that encourage us to play it safe and avoid further stress.

It goes without saying that this is easier said than done. We've been running away from fear for as long as mankind has existed. Long ago, when our cave-dwelling ancestors had to deal with dangerous wooly mammoths and saber-toothed tigers, being able to react fast to danger could mean the difference between life and death. Fortunately, through exposure, we can create positive experiences and learn new skills to reduce our fear. The benefit will be a reduction of fear's grip on us, and we will be less avoidant of that which we fear. There are likely limitless ways we can get exposure to a stimulus we fear, reduce our distress, and enhance our courage.

Five Approaches to Enhancing Courage Through Exposure to Feared Stimulus

1. Cognitive Reappraisal
One technique used by psychotherapists is called cognitive reappraisal. During periods of high stress, we can learn to re-interpret the meaning of an emotionally upsetting adversity. By revisiting how we responded emotionally to the event, we may be able to modify our view of what happened, and end up decreasing our stress.

For example, assume a little boy walking down the street encounters a large dog wandering around off leash. The boy is scared and runs off. The dog, upon seeing the running child, responds instinctively, chases the boy and bites him in the leg. Remembering this incident, the boy now develops an irrational fear of all dogs. The brain is not considering the fact that small dogs, or walking instead of running by dogs, or dogs on leashes across the street, do not pose a threat.

There are three new thoughts that must accompany our revisiting of these stressful situations, and timing is critical. First, as soon as the negative thought comes in, we should immediately adopt a better perspective. An example is going from thoughts that "That dog is going to bite me," to redirected thoughts of, "That dog is wagging his tail and looks perfectly happy." The second step is to find a better outcome. An example is changing our perspective by going from feeling like a victim and thinking, "I'm powerless against dogs," to "Dogs respond well to me when I consider their instinctive reactions as well as mine." The third step is to redirect our focus by believing the future will be better. An example is going from, "I need to avoid all dogs," to "Dogs are like people; some are nice and some aren't."

2. Flooding
Another practical approach used by behavioral psychologists is termed flooding therapy. It consists of repeatedly exposing a person to that which they fear. The goal is for us to learn to face, rather than avoid our fear. We will be very upset, and even overwhelmed, when exposed to the stimulus that created our original fear. But adrenaline and fear response has a time limit, and when

we calm down, we will realize that our extreme anxiety was unnecessary. After repeated exposure, we will become desensitized to the stimulus and the emotional hold it had on us will be either diminished or resolved.

An example of flooding can be explained by the fear of spiders. A big spider, like a tarantula could be brought into the room, providing you with the opportunity to see it up close. Your heart will race, and your amygdala will be advising you to hightail it out of that room. But if you stay, you will slowly get desensitized to the spider, lessening the power of the spider, and reducing the amount of fear you are experiencing.

You may never want to become an arachnologist, but through flooding, you have successfully re-wired your deepest instincts of fleeing, and have learned the skill of facing rather than avoiding your fears. This skill is valuable in finding the courage necessary to push through fears when overcoming adversity.

3. Differential Reinforcement
We have the ability to learn courage all the time, and often do so in our everyday lives. We learn by observation, reinforcement, and encouragement by others around us. One approach psychologists find success is called differential reinforcement.

Differential reinforcement of courage means that people can teach others to be courageous by supporting wanted behaviors, and extinguishing the unwanted ones. Reinforcement can be whatever the individual desires, like attention, pleasure, money, etc. Reinforcement is time sensitive because it must be provided consistently, and ideally, verbally and with eye contact. It's like lying in wait to catch the person doing something that we want to reinforce and then happily pouncing on that behavior.

The behavior that is not desired is ignored. This is different from punishment. Ignoring unwanted behavior is difficult, but can be achieved by breaking eye contact, using silence, or ignoring the person immediately following the event. By ignoring the behavior, the reinforcement of attention is removed, and the negative behavior goes away.

I can draw from a personal experience as a parent using differential reinforcement. When my daughter, Rachel, was three years old, I had a predictable nighttime routine for her; bath, book, bed. But that is when the nightmares for me often began. Many children are afraid to stay in bed alone at night. There is so much going on; the boogeyman is hiding under their bed, the stuffed animals are looking at them funny, or it is too dark/light/noisy.

Rachel would often pop out of bed and come to my room at all hours. Night after night of this left me quite un-amused. I became aware that I was likely reinforcing this nerve-wracking behavior by talking sweetly to her, rubbing her back and giving her loads of attention when she showed up in my room. Sometimes, I gave her negative attention, because I was annoyed that after all the time I devoted into her nighttime routine, she would bounce back like a boomerang. But be it positive attention or negative attention, it was attention that this three-year-old wanted. Either way, when I sent her back to her room, she'd howl like a wet cat.

I decided to reinforce the behavior I wanted with the invention of the 'surprise drawer.' I filled a drawer in my bedroom with very inexpensive, often less than a dollar, items that would interest her. If Rachel remained in bed throughout the night, she had the privilege of selecting one item from the surprise drawer the following morning. If she came out of bed in the middle of the night, she would forfeit her right to the surprise drawer. We discussed the rules, and Rachel understood. She also understood that if she was ill, she could get out of bed without sabotaging her eligibility for a toy the next morning.

The program worked like magic. Rachel wasn't perfect, and one in a while, especially initially, she popped out of bed. In a very even, flat, non-judgmental tone I would inform her that she wasn't eligible for a gift the next morning and that she had to go back to bed. I would remind her that tomorrow was another day, and she'd have a brand new chance to earn a toy the following night. That gave her hope while I gave her nothing regarding emotional reinforcement — no backrubs, little eye contact, and no chitchat — for coming out of bed.

Mornings were fun because I got to 'catch my daughter being good.' By rewarding the positive behavior of staying in bed with a token toy, praise, and smiles the following morning, and extinguishing the negative behavior of showing up in my room at all hours of the night, Rachel quickly found the courage to stay in bed all night long, exemplifying how easy the differential reinforcement process can be.

4. Modeling

Modeling is another way we learn courage, as we imitate what we see and like. Modeling of courage can come from direct contacts, such as close relationships, or it can be found indirectly, such as learning about a person's courage through history, movies or books. From the time we are toddlers, we are modeling or imitating the courageous behavior of others whom we admire.

With time, we build up our ability to make courageous decisions about dealing with adversity by patterning courageous behavior of others.

It has been established that for combat soldiers, one of the most important influences in their ability to survive on the battlefield is having a leader who demonstrates both moral and physical courage. Observing how, in adverse times, their leader uses stubbornness, imagination, and discipline, helps provide the soldiers with a model for skills on acting courageously during critical wartime experiences.

5. Trial And Error

The willingness to venture into the unknowns of trial and error is how we courageously become the person that we were meant to be. This means we feel safe enough to question what we previously believed, and have the personal choice to change our views if we have new information. In a nutshell, it is about becoming self-confident in being able to admit and accept our thoughts, feelings, and behaviors. When we courageously resist conformity, we become individuals. And once we do, we are never the same again. Scientists have determined that the plasticity of our brain — the amazing ability to reorganize and develop new pathways in our brain throughout our lives — is a key player in this growth.

In a three-month study on the development of mice, German researchers found that there was a change in the structure of their brains, depending on whether the mice explored their vast and complex enclosure a lot or just a little. Even though the mice were inbred and nearly genetically identical, they developed very different personalities. The exploring mice became more self-reliant, more independent, and explored even more. This occurred because the exploring mice grew far more new nerve cells in their hippocampus than the less exploring mice. The hippocampus is a brain region crucial for emotions, learning and memory. This study shows us that brains can change when we have new experiences. Whereas the mice all started out being very similar, trial and error made some more capable and self-reliant. In other words, the adventuresome and less adventuresome mice became less similar and more unique. Confucius made this observation over 2,500 years ago, when he said, "By nature, men are nearly alike; by practice, they get to be wide apart."[11]

Like the adventuresome mice, if we venture out of our comfort zone, we can learn new skills that will help us become more capable, self-reliant thinkers. These new skills, learned through trial and error, support us in becoming increasingly better equipped to be courageous.

Personality Traits

Personality traits make up who we are. They are observable behaviors that we can easily see in others. For instance, they are exhibited in that person we know whose personality is warm, and in another whose personality is detached, in the one who has high energy and in another who is relaxed.

Dr. Salvatore Maddi, professor and founder of the Hardiness Institute at the University of California, Irvine, discovered the personality trait of hardiness to be a core influence in our ability to have courage in times of adversity. It is well known that intense or prolonged stress can wreak havoc on our bodies and our minds. In 1981, the Illinois Bell Telephone Company experienced a deregulation and divestiture and had to fire half of the 26,000 employees in less than one year. Nearly two-thirds of the terminated employees suffered emotionally, including depression, anxiety and burnout. They suffered physically with heart attacks, strokes, and obesity. They suffered socially with divorces and substance abuse, and they suffered professionally, with burnout, poor performance reviews, and demotions.[12]

Interestingly, Maddi, who worked with the divestiture, found that the remaining one-third of the terminated employees had fewer physical illness symptoms, and their family relationships were not negatively impacted. Their perspective on dealing with adversity, along with their coping mechanisms differed from the other two-thirds of the terminated employees.

Maddi determined that the individuals who dealt well with adversity had healthy coping strategies, which he labeled as 'HardiAttitudes.' The three components of HardiAttitudes consist of commitment, control, and challenge, all which give us the courage to grow following traumatic events. Commitment is the belief that we have value and importance. It means that no matter how rotten life can seem, it is still best to hold onto a strong sense of meaningful purpose, and stay involved with people and events around us rather than to become alienated or isolated. Control is about not expecting that good things will be handed to us. Rather than feeling passive and powerless, control is an attitude of staying put in the driver's seat, so to speak, and doing what we can to make things happen to our advantage. And last, challenge is about believing that nothing remains the same forever; that life happens, and in it will be stressful experiences. But we can use these stressful experiences as an opportunity to learn and grow.

These 3Cs — commitment, control and challenge — helped employees of the Bell Telephone Company find resilience under stress and the courage to keep going. We can experience the resilience to adversity as well. If we adapt the HardiAttitudes mindset, we will experience less strain when dealing with a long and protracted hardship, and be flexible and willing to step outside of our comfort zone during times of change. By doing so, we will be able to look at the bigger picture, a perspective which always helps with problem-solving. We will be able to think clearly and problem solve rather than feeling powerless and inclined to withdraw from them. We can turn problems into an opportunity to learn and grow as we work our way through adversity.

The HardiAttitudes are directly related to the three spheres vital in overcoming adversity; Self, Society, and Spirituality. Our Self (physical and mental health) will be enhanced through the attitudes of control. Our Society (social relationships) will be improved through a commitment to others. Our Spirituality (a deeper sense of meaning) will help us have the courage to address things beyond our control.

Neuroplasticity

Research in neuroscience in the past two decades has debunked the long-held belief that our brains are fully formed in that critical window of birth to five years old. It turns out that our brains are more social and flexible than previously thought. They continually develop and change throughout life, being shaped and reshaped by our relationships; how we communicate, interact and feel about others. As noted by Dr. Charles Nelson of the Harvard Medical School, "Our genes supply the basic blueprint for brain development, but experience adjusts the underlying brain circuitry based on the unique environment in which each individual lives."[13]

As mentioned earlier regarding the brains of mice changing through trial and error, this process of the brain being able to change and create new pathways and connections is called neuroplasticity, and it is very helpful to us when facing difficult times. If we use positive approaches when dealing with adversity, positive changes in our brain will be triggered. We can intentionally change our thoughts about what we fear. We can change the self-limiting stories we have in our head that tell us we aren't capable of achieving a goal. The end result of this marvelous process is that we will be rewiring our brains and developing valuable 'courage muscles.'

Vulnerability

The French word for courage essentially means 'from the heart.' If you have ever experienced a meaningful relationship, then you realize that to have heart requires the willingness to be vulnerable. Dr. Brene Brown, the author of *Daring Greatly*, writes that courage and vulnerability are closely associated with each other. She has found that innovation, creativity, and change are possible because we have the courage to drop our guardedness, allow ourselves to be vulnerable, and step outside of our comfort zone.

It is entirely understandable why we choose to shield ourselves from vulnerability — we want to protect ourselves from being hurt. By playing it safe and not taking risks with uncertain or uncomfortable feelings or events, we don't have to risk failure. But there is high cost we pay in playing it safe. We cut off the opportunity to be honest or genuine when we try to resolve our adversity. We then lose our ability to be connected to our true selves and end up becoming frustrated. The result is we lose our heart, or courage.

Vulnerability in problem resolution is important in all spheres of our lives. Seth Goldin, in his book, *Tribes: We Need You To Lead Us*, sees the relationship between vulnerability and leadership, and the importance of allowing people to see who we really are. He writes, "It's uncomfortable to propose an idea that might fail. It's uncomfortable to challenge the status quo. It's uncomfortable to resist the urge to settle." Yet he emphasizes that without allowing ourselves to move into that position of vulnerability, " … it's almost certain you're not reaching your potential as a leader."[14]

Not only is vulnerability a highly regarded element of uncovering courage, it is clear that vulnerability begets vulnerability in others. In a doctoral research project Peter Fuda, Ph.D. and Richard Badham, Ph.D. found that when business leaders find the courage to allow themselves to be vulnerable, a "snowball effect" occurs, with subordinates quickly following suit. No longer viewing vulnerability as a weakness, protective barriers of perfection that people assume in the workplace are replaced with increased collaboration and relating in a more honest manner. As Fuda and Badham's snowball theory describes, this vulnerability starts from top leadership, and rolls throughout the company, gaining momentum and providing benefits.[15]

The consensus, in both personal and professional relationships, is that vulnerability and courage work hand in hand in helping us step outside of our zone of safety to develop resilience in times of adversity.

Compassion And Mindfulness

Dacher Keltner, Ph.D., author of *Born To Be Good*, finds compassion to be "a progenitor of courageous acts."[16] How? Courage is about the mind and heart, and compassion is the glue that binds them.

When we are consumed with fear, our courage shrinks. When dealing with adversity, this is akin to pouring gas on a fire. Compassion for others and ourselves calms our internal fires. It impacts on how we relate to the rest of the world by keeping us more aware, less judgmental, and more forgiving of what others say, feel or need.

It helps us recognize the importance of opening our hearts, and focusing on the meaning and purpose of life, rather than putting up barriers. When compassionate we remain aware of positive feelings. This gives us the courage to push forward and take risks rather than avoid connecting with others.

Stephen Madelon, 23 years old, of Amsterdam, New York, knows firsthand the power of compassion in times of adversity. In 2014, Mr. Madelon was laid off from his job the day after Christmas. He was feeling stressed, worried about being able to care for his 3-month-old daughter and his fiancée. He recalls feeling, "down on my life, and never experiencing anything as burdening as this before."

"I was feeling powerless. I just lost my job but there's nothing I can do. You can walk around and try to find a job but it is such a small town, where is there really to go?" A couple of months later, still unemployed, unhappy, and sleeping on the cold floor — the couple could not even afford a bed — Mr. Madelon woke up to a massive snowstorm. He thought, "I'm wasting my day, so why not make that day for somebody else?" He posted a notice on Craigslist offering to shovel the driveways of people who needed it.

By the end of the day he had shoveled 20 driveways and sidewalks. He refused all offers of payment but engaged in conversations with the homeowners. He was tired, but noticed, "the struggles weren't there" anymore. "I just feel amazing when I go out and do something for people," Mr. Madelon recalls. "Anytime I give to somebody in need, I feel great. I did a lot of giving so I felt really good at the end of the day."[17]

When we are compassionate, we reap the benefits similar to those experienced by Mr. Madelon. In fact, we are hardwired to be compassionate, and the evidence has been proven through multiple studies. Neuroscientists have discovered that alarm signals in the brain are set off when we detect stress in others, activating portions of the brain to respond empathically with offers of help.

Nowhere is this more evident than in the behavior of new parents. Emory University neuroscientists discovered that there is a reason that otherwise unemotional parents get all googly-eyed when talking to their babies, and become obsessively worried about their health and safety. Parents that are deeply involved with their babies experience an increase in activity in the parts of the brain that control empathy, anxiety, and social interaction. This activity is so consistent and repetitive that their brain anatomy changes. They experience a rise in compassion as a stronger connection between the mind and the heart is established. While the pathways for developing this compassion differ by gender, both men and women experience similar changes in their brains.

Our olfactory system is further proof of our being biologically designed to experience compassion. Were you ever told as a little child to act calm around a scary dog because it can smell your fear? It turns out that all mammals can smell fear because stress or anxiety can rewire the brain. This process, which occurs unbeknownst to us, is fascinating. When we are stressed or anxious, chemical changes occur inside of us, and we emit an unpleasant odor. These smells usually fall below our radar, but the noses of others smelling us know stress and can't be so easily fooled. This information about our anxiety is sent to the section of the brain that controls empathy towards other people. Through this process, others can subconsciously 'read' us when we are upset and understand our feelings and thoughts.

Compassion can be learned, and mindfulness is a tool for doing so. They are so closely intertwined that they have been described as 'two different wings of the same bird.' Mindfulness refers to the ability to be aware of the present, without judgment. By being in the present, we can be more open to new experiences. We're not worrying about tomorrow and we're not making judgments about yesterday. Free of worry and judgment, we are able to expand our ability to be kind to and accepting of ourselves, have more compassion towards others, and have a broader perspective of humanity.

The blend of compassion and mindfulness results in a positive rewiring of the brain. The brain of a Tibetan monk, who spent decades practicing mindful and kindness related thinking was found to measure the highest level of compassion-related neural communication in the left frontal lobes, which is where emotion regulation and positive emotions, is stored.

Compassion and mindfulness provide an essential foundation on which courage can be developed. It is promising to know that we don't have to go to the extreme, such as living the life of a monk and devoting our lives to mindfulness, or shoveling snow off of driveways all day, to develop compassion. Engaging in compassion meditation for only 30 minutes each day has been found to result in changes in the regions of the brain responsible for empathy, understanding others, emotion regulation, and positive emotions. This is able to occur, according to Donald Altman, a former Buddhist monk, and author of several books, including *101 Mindful Ways To Build Resilience* and *Clearing Emotional Clutter,* because when the brain gets emotionally upset, "all of the blood from the thinking (part of the) brain goes down to the inner core of the brain. In times like this, we are not necessarily thinking very clearly, and can become over-reactive and behave in ways that in retrospect do not make us very proud. Daily meditation allows us to reactivate the thinking brain when we get emotionally upset by helping us notice our emotions and constructively distance from our (negative) reactions."[18]

Learning to regulate our emotions not only helps us have clarity of thinking, which helps us with compassionately approaching our suffering and the suffering of others, but it can help us spiritually by increasing our sense of meaning and life purpose. As a result, we become more resilient when encountering adversity.

Creativity
Creativity is necessary for courage, because it enables us to step out of the box of what we already know, and figure out a new way to resolve our problem. To move into the realm of being creative, we have to let go of the familiar way of looking at addressing a problem and be open to trying new approaches. We have to value the process of learning, and accept that we may stumble a few times but believe that with tenacity we can find the resolution we are seeking.

Creativity is precisely what Alain Basto drew on for his survival. Born and raised in Cuba, Mr. Basto loved his extended family, his friends, and his seaside home. But he also realized he had no control over his life while living under Fidel Castro, the president and dictator of Cuba. Following the Revolution, family farms were nationalized, and the government determined what food the families were permitted to keep for themselves. As a result, Mr. Basto witnessed his family going without food at times, despite the fact that the family had livestock and grew an abundance of bananas.

When he was 16 years old, the government sent Mr. Basto to serve in the armed forces in Angola, as part of the Russian navy. After discharge from the military, Mr. Basto was expected to sign paperwork, pledging his commitment to the Communist party. He refused. Over the next several years, he repeatedly rejected the government's expectation that he commit to communism, suffering a greater loss of control over his life with each refusal.

His first refusal of communism resulted in the government denying his career choice of becoming a marine biologist, despite ranking number six in the entire city of Havana in his test scores. He was ordered by the government to go instead into medicine. The second time he refused to sign his allegiance to the communist party the government abruptly halted his medical training. Having to change his career again, Mr. Basto found work as an optometrist in a large hospital. But in 1993 his uncle, who also worked in the same hospital, escaped from Cuba. "When he left, they made my life miserable. The secret service called to see if I knew about it, and why he did it. I was blindsided. I didn't know my uncle was planning to leave. So I had to leave the hospital. I went to a new job and started welding."

Mr. Basto was finding life in to be overwhelmingly stressful. His attempts to find security in a career, to be confident of having enough food to eat, and to make his life work within the existing political system repeatedly failed. He realized that his values alienated him from the communist government and that if he continued, he would have either lived a life of meaninglessness or locked up in prison.

In his despair, he realized he needed a more creative solution for his life. "In 1994 my neighbor, who used to be a very good friend of the Coast Guard, said, 'You know, for a week, the Coast Guard is not going to be patrolling the coastline. So if for any reason you want to go, this is a good time to leave Cuba.' On August 01, 1994, I put an inner tube in the water and left."

Creativity, when applied to adversity, is often solitary work. This is because the process of working through adversity is very personal. It requires reflection and the building of confidence. Sometimes, being social can inhibit the opportunity for reflection because we are inhibited or influenced by others. Mr. Basto recognized that he had to choose an independent path with no feedback from others, so as to not be distracted from his goal. Mr. Basto realized that by going against the status quo, he was engaging in a dangerous act and that to disclose his plans to his family was to place their lives in danger. "I told no one I was leaving. I left everyone, the whole nucleus of my family, my mother, father, sisters, uncle, two grandparents, all my childhood friends."

Mr. Basto's courage carried him through five days of ensuing hardship. He was terrified but drew on considerable mental stamina and physical strength to survive the harsh conditions. Knowledge that setting out on an inner tube was his one hope of not being defeated by the communist regime helped him overcome his fear of being captured or perishing at sea.

"The sun was horrible," he recalls. "I had a bandana on my head. On it, I put my name and date of birth. If I died, I'd float for a few hours. They take your name and notify your mother. You have probably a 60 percent chance to be dead in two days, and a 40 percent rescue. The first day was fine but the second day there was a storm. The sun really kills you. You have to cover your eyes because the reflection of the water goes into your eyes and burns the retina."

"I was worried the second day, because I could still see the mountains of Cuba. If you got caught by the coast guard more than 12 miles out, they would kill you. Sometimes they go into the international water, tie bags of sand to you, and drown you. Many, many of those cases occurred. I know, because, in the military, they tell you those things. It was illegal to leave Cuba. Cuba was called the biggest prison in the world, 11 million people."

His fear, channeled into courage and creative problem solving, reduced his vulnerability at sea and increased his chances of survival. "On the third day, I started seeing buses, bus stops, and people walking around. I knew half of my brain was going out, so I tied myself in with rope. That is what happens when you get dehydrated; you start seeing things that aren't there. Many people pass away after four or five days because of dehydration."

After five days at sea on an inner tube, Mr. Basto was picked up by rescuers and transferred to Guantanamo Bay. "I was there one year and three months. I was one of the first ones to get there and pretty much the last one to leave because I didn't have a sponsor."

Mr. Basto's struggle to search for an existence that had meaning rather than surrender to a life of powerlessness, and to not be afraid of creatively stepping outside his comfort zone helped his ability to push through hardship and overcome adversity. His commitment to persevering is summed up in his reflections about deciding to leave Cuba. "On the raft, I had only one thing on my mind, and that was to leave Cuba. I would have loved to die if I had to go back. I didn't want to see land."[19]

Flexibility

The quote, "It is not the strongest of the species that survive, nor the most intelligent, but the one most responsive to change," is often attributed to Charles Darwin, evolutionary theorist.[20] Responsiveness requires flexibility or compromise. Resistance to flexibility occurs when people are uncomfortable and afraid of altering the way they are used to operating their lives. Instead, they prefer a familiar status quo, even if their current way of approaching a situation is not working.

Openness to change is a vital component of courage. Without consideration of the idea that there might be another way of viewing a situation, the possibility of moving forward is unlikely. If we do not think about different options, we will find ourselves unable to get beyond obstacles blocking our path and preventing us from reaching our goals. To be flexible is to relinquish control to a certain extent, step outside of our comfort zone, consider other options at a time of uncertainty, and be open to responding differently than we have done so in the past. It means to not let our current beliefs, attitudes, traditions or knowledge get in the way when what we really need most is to be flexible. For it is flexibility that will help us remain agile, open to learning, and able to develop creative ways to find resilience.

Silvio Scaglia, 56, didn't step out of his comfort zone as much as he was pushed. On Forbes Magazine's 2010 list of 1,000 wealthiest billionaires in the world, founder of Fastweb, and owner of companies including Elite Modeling and La Perla, Mr. Scaglia was accustomed to having control over his destiny. That all changed in February 2010. While vacationing and working in Antigua with his family, he learned the Italian government had issued a mandate for his arrest, accusing him of money laundering and international tax fraud. He promptly returned to Italy to cooperate. What followed were three years of adversity. He was incarcerated in prison for three months and then placed on a stringent house arrest for another year. He had to endure 147 legal hearings and millions of dollars in legal fees before he was acquitted of any criminal involvement with tax evasion and declared fully innocent of all charges.

Mr. Scaglia used flexibility throughout his ordeal as a way to stay in control and to maintain his integrity, values, and perspective. Believing he had done nothing wrong and wanting to "clear my name," he returned to Rome on his terms, hiring a private jet rather than risk facing the public spectacle of being arrested at the national airport.

Arrested upon entry to Italy, he was immediately sent to jail. Finding himself in a dire situation, Mr. Scaglia recalled stories passed down in his family about adversity, and lessons from his religious faith, all which helped him create the right mindset to be flexible in an inflexible environment. "When you hear parents telling you about World War II, or grandparents telling you about World War I, then you think, this is nothing. It helps to have the awareness that these things happen and that you really have to endure some difficult times in your life." He similarly credits Christianity, stating, "you understand that suffering is a part of life, and is a precious part of life. Through suffering you better understand yourself, you better understand the meaning of life."

Mr. Scaglia was open to change. "The biggest difficulty in jail is spending time, to not let the boredom kill you. So I studied Chinese. I had an interest in China, so I decided this is my chance to dedicate some time and learn something. I did quite well."

More accustomed to thinking long term about the structure, trends and uncertainties of his many businesses which employed over 30,000 people, Mr. Scaglia quickly recognized that he had to adapt his way of thinking to the current situation if he was going to survive emotionally in jail. He states that he learned to "try living moment by moment. To not to look too far in the future but live every single moment, trying to find a good moment, an interesting moment. Even in jail, it is possible, if you look hard."

The emotional flexibility Mr. Scaglia exhibited during his protracted legal battle served him well. "I feel stronger. I am happy to have faced the tough battle. I am even happier to have won it. But I would have been happy to do it, to come back to Italy, even if I would have lost my battle. I tend to be more sure of myself, of my values, of what I consider to be right or wrong."[21]

Society

Dr. Adler, a physician and psychologist, believed that everything about our existence is socially related and that we are all intimately connected with other people. If all of our problems have a social component, then involvement with others will provide us with the courage we need to resolve them.

Encouragement

Encouragement is the nonjudgmental recognizing and accepting of another person. It helps cut through our fear of the unknown, which creates inaction and a feeling of powerlessness, and increases confidence in our ability to cope with stress and overcome obstacles. As the recipient of encouragement, we feel valued, as is evidenced widely, from parenting to the military. Parents who provide support to their children raise them to perceive themselves as being able to cope with life's challenges. They will have an easier time handling conflicts, relating well with others, and view the world as a safe place in which they can interact.

A study of World War II revealed that aircrews received four times as many medals as combat soldiers. What was in the special sauce? Encouragement. Encouragement gave them the confidence to make tough decisions, try something new and face unknown risks. It also led to high motivation, high morale and self-confidence, thereby influencing more courageous behavior. The aircrews were willing to risk failure and make decisions in the hope of finding a solution to their problems.

During challenging times, when we feel vulnerable and lose confidence in ourselves, encouragement from our social relationships reminds us of our strengths. Social support helps us feel safe enough to let go of our fear, confident enough to be vulnerable, and courageous enough to step outside of our comfort zone in times of adversity.

In the 1990s, Ron Lum Shue Chan was in training to become an Advanced Combat Leader in the Canadian army, The Commonwealth Regimental System. Mr. Chan describes himself as not having the strength or endurance of others in the training. But he made friends easily; was amiable and often helped others in his barracks by ironing their uniforms to meet the strict requirements of the army.

During a 30 km training march with a full backpack designed to weed out the weak, Mr. Chan was tested beyond his ability. Because the sergeants "knew I was physically weaker, they had me perform duties that required more physical strength, especially on a long march. While others had to carry the rifle and backpack and helmet, I was the one who had to carry the light machine gun, which is a heavier piece of equipment, and munitions, and was a part of the machine gun crew," recalls Mr. Chan.

"They would have this march, and they would say, 'you can get on the truck if you want, but as soon as you get on the truck you are going home to your home unit. You have failed the course." As he approached the last five kilometers, Mr. Chan recognized that he did not have the physical capacity to complete the course, and feared that, "I wasn't going to make it." Giving up became a possibility. But, "at the last 5 kilometers one person took the machine gun from my arms, and the ammo went to someone else, another two of my buddies pretty much dragged me across the finish line." This encouragement boosted his confidence, giving him the courage to try harder and endure the challenge. "I passed the course," he proudly recalls.

Mr. Chan attributes the support he had extended to the others in his troop as a causal factor in his being able to overcome his adversity. "My particular strength wasn't in being able to do it all myself, but it was my ability to get along with others and show that I had value."[22] He knew the battalion recognized his strengths and contributions, and regarded him highly as a part of their community. The confidence they had in him was contagious. It raised his morale, which in turn helped give him the courage to control his fear and self-doubts. Supported and knowing he was not alone, his resolution to endure and successfully complete the grueling military exercise ended positively.

Advice And Information

Sometimes the support offered us from others in society is found in advice and information. Self-help groups in the community provide support in the form of guidance from those who have been through a similar experience and have felt a similar stress and pain. It is comforting to know we are not alone and that we belong to a greater community.

One such organization is Reach to Recovery International. Reach to Recovery comprises volunteers who have survived breast cancer themselves and now offer emotional support and information to women experiencing a new diagnosis of breast cancer. These community-based organizations can help people with a newly diagnosed cancer find the courage to confront their fears, feel more in control of their lives, and move towards their goals. Such guidance improves the level of optimism in breast cancer survivors, giving them the courage needed to adapt to the changes in body image, sexuality, and physical health.

The value of belonging to a group is the interdependence and vast availability of resources it offers a member. Members can rely on others for competence in areas in which they do not have self-efficacy, improving their confidence.

Goods And Services

Sometimes the support a community can offer is financial help, material goods or services.

Communities frequently develop programs aimed at helping reduce risk to individuals by meeting these needs. Some, such as the elderly, may have difficulty overcoming adversity because they are inundated and burdened with multiple traumatic events, and in need of community resources. For example, older people may have less resilience due to decreased cognitive functioning, loss of supportive relationships due to friends dying, lower mobility resulting from physical impairments, and social isolation due to retirement and family living far away. They may have fewer financial resources and inability to obtain necessary goods and services. Community-based programs aimed at providing both concrete services and compassion can bolster social connectedness, which in turn improves optimism, a sense of purpose, emotional support, and ultimately, courage to tackle difficult life events.

Societal Groups

An unusual but important social group is that which develops for people who have the courage to speak out against harmful regulatory or institutional practices. No one has the potential to benefit more from association with societal groups than whistleblowers and grassroots environmental activists, who confront social problems like chemical contamination or sea life pollution. These are individuals who typically challenge the unethical or illegal behavior of another person or organization. In doing so, they courageously seek justice, which often draws the ire from those whose behavior they oppose. They may risk retaliation, exclusion in the workplace, criticism of their credibility, legal consequences, transfers, demotions or loss of jobs, physical attacks, and ostracism by the industry.

Studies have found that whistleblowers that do not have social support from the community, management or like-minded organizations risk experiencing severe negative emotional outcomes. The pressure places them at significant risk of feeling marginalized and vulnerable, suffering deteriorating marriage and family relationships, and all too often turning to drugs or alcohol.

When whistleblowers and activists are able to associate with groups that reinforce their beliefs, they are protected from feeling isolated or frustrated. The anger they experience about their issue is validated. Their vision for change is shared by the organization, providing cohesion, a group identity, and emotional support. Strengths from group members can compensate for the limitations of individuals. This helps provide protection from fear of failure that could result in panic attacks or feelings of unworthiness when challenged by others during the ordeal. The societal group cushions them from the hurt of backlash and retaliation by others, because there are others to offer emotional support as well as to react against the offenders. In other words, the activist knows he is not alone. This helps prevent burnout and propels his sense of purpose. The courage many social activists display would not be possible if it was not for the support they receive from society.

Social groups needn't always be large, or selected by choice. Our families are the first social group to which we belong. While many types of courage can be learned in the family setting, it is the primary place in which moral courage — which is about doing the right thing, even at the risk of rejection, loss or ridicule — is developed.

Life is more difficult today for families than it was in the past. Families are isolated. Extended and even nuclear family ties are stretched and fragile. Parents are scared for their children's safety in an uncertain and conflict-ridden world. While parents want to model courage, it is understandable why parents feel challenged and unprepared to do so in their day-to-day communications with their children. They may not know how to provide their children skills such as assertiveness and negotiation strategies, which would be helpful tools in overcoming their fear of risk.

Children can learn about courageousness not only from parents, but also from associating with other social groups; including clergy in religious organizations, school administrators and friends cultivated from the neighborhood or community clubs. All can help prepare children to become resilient adults. This can be accomplished by conveying respect for the children's feelings, encouraging development and ownership of real emotions, and supporting belief in themselves as opposed to yielding to the pressure of others in peer groups or the neighborhood. By feeling empowered, confident, and self-directed, children will grow up to have the courage to overcome challenging experiences throughout the years.

Spirituality

Marcus Tullius Cicero, a Roman statesman from 106 BC, is quoted saying, "A man of courage is also full of faith,"[23] indicating that the view of spirituality and courage working hand in hand has been around for centuries. Spiritual beliefs provide us with a sense of hope, comfort and meaning, which helps us have courage to deal with adversity in our lives.

Purpose

Having a sense of purpose in our lives has to do with aligning our values with our goals. When adversity strikes, a sense of purpose can uncork the courage within us. It is a positive driver in our lives. It motivates us to take constructive action because it provides us with a clear goal of what we want. Business executives emphasize the importance of having a sense of purpose in order to meet work-related objectives. Doctors see those who have a sense of purpose following retirement as living a healthier and longer life. Having a sense of purpose gives us the courage to cope with challenges in our lives, and keeps what is valued in sight.

If we don't have a purpose, we cannot expect to obtain our goals. For example, if needing groceries, going to the store without thinking about the purpose for this trip will likely result in guesswork as we walk up and down the food isles, and we'll come home with random and meaningless impulsive purchases. If, on the other hand, we go to the grocery store with a shopping list for recipes being cooked that week, we will have a sense of purpose, and more likely will come home having achieved our goal. Just as a lack of purpose is a blocker to proper grocery shopping, so is a lack of purpose a blocker to courage. Without purpose, we will lose our inner connection and become unfocused, making it too difficult to overcome adversity. We will find overwhelming fear replacing hope and we will remain in a chronic state of apathy or dissatisfaction.

Reframing

Believing in something greater than ourselves helps us accept what does not make sense and what we cannot understand, and provides us with the courage to go forward in spite of these uncertainties. Faith that everything has a reason for happening allows us to reframe events that feel out of control, and to believe that eventually, things will work out. It gives us freedom from regret, and comfort to believe that we can overcome, rather than surrender to, our adversity. Spirituality gives us that sense of humanness, and what could be more human than the ability to connect with our hearts?

Stephanie Parker's personal experience with loss exemplifies how, through spirituality, she found courage and connectedness to something beyond herself. In 2013, Mrs. Parker, pregnant with her second child, was devastated when she was told by her obstetrician that "I had a grapefruit sized baby growing in my fallopian tube, was bleeding internally, and had to go in for immediate surgery, or I would have died within 24 hours." She miscarried the baby. After her surgery, she recalls: "The loss I experienced was overwhelming … but I knew that … I had to trust that God had the best in store for my family. Although I was crying, and I sobbed many times, I had this odd sense of joy that lasted literally a week after my surgery. And then it went away. It carried me through one of the most difficult times of my life, and I can honestly say I give God the glory for it, because I would not have made it without that joy, without that refocus on where my trust and hope should be." Mrs. Parker adds," … people need to be willing to open up … so that they can heal and allow God, family and friends to help them heal. Because doing it on your own is destructive, it is absolutely self-destructive."[24]

Spirituality enabled Mrs. Parker to reframe her loss in a way that was significant and understandable to her and her life. It restored her sense of need to connect with God, family, and friends. It provided meaning, purpose and hope, reducing her feelings of anxiety, depression, and despair. It helped her find the courage to cope with this tragic event.

Compassion

Spirituality is connected to compassion for others and ourselves, which is central to overcoming adversity. Preliminary research suggests that we are hardwired to experience compassion and spirituality. Running from the brain to the stomach, the vagus nerve collects and sends the 'feel-good' hormone, oxytocin, throughout our body to many important organs and nerves. When we experience an event that stirs up emotion, oxytocin travels through this nerve, from our brain to our heart.

The vagus nerve, also referred to as the 'nerve of compassion', linking the brain and heart, likely triggered Mrs. Parker's feelings of love and trust, and deeper connections with compassion, gratitude, and spirituality. Along with the reframing process, her feelings of compassion contributed to Mrs. Parker's ability to find the courage she needed to get through each day when she felt her world was crashing in around her.

Rabbi Richard Steinberg, of Congregation Shir Ha-Ma'alot, in Irvine, California, views spirituality as being significant in finding the courage to go up against obstacles. "At its core, spirituality is about accessing the full potential of one's best self. Perhaps no other virtue best exemplifies this than "courage." To be able to face one's fears and act constructively in the face of those fears is a spiritual feat of immense proportion. We all have the potential to face our fears, but the spiritual person knows he is not alone in the process. There is a spirit of God-given potential that can be accessed, celebrated and used to further one's life towards meaning."[25] This combination of trusting in a higher power, along with using our own resources, enables us to have the courage to cope with formidable tragic events.

Religion

Spiritual belief can be separate from formal, organized religions. Yet all major world religions communicate to their followers the importance of turning to a spiritual belief as a source of coping when needing courage to overcome fear. Benevolence is encouraged and hatred or indifference, which is the opposite of finding and embracing compassion, discouraged. Compassion, one of the cornerstones of discovering courage, is achieved through prescribed beliefs, practices and rituals.

Judaism

Jewish values such as showing compassion and caring for others, doing what is just and merciful, and seeking truth and self-respect is captured in the Talmud (the basis for all codes of Jewish law), where it is written, "To save a life is equivalent saving the an entire world." This phrase speaks to Judaism's focus on how people should live their lives, care about each other and God, and contribute to the well-being of the world.

The Tanakh, or Hebrew Bible, has many instances in which followers are encouraged to follow their moral convictions, overcome their fear and be courageous, and help others. God tells Joshua to not be afraid of being a leader, "Did I not command you, be strong and have courage, do not fear and do not be dismayed, for the Lord your God is with you wherever you go." (Joshua 1:9) And Joshua, in turn, encourages the people to not be intimidated by the Canaanites. "Do not be afraid; do not be discouraged. Be strong and courageous." (Joshua 10:25)

Buddhism

Buddhists do not worship God. Their religious principles emphasize the importance of striving to reach one's potential, which is referred to as spiritual enlightenment. Followers are encouraged to embrace both faith and courage in their efforts to let go of all yearnings and do the right thing. Meditation helps followers find wisdom, which is viewed as the way to conquer worldly suffering and challenges. Daisaku Ikeda, a Buddhist scholar and spiritual leader, provided the essence of Buddhism by saying, "Life is not expected to be easy. One who has the courage to speak the truth lives a truly splendid and fulfilling life."[26]

Christianity

Christianity teaches that everything in life is according to God's plan. It is taught that by developing a stronger belief in God, a path is paved for the growth of courage. Through this process God's plan will be more understandable and immobilizing fear can be overcome. Christianity provides comfort for people who are afraid because it explains that if one lives life as God designs, they will go to heaven. Two examples include: 'The Lord is my helper, and I will not fear what man shall do unto me'. (Matthew 10:28, [King James Version; KJV] Bible), and "Be on your guard; stand firm in the faith; be courageous; be strong." (1 Corinthians 16:13)

It took decades for David Klein, known to many as The Candyman, to learn this. Mr. Klein loves candy. His love of candy changed the industry but nearly destroyed his life; resulting in his being immobilized by fear, vengefulness and regret. It was finding a higher power in the structure of religion that restored his ability to want to live again.

The beginnings of his problems can be traced back to "one Thursday night, when I came up with an idea — what if a store were to open up just selling jelly beans? No liquorish, no gummy bears, no jawbreakers, no chocolate. Just focus on jelly beans," recalls Mr. Klein. Mr. Klein's vision was to create recipes for jellybeans that had exotic tastes and names. He named these flavorful jellybeans, 'jelly bellies.' His vision took off, largely due to his wildly creative marketing which included appearing on Mike Douglas's television show and posing for ads in a colorful jellybean filled bathtub. "I was Mr. Jelly Belly," states Mr. Klein. Soon, jelly bellies were everywhere, including candy stores, on President Ronald Reagan's desk, and even accompanying astronauts aboard the Space Shuttle Challenger.

Mr. Klein's success was short lived and soon came to a crashing halt. "The company I found to manufacture my jellybeans took it from me in four years. During this time I was blackmailed, there was extortion, and people I had trusted wanted to wrestle away from me whatever I had. It got to the point where they were making the beans, but they had me over a barrel. They basically threatened me, saying, 'If you don't sell us the name, we're going to stop making the jellybeans. You'll be backed up for a year and a half in orders and people will sue you because you couldn't provide them with the product.'

There was nothing I could do about it. I sold because I had no choice. I knew for a fact that I would be cut off," cites Mr. Klein sorrowfully.

"Two minutes after they took over they removed my Mr. Jelly Belly signature, which was on the back of every Mr. Jelly Belly product. They came out with a book, *The 30 Year History of the Jelly Belly*, and I wasn't even mentioned in there. They totally erased me from the history of the product. I was furious."

What followed was nearly 30 years of adversity. "Anger wears you out beyond belief. I was always wishing I was dead. I used to tell my son, Bert, 'I can't wait until the day I die. It will be the happiest day of my life.' I was a train wreck. I put a lot of curses on people. I went crazy. I was driving a car and wanted to drive into the median. I acted in a way that drove a rift between my son and me," recalls Mr. Klein. "It wasn't just passing anger," recalls his son, Bert Klein, "the type that comes and goes. It was the type that builds and doesn't go away."

After three decades, Mr. Klein found the resilience that had been eluding him. "Picking up a bible changed the course of my life. In 2008 I turned to the Lord, converting to Christianity." He found that at a time of great personal suffering, the fellowship of others pulling and praying for him " ... brought me back to life. Ninety-five percent of the support came from being around other people to support me, people with like feelings, values, and beliefs. Before that, I was very isolated, like a hermit. I actually kept my phone off the hook most of the day because I didn't want any contact with anybody," recalls Mr. Klein.

"Now I'm a better person. I couldn't stand the old me. My relationship with my family has improved. We talk more. We laugh more. I'm learning more about what they're doing in their lives and enjoying their company. I have a much closer family. I've learned coping skills. I learned about not getting angry, not getting disturbed by people's comments, accepting people as they are instead of trying to change them, just being much more happier and outgoing and genuine and just enjoying life and all the pleasures life gives you. It permitted me to just be me," he states with a smile.

"Financially, things are a disaster today, but I can handle it. I might end up with less earthly things, and less money, but I don't really care. My view of it is different. I feel very optimistic because I'm focused on the eternal. If I hadn't lost Jelly Belly, I wouldn't have found God. If I hadn't found God I would have been dead long ago, even with Jelly Belly. For that reason I wouldn't change it.

I'm absolutely 100 percent good with it. I didn't lose anything, but gained," adds Mr. Klein.

"There are still temptations to stir things up. My wife wants to know when I'm going to sue Jelly Belly. I really don't want to, between you and me. Jesus Christ says if there is something that is going to cause you to stumble, stay away from it."[27]

Research over the past decade has found that spirituality and religion benefit nearly every aspect of our lives by providing ways of coping with hardship. As seen with Mrs. Parker's spiritual faith, and Mr. Klein's religious affiliation, they developed the courage to examine how they viewed their life circumstances. They discovered hope, resulting in a higher level of self-esteem and personal happiness. They felt more in control and established better coping skills, leading to resiliency in the face of adversity. Even more significant, their experiences taught them lessons about life that they would not have otherwise learned, resulting in their finding deeper meanings in their experiences.

Impediments to Spirituality

Despite the evidence that spirituality provides emotional benefit and personal growth to those who would otherwise lack the courage to negotiate an adversity, challenges exist for some people. Some may feel uncomfortable discussing or seeking spirituality because they do not understand what it is, and are embarrassed to ask others for guidance. Some feel embarrassed by their role in the adversity and may feel unworthy of turning to their religion. Others may feel abandoned by God, and pull away in anger. Or others may have unresolved feelings arising from their upbringing, resulting in a stigma on the entire concept of spirituality and religion. And even others, who sought spirituality in their time of trial, were turned off by a spiritual practice or the clergy, and turned away from might what otherwise could have been helpful to access their courage.

In such circumstances, it can help to talk with someone, be it a friend, therapist or spiritual counselor. They likely have spoken with others who have had a similar experience, and may be able to help with the individual's concerns. Sometimes, just being able to express one's feelings of anger or disbelief out loud can provide clarity and answers.

Conclusion

Adversity is exhausting. It uses up much of our emotional strength, leaving us overwhelmed by fear and unable to move forward. After all, we need to be safe and take care of ourselves if we are to survive in times of difficulty. Finding the courage to go forward when the future is unknown and there are no guarantees is frightening. To do so involves a deliberate and courageous choice on our part. We venture forward knowing that to remain stuck in a place of fear, unhappiness or danger is to leave ourselves unfulfilled or at risk for further harm.

It takes courage, but courage is complicated. Courage is the blend of the emotion of fear as well as the cognitive aspect of understanding the risks involved with pursuing an action. When we choose courage we understand that we might not succeed in reaching our goals. But we pursue these goals anyway because we have weighed the situation against our value system. The desire to have a better life helps give us the motivation to move outside our comfort zone and not give in to our natural risk-avoidant tendencies.

Our support systems help us by providing encouragement to succeed when we don't have the confidence, or if we question whether we deserve to have a better life. Others in our social network can provide strategies on managing fear, and contribute resources that will improve our skills and ability in reaching in our goals. They are there to help pick us up when we fall, help keep our discouragement from ratcheting out of control, and offer alternative pathways to our goals when we get discouraged. Our spirituality helps us hold onto faith that we are worthy, and that our conflicted feelings are a normal part of being human. At a time when so much in our lives seems uncertain, spirituality helps calm our fears. It helps us feel confident and strong, and that we can do what we previously had believed we could not do.

We all need courage when we are struggling with a conflict. When we make the calculated choice to act courageously, we are rewarded with belief in our ability to make decisions that will help us find resilience in our adversity.

Suggested Exercises for Using the Three Spheres of Support to Enhance Your Courage

Finding the courage to tackle adversity is more probable when encouragement is provided to the struggling individual. Too often encouragement is what people are missing the most when practicing to be courageous. Starting with small steps will provide you with confidence and skill building. Achieving some success will empower you and building new skills to deal with larger adversarial issues will not be as daunting. You will find you can develop your courage muscle by being courageous. Below are some suggested exercises to achieve courage.

Self

1. *Visualize Success*

   You have to be able to see where you are going to get there. Think of a time when you were afraid, but you pushed through your discomfort and succeeded. What were you thinking at that point? Were they negative thoughts of how you may fail? Or were they positive thoughts of encouragement and believing you could succeed? How did it feel after your success? Try and replicate that experience when you need to find the courage within.

2. *Redefine Obstacles*

   Decide what you would like to accomplish and break it down into manageable, bite-size tasks. Focus on successfully addressing each task before moving on to the other. After each newly achieved task, pause and appreciate your accomplishment. Consider what you have learned about yourself. Perhaps you will discover the obstacles are not insurmountable. With each small accomplishment you may find greater courage to push forward to the next task.

3. *Review Past Accomplishments*

   On a sheet of paper, list previous situations in which you have successfully drawn on personal courage to accomplish your goals. What types of problems did you encounter? What did you learn about yourself from the past experiences? How can these past experiences and knowledge obtained help you with future obstacles in your life?

4.   *Learn About Courageous People*

Courage can be contagious. Read, watch television, movies or YouTube to learn about the courageous undertakings of others.

5.   *Be Angry*

Get comfortable feeling angry. Anger is often a motivating emotion, a precursor to being courageous.

6.   *Relax*

Therapy, yoga, meditation and gratitude exercises help with mindfulness. They help us avoid the burdensome clutter of worrying about tomorrow and fretting about yesterday, which commonly creates anxiety. These activities help us be present and nonjudgmental of ourselves. They help us to have clarity of thinking and make better decisions.

7.   *Step Outside Your Comfort Zone*

It is likely you will feel awkward. Once you do so, assess how it feels to you, and what you learned about yourself. Do you have more confidence? Self-confidence helps propel us forward into courageous acts.

8.   *Change Your Habit of Fear*

Allowing fear to inhibit your ability to be courageous can result from the formation of habits. When an event triggers your brain, you will respond emotionally, physically or mentally. If you find this reaction to be beneficial, then your brain releases serotonin and dopamine, the 'happy' hormones. In other words, you are rewarded for making the decision you chose. Over time, this reaction becomes more automatic, and a habit is formed.

Unhelpful habits that may be inhibiting courage can be changed by deliberately choosing to not respond to behavior in the same fearful manner. Identify one behavior or reaction you would like to change. By addressing the following questions, you can identify why you've been reacting with fear and learn to respond more courageously.

What is happening when the fear arises? (Time of day/week/season can trigger unconscious associations for you. Or perhaps certain individuals or locations increase your distress. Knowing this can help you modify your habit by doing something different for yourself at these times. Consider interrupting your fear by listening to music, exercising, or laughing at a sitcom, all which will raise your serotonin and elevate your mood. You will then be better able to examine the matter.)

How are you feeling emotionally? (Take several deep and slow breaths, and turn your attention to your body. Be curious about what you are feeling, and then ask yourself when you first felt that emotion. What was happening? Today's painful feeling may be connected to a previous unresolved hurt. That hurt is ground zero and affecting your ability to be courageous today. Examining your feeling in a self-compassionate manner will help reduce your fear.)

Understanding the connection between the event and your fearful reaction will provide you with new insights about why certain emotions are triggered. You will now have the ability to purposefully view situations differently and choose more positive thoughts, emotions and reactions. If repeated regularly, your old habit of fearfulness will give way to the development of your new deeply ingrained habit of successfully facing obstacles.

Society

1. *Question Jar*

    Parents model courage through every day actions and conversations. Sometimes we have to manufacture such events so that we can facilitate the learning process. A fun exercise can involve the creation of a jar in which all family members are encouraged to insert questions they have about courage. This is a broad category, and can include such wide ranging topics such as what to do if you see that someone was discriminated against, or who is your hero (and why), how to handle a situation that made you scared, or what you think about a current event issue in which people are being viewed differently? With parents sharing their views and encouraging children to share theirs, the children are learning how to courageously express their feelings. Through this family sharing exercise children acquire new skills and strengths to work through adversity.

2. *Surround Yourself With Positivity*

Surround yourself with people who will support your efforts and gently challenge you to push through your fears. These people may be in your inner circle, such as friends, and family, or may be in your professional circle, such as colleagues. Likewise, identify and remove toxic people who inhibit or sabotage you by dwelling on the negative.

3. *Share Your Own Past Struggles With Fear With Your Children*

Children benefit by learning from their parents how they went through the process of developing courage. Their parents' former struggles, self-doubts, and perseverance will provide the template for their challenges with courage later in life.

4. *Identify Heroes*

Parents are a child's first 'bigger-than-life-all-knowing-God-like' heroes. When children have a problem, they naturally look to their parents and wonder, 'what would they do?" Help children learn to look for heroes in every nook and cranny in their lives: on television, in bedtime stories, in the school classroom and in current events. Explore together what feelings and values must have taken place for courage to conquer fear.

5. *Organizational Support of Courage*

Organizations, such as employers and schools, can identify their important values, and develop programs to assist their members become courageous in achieving them. Programs including mentoring, training and rewards, to name a few, can provide awareness and skills to members. For example, taking personal responsibility for what one sees going on in an organization may be a value. If it had been so for members in the Catholic Church, and employees had been given the tools to be courageous, events of sexual abuse of children by priests would likely have not lasted for decades. Likewise, had clients of Bernard Madoff had the courage to question rather than trust the high payoffs, the financial ramifications of Bernard Madoff's Ponzi scheme may have been halted years earlier. Instead, innocent people lost their life savings, community based charities were forced to shutter their doors, and Madoff's own son committed suicide.

6. *Community Interventions*

People who have a sense of purpose in life have better psychological health and are potentially able to be more courageous when experiencing setbacks. Contribute to the development of programs that will improve social connection with others in the community. Volunteer in existing activities that will help you connect, such as civic involvement.

Spirituality

1. *Remember That You are Not Alone*

"The Lord is your Helper. So long as God is our Helper there is nothing that man may do to us that He cannot over rule to our good." (Romans 8:28) Carry this saying (or a similar one that resonates with you) on a piece of paper in your pocket, in your wallet, tape it on the cover of your computer, on your car dashboard, or on your mirror so you can remind yourself, throughout the day, every day, that you are not alone.

2. *Model Turning to Your Higher Power*

Parents can empower their children by letting them know that they draw strength from turning to their Higher Power. Provide specific examples. Children will learn that they, too, can reach to a spiritual source for loving and supportive help when they are fearful.

3. *Listen to Your Inner Voice*

Close your eyes and allow yourself to commune with your inner feelings and thoughts. Finding your voice is imperative when needing courage to speak up for yourself or others. Trust yourself rather than doing or saying what you think others expect of you. Your voice will become louder, prouder, and truer to who you really are.

4. *Practice Dropping Judgment*

    If you do not judge yourself, you will find yourself becoming more tolerant of your imperfections. Accepting your human flaws is important and can be achieved by turning any need for judgment to God. You'll find it easier to be courageous, because you will not worry about risking being wrong in what you say, or taking a risk and trying something new.

5. *Love Your Children*

    Love from parents and siblings gives young children the courage to tackle daily challenges. The trust that others love them lets children grow up knowing they are not alone. The knowledge that they received unconditional positive love when young can, in adulthood, transition into faith in one's higher power. Believing that we are not alone helps us overcome our fears and gives us courage.

6. *Link Spirituality to Courage*

    Provide encouragement for people who want to increase their understanding of how to find and use spirituality in being more courageous. It may be a matter of suggesting books to read, guiding them to available resources in the community, or simply talking with them. Too often people mistakenly believe that it is circumstances or physical resources that provide empowerment. Spirituality helps people discover meaning and purpose, which gives us the courage to transcend our darkest moments.

Chapter 3

Perspective

"Everything we hear is an opinion, not a fact.
Everything we see is a perspective, not the truth."
— Marcus Aurelius (Philosopher and Roman Emperor, 161 AD – 180 AD)

Historically, adversity has been viewed as a negative, traumatic event that causes immense suffering. We now know that is not necessarily true for all of us. While an adversity can be so disruptive that it rattles our beliefs about how we view our world, it also can be the catalyst for personal growth. Adversity can be the stimulant that causes us to re-examine our priorities, values and relationships, and shed that which is not working well.

One of the key mechanisms for influencing our resilience to adversity is known as "perspective taking." We form perspectives daily, even before we lift our head to get out of bed each morning. From there we go on to create, modify, abandon and challenge our perspectives numerous times during each day. We couldn't live very efficiently without doing as much. We wouldn't be able to solve any of our personal problems. Political leaders wouldn't be able to resolve domestic conflicts or international battles if their perspectives were not being continually re-evaluated. New inventions, including the light bulb, would not be created if Thomas Edison had not explored different perspectives — 1,000 times. And as any married couple will readily confirm, viewing an issue from one's partner's perspective typically brings a halt to bickering and instead, rewards of greater trust, intimacy, and satisfaction in the marriage.

What is Perspective?

A perspective has to do with how we assess something. It is intangible, entirely subjective, and has the ability to change. It is 'the story' we develop in our head about something based on our beliefs, attitudes, experiences, and knowledge. Perspective taking is a process of looking at an issue from more than one point of view, attaching a meaning to these facts, and developing feelings about them. This process can influence the difference in making a good or bad adjustment following an adversity.

For example, 88-year old Joyce Stromberg was despondent following an illness that resulted in losing her ability to ambulate independently, thereby requiring a walker to get around. An active woman, she resented the walker, finding it annoying and cumbersome when getting into the car or walking through a crowded room. The walker was a continual reminder that she had lost some of her independence and was growing old. With each passing month, her bitterness increased.

One day, at a routine orthopedic appointment, Mrs. Stromberg observed another patient in the waiting room who seemed worse off than she. The patient was a man, appearing to be in his early 30's. He had only one leg and was sitting in a wheelchair beside his wife and infant daughter. During the wait for her father's appointment with the physician, the little girl reached out her arms, signaling she wanted to be held by her father. Mrs. Stromberg noticed a subtle but well-rehearsed eye contact between the parents. Unable to deftly pick up his daughter himself due to the constraints of the wheelchair, the man was communicating to his wife that he wanted her to do so for him.

Mrs. Stromberg's perspective, or point of view, on her ambulatory limitations, underwent a significant change after looking at her losses from another person's view. She developed an increased awareness of what she had to be happy for in her life, realizing that she could have lost much more than the ease of mobility. She recalled the simplicity, when she was a young mother, with which she had been able to reach over and pick up her own children.

She realized that others are worse off. She developed the insight that her situation, when considering more facts, needn't be debilitating. Instead, perspective taking opened up her view of her life. She started focusing on the activities she could still do, such as taking an art class and playing bridge, which helped her see her loss in a more relative degree of importance. [1]

Why is Perspective so Important?

Failure to perspective take can inhibit us from building up resilience when we face a hurdle in life. Perspective taking is one of the single most powerful dynamics available to us in successfully overcoming life's obstacles. The benefits are numerous and far reaching, as listed below.

Shifts Our Thinking

When something happens to us, we have thoughts that immediately stream through our head, which in turn triggers our perception about this event. What we think about it, and what we say to ourselves about the event, influences the importance or meaning the event will have to us. Even a small shift in thinking can change how we perceive ourselves and interpret the event. This can influence our ability to deal successfully, or unsuccessfully, with the task at hand.

Considering our adversity from different perspectives pays off in spades. When reflecting on other viewpoints or information, we are better able to re-evaluate the issues. We will be more empowered to develop more successful problem resolutions. The real life situation is the same; nothing has changed concerning the situation. But by thinking differently about the event, we can benefit from having access to additional choices and resources.

Resolves Problems

When we want something different from what someone else wants there is a high likelihood that we will clash. Being able to consider additional information and views from each other can go a long way in resolving such conflicts. When each of us can truly hear the other person's point of view and emotional feelings, we are better able to walk in each other's shoes. The opposing party feels validated and as a result will be less defensive. This is paramount, because when a person is defensive, he stops listening to the other person. He is too busy preparing his defense. On the other hand, if the other person feels validated, he will not need to be defensive and will be more amenable to listening to the others' perspective. Because each opposing party is listening to the other, they will more likely be able to consider the perspective of the other person. Unhealthy reactions of defensiveness, anger and judgment are replaced with a readiness to consider different outcomes and problem resolution. The adversity is better managed, even if there is no resolution, because we can let go of our anger, and reduce our feelings of being wronged and wanting revenge.

Promotes Information

Perspective taking is the process of understanding something from a different point of view. We achieve this by first collecting information. After all, the more information we have about an issue, the better we will understand it, and the more improved our decision-making will be.

But it isn't easy to take in new information, because we automatically apply our values, judgments and beliefs to this new information. We do this instinctively, without realizing we are doing so. This will impact on how we feel or think about the other party. If we are successful at putting our point of view on ice temporarily so that we can consider that of someone else, we will be successful at taking in new information. We will be able to question our stereotypes or biases that may be getting in the way of our assessment, understanding, and management of the adversity. This additional information is improving our perspective taking, and aiding us in selecting the best path for us to take in resolving the resiliency.

Self-Empowering

People struggling with adversity will often feel that they have lost control of their ability to steer their ship. Yet each of us has the capacity to decide whether we want to view the obstacles we encounter as problems to be endured, or as unexpected opportunities to experience, learn from, and grow. Once we begin to accept that we are in control of our perspectives, we can see that while life is challenging, it can still have meaning. Instead of viewing the misfortune through a lens of victimization and hopelessness, we can begin to feel empowered. We are then able to shift how we perceive adversity, which enables us to take charge of our lives.

In 2002, on a typical hot summer day in Southern California, a stranger abducted five-year-old Samantha Runnion from her front yard. Tragically, despite a manhunt consisting of more than 500 police and FBI agents, Samantha's sexually molested body was found discarded in a nearby national forest. Overcome with agony and anger at her loss and this incomprehensible violence, it took Samantha's mother, Erin Runnion, years to experience a shift in her emotions. "It felt like time stopped when she died," recalls Ms. Runnion.

"Looking at her pictures would make me cry. Up to that point, nobody had ever given me that much joy."

Ms. Runnion's viewpoint began to change one day when she realized that, "for me to dissolve into tears and to feel that much pain every time I thought about her was doing a disservice to her memory." Her assessment of her tragic loss changed slightly, as she began considering other perspectives. "Nothing happened to me. It happened to Samantha. She is the one who suffered," she observed.

"For three years, leading up to (the murder) trial, I knew I would have the opportunity to give a victim impact speech during the sentencing. I really wrestled with what I was going to say ... to him. I remember waking up in the middle of the night, countless times, having nightmares about hurting him, about saving her life, and exacting revenge on him. I had to let that go. To me, it was distracting from my love for her. Such an acid, that I thought it was corroding who I was and how I wanted Samantha to be remembered." Ms. Runnion recognized that she needed to change her perspective so that she could detach from the murderer and go forward with life.

Ms. Runnion found addressing the perpetrator and the judicial system helpful. "Being able to tell him how I felt was an enormous release. I felt physically lighter after that sentencing day. I was able to express the frustration and anguish from what he did. It was very helpful to be able to say how I felt and be able to let it go." Broadening her perspective, she also felt that "understanding that (the murderer) had a history as a victim of ongoing abuse as a child, and accepting that he is who he is," helped her move forward. Ms. Runnion reflects that, "It makes it plausible even though it's so unfathomable to a normal person." Viewing the perpetrator in this broader manner helped her in "setting him aside. It's not about forgiving, it is accepting," she recalls. It was about changing her story from being the victim to viewing her daughter as the victim. This change in perspective enabled her to look for and discover how to cope with her emotions and live her life in a positive way.

Ms. Runnion realized that becoming a child safety advocate was a route that would empower and enable her to move forward. She states that, "for me, that was like a continuation of my parenting, that I had to honor her and find a way to survive and not let it destroy me as well."

Ms. Runnion discovered that the last step to take in resolving the loss of her daughter was not to allow grieving to become an end in itself. By broadening her perspective, she was able to see a need for child safety that was going unmet in the community. "When Samantha was taken, the massive public response was overwhelming. We received probably 10,000 letters and donations. People were sending money, and that was the money that ultimately seeded the (Joyful Child) Foundation,"[2] a non-profit organization she founded that provides education in the community on safety and empowerment tools for children and parents. Ms. Runnion found that in her grief, she could help both the community and herself.

Offers New Meanings

Being open to developing new and broader perspectives enables us to learn to attach fresh meanings to the painful event. When we do so, we are more likely to think and feel differently about others and ourselves. In the process, we can discover personal benefits to the current challenge. Even though our circumstances haven't changed, the way we feel about them changes. These changes in our thoughts and feelings about life will help us with not only our current but future experiences with adversity.

As described earlier, Ms. Runnion's perspective was broadened when she was able to transition from ruminating about her pain to considering other information. Setting her feelings aside and looking at the perpetrator's situation, she recognized that the perpetrator was trapped by his demons, damaged as a result of his abusive childhood, tragically causing him to be on a life path of destruction.

She changed her focus from looking backward at the cause of her agony, to focusing on her response. Deciding to dedicate her life to preventing crimes against children was an important shift. For years, she had dwelled on looking back at the cause of her sadness. Accepting that she had no control over the past, Ms. Runnion realized that a more constructive response was to look at what she could control.

Reflecting on her work with the Joyful Child Foundation, Ms. Runnion says, "I didn't really know that going into it, but an enormous blessing is that I get to think and talk about Samantha and bring her into my every day without me living in the past. I'm giving to every child what I wish I'd given to Samantha. I feel that this is what I should be doing, and I'm lucky I get to do this job."

Improves Physical Health

Our perspectives affect our physical health. Many of us have heard the adage "an apple a day keeps the doctor away." It appears that a broadening of perspective can keep the doctor away as well, by helping us prevent and recover from physical illness.

When we expand our perspective, we think about others, and not just ourselves. We tend to find ourselves appreciating what they have done for us, and as a result, we become kinder to others. This is known as developing a grateful attitude. Robert Emmons, the world's leading scientific expert on gratitude, discovered in his research that while it is easy to feel grateful when life is going well, it is essential to feel gratitude when adversity strikes.

In times of adversity, gratitude helps us understand that there are things in our lives that are still within our control. This helps us to be thankful, which in turn helps us create and maintain an optimistic perspective. This optimism helps us become more resilient when coping with adversity.

Studies by Martin Seligman, known as the father of positive psychology, and others, have conclusively shown the benefits an optimistic perspective has on our medical well-being. They have found the impact of optimism to include a higher quality of life, reduced risk of depression, and greater longevity. Patients are less likely to feel overwhelmed when faced with serious illnesses. Many studies have found that coronary artery bypass surgery patients recovered faster from bypass surgery when focusing on the positives in their lives. They experienced better recoveries, fewer physical symptoms, and fewer incidences of angina and heart attacks. Watching movies that made them happy resulted in lower readmission rates to the hospital. Senior citizens who were thankful adjusted better to their illness, had fewer complaints, exercised and slept more, and had a lower mortality. Optimistic women experienced a slower progression in carotid atherosclerosis and a better quality of life for those with breast cancer. Studies have also found optimism can improve the immune functioning in optimistic people, contribute toward suppression of disease progression in those infected with HIV, and reduce depression following surgery for patients with AIDS.

Optimism opens us to the feeling of being connected to others. Scientific evidence has found that the varied social relationships; parent-child, marriage, peer groups, and religious or secular organizations, all help us during challenging times, and help save lives. This happens, in part, because when we have the perception that others are there for us, we are more likely to take care of our health. Our health behaviors, like eating well, exercising, and avoiding excesses in drugs or alcohol, are influenced in a way that promotes health and inhibits detrimental behavior. Examples include starting an exercise program following concern from a spouse about becoming too sedentary and over-weight, pressure from a peer group that frowns on excessive drinking, or encouragement to seek medical attention for a noticeable ailment.

On the other hand, when people have the perception that they are socially isolated, they are less equipped to cope with adversity. Research shows they are at greater risk for heart attacks, high blood pressure, an impaired immune function, and twice as likely to die as those with robust relationships.

When we broaden our perspective and experience gratitude and optimism, we are provided with a softer landing when experiencing hardships in our lives. Our problems are the same, but we develop resiliency through new coping skills, medical health benefits, and often find new pathways through our adversity.

Increases Empathy

A lack of empathy can create toxic emotions and a narrowing of our perspec-tive, making resiliency following adversity impossible. In 1923 two scientists, Frederick Banting and John Macleod won the Nobel Prize in Medicine for dis-covering insulin, a treatment for diabetes. But this prestigious honor was tar-nished by a lack of empathy that played out in an escalating professional rivalry and personal conflict. Articles on the topic reflect Banting's belief that sharing the Nobel Prize with Macleod was unfair. Banting perceived Macleod's role in the discovery of insulin as minor.

Driven by an increasing anger, Banting even threatened to not attend the ceremony in Stockholm. Vengeful, he told the scientific community that Macleod's involvement had amounted to little more than the contribution of lab space, ten experimental dogs, and a medical student assistant. Their conflict was never resolved, and the animosity continued throughout the rest of their lives. Only decades later did an independent review confirm that without Macleod's supervison, corrections and contacts, Banting would not have been able to carry out the research that resulted in the discovery of insulin.

Much like the story of unfairness in awarding the Nobel Prize, the percep-tion of unfairness is a common barrier to overcoming adversity. Empathy is the crown jewel of breaking down such barriers. When we attempt to understand the feelings of the other person, we broaden our viewpoint. Even without having to change our opinions, we may begin to understand the other person's feelings and develop some positive thoughts. We start to become less focused on our previous sense of unfairness and anger, and in its place develop a growing compassion for the other individual. This change in perspective is likely to create feelings of empathy, an essential element in forgiveness, and a critical component of overcoming adversity.

Bantings' narrow perspective towards Macleod and the Nobel Prize selection committee never changed. Unwilling to shift his perspective, his feelings of anger and victimization escalated, creating further distortions of Macleod's role in the discovery of insulin. He became backward-focused, dwelling on factors that were out of his control, and blaming Macleod. This caused Banting and others to create errors in their perceptions of Macleod, prevented Banting from developing empathy, and resulted in his failure to cope successfully with adversity. Had he questioned his thoughts, he may have been able to develop a broader understanding and expand his beliefs, correct inaccurate viewpoints, and think in a different, more positive manner. Instead, his lack of empathy resulted in considerable anger and resentment, when awarded the highest honor for professional scientific achievement.

Promotes Forgiveness

Forgiveness was discussed at length in chapter one. In brief, self-forgiveness consists of the offender admitting wrongdoing, expressing remorse, and trying to perform corrective action. Forgiveness of others consists of the victim replacing their negative reactions with positive emotions. A way to achieve forgiveness is through developing a broader perspective, as perspective taking begets empathy, which begets forgiveness.

Understanding the other person can help reduce anger, which is a barrier to developing empathy and forgiveness. A broader perspective can reduce or help us be aware of any stereotyping we may be experiencing that creates prejudice and bias towards others. While forgiveness is much more complicated to achieve than simply developing perspective, if it is going to be achieved, perspective is certainly a necessary ingredient in the recipe.

What Perspective is Not

Facts

While perspective taking may be influenced by facts, it is not exclusively about them. Facts force us to look at things in a black or white fashion. This is too narrow because perspectives are about our emotions and how they relate to what we think about something. We need to have more than facts to help us resolve our issues or problems with others. Perspective taking enables us to include the facts along with our prior knowledge and experiences related to the event. The combination of all of these ingredients comes together to help us form meaning and beliefs about other people's motives.

Facts and perception often collide with each other, even in our courtrooms. A study evaluating the impact of jury empathy towards defendants found that if jury members were encouraged to develop compassion and understanding towards the defendants, they became more empathic towards them. However, when the same jury members were instructed to pay attention to just the facts, they experienced a reduction in their empathy for the defendants. In other words, when emotions are deleted from the equation, the perspective taking process looks very, very different.

Barriers to Perspective

Apathy

Apathy is indifference. When apathy raises its useless head, we lose our ability to benefit from perspective taking. We close our hearts and become disengaged from others, emotionally, spiritually and socially. We check out and do not have interest, concern or feelings about others. It is not possible to understand the viewpoint of others if we are not curious about the other person.

Culture

Perspective taking is dependent upon understanding people's feelings, beliefs, values, and thoughts. It can be challenging enough to 'put ourselves in someone else's shoes' that comes from a similar background. It can become even harder when we attempt to understand the viewpoint of someone from another culture. We grow up learning to see the world in one particular way. Unfortunately, most people fall victim to the belief that someone from another culture likely thinks and communicates just as they do. This can result in communication errors, such as when words and phrases that have double meanings are not understood. The result can be a failure to understand the other person's perspective accurately. Communication is so much more complicated than just the use of words; it includes perceptions, interpretations, and body language. It is no surprise that we perceive communication that does not exist and mis-perceive communication that did occur.

Examples of difference in perspective taking are the two very different cultures of China and the United States. China is collectivistic, or group focused; a culture that has a perspective of viewing relationships and social obligations in the community as being important. The United States is an indi-vidualistic culture, with a focus on individual achievement and desires.

The importance of focusing on the other person's perspective is ingrained into the everyday lives in the Chinese culture. For example, a Chinese mother will likely refer to herself as 'mother,' if she is in the presence of her child, as she is thinking about her identity from the perspective of her child. The ability to better understand patterns of perceptive taking between cultures was tested a few years ago in an experiment conducted by researchers at the University of Chicago. It found that while sometimes the Americans failed to understand the perspective of the Chinese, the Chinese never erred in their ability to under-stand the perspective of the Americans.[3]

This is not to say that the American culture is flawed. Individualism fosters independent thinking, creativity, and imagination, and was one of the core underpinnings of our founding fathers. But it is worthwhile when dealing with adversity, to factor in the patience and time that may be required to perspec-tive take and understand people from dissimilar cultures. To paraphrase humanitarian entrepreneur Connie Duckworth, 'it's very hard to parachute into another culture.' People from other cultures may have different ideas, beliefs, values or actions. But once we broaden our perspectives and become more inter-culturally sensitive, we will be able to bridge the cultural divide.

Social Isolation

When we are socially connected with others in trusting relationships, we have people who will provide us with feedback regarding our thoughts, feelings, and behaviors. Sometimes, just the process of speaking our thoughts out loud, and conveying them to someone, helps provide clarity for us. In other words, our thoughts can become clearer, and our perspectives can change. This can happen naturally through the process of engaging our brain in speaking, even if the other person did not provide any advice. We gain so much through our relationships with others; hope, optimism and clarity, all which contribute to our ability to establish new perspectives.

Social isolation prevents us from being able to get information or advice from others. Without this feedback, our ability to perspective take is hindered. If we do not engage in perspective taking, then we are unable to understand how someone else's behavior would be different from our own behavior. We will be like the little boy who suggests his father buy his mother a baseball mitt for her birthday, assuming she will want it because he himself is passionate about the sport. Unable to perspective take, the child will not be able to understand that his mother has different interests, abilities, and feelings than he. When we are socially isolated, we are handicapped in bridging that gap of misunderstanding, and will miss an opportunity to correct our feelings, thoughts or behavior. This can hinder our ability to move through a challenging period in our lives.

The human species is a social species, and when we are cut off from others, either because we live alone, have a negligible social network, or engage in few social activities, we are likely to feel lonely. Our stress level will rise. We will experience emotional and physiological changes, creating further challenges to our ability to develop healthy perspectives. Social isolation taken to the extreme causes disabling depression and despair. In an experiment dating back to the 1950s, a study of the impact of isolation on rhesus monkeys resulted in profoundly disturbed behavior, even self-mutilation. The effect on humans has similarly devastating consequences. Researchers studying the consequences of social isolation at the turn of this century found that nearly half of all prison suicides occurred in prisoners who spent most of their time in solitary confinement.

On the emotional level, if we are socially isolated our self-esteem will suffer. We may have difficulty coming to terms with our feelings of fear, anger and sadness when coping with adversity. As all of our energy is focused on ourselves, we will become preoccupied with our feelings. Our self-absorption will increase and our perspective taking decrease. Physiologically, numerous studies have linked social isolation to worse health in all age groups. People will likely feel more tired, have more difficulty sleeping, and get sick more often. They will be more vulnerable to infections and take longer to recover than those who are not socially isolated. They will be at risk for chronic medical problems such as depression, high blood pressure, and even an increased like-lihood of developing cancer and dementia.

Without meaningful relationships, we will find it challenging to maintain our optimal mental and physical level of functioning. We will find it more challenging to have the ability to look beyond ourselves and broaden our perspectives in times of adversity. As a result, our resilience, as well as our level of happiness with life, will be diminished.

Instinctive Basic Needs

Visceral factors such as hunger, thirst, pain or sleep deprivation impact on perspective taking. We are likely to experience less self-control, more impulsive behavior, ineffective decision-making, irritability and anxiety when deficit in any of these areas. Our desire to satisfy these basic needs will pose a barrier to our being able to develop accurate perspectives on our adversity. We are suffering because our body wants to grab our attention and turn our attention towards goal-specific, inwardly focused factors rather than the broader-based focus required for perspective taking.

Egocentrism

It's hard for egocentric people to set aside their views or needs when considering the thoughts and feelings of others. This self-focus causes them to over-simplify the differences between themselves and others because they believe that others think like they do. Being close-minded to the thoughts and feelings of others damages their ability to listen, view ideas and concepts from different vantage points, and develop perspective taking.

Mood Altering Chemicals

Uncontrollable situations resulting from adversity may lead to people searching for something that will reduce their chronic stress. They are looking for a sense of balance in life and escape from the emotional pain. Drugs and alcohol are sometimes used as a self-medicating method of coping with the overwhelming burden of emotional distress.

Mood altering chemicals are an example of maladaptive attempts to gain a sense of control in one's life, or to obtain positive gratification at a time when despair rather than contentment is the norm. Drugs and alcohol negatively affect perspective taking because judgment is promptly impacted. Decisions are likely to be made without acquiring enough information and not paying proper attention to details. They are muddied with cravings, mood changes and impulsive decisions often made against one's best interest. Being under the influence of mind-altering chemicals blocks one's ability to consider another person's viewpoint, and understand what they are thinking or feeling. This makes perspective taking impossible and one's struggle for resiliency diminished.

Negative Emotions

Perspective taking can be challenging under the best of circumstances. But negative emotions, such as anger, anxiety, hostility or depression can obstruct our ability to respond well to adversity. It makes our thinking less flexible and narrower, and perspective taking even more difficult.

Negative emotions are self-esteem deflators. Self-esteem is important in developing resiliency because it helps us feel optimistic, trust others, and feel confident in our ability to solve problems. With negative emotions, we are more likely to view challenges with others as being an 'us' against 'them' situation, in which there is a winner and a loser.

One way to protect our self-esteem is to avoid experiences that are similar to the painful one that brought on the negative emotions. While avoidance protects us from further hurt, it typically is not beneficial in overcoming adversity because we end up narrowing our perspective. When we avoid an issue, we are simultaneously avoiding not only our painful feelings, but also our ability to understand the feelings of the other party. We will miss out on the opportunity to engage in the sharing of facts or beliefs, clarify and better understood a situation, or enhance our perspective of the adversity.

Negative emotions also impact on our neurological ability to broaden our perspectives because they inhibit our brain's executive function. The executive function consists of the skills that help us sort out good and bad memories and conflicting thoughts, figure out what needs to be done, regulate our emotions, and identify how to carry out the plan to move beyond our adversity. The executive function is like the captain of our ship, and our ship does not sail as smoothly with a self-immersed captain, who is experiencing narrowed decision-making abilities.

By addressing our negative emotions, we enhance our ability to being open to looking outside of ourselves and see multiple views or perspectives of others, and increase our ability to understand and resolve our problems.

Pessimism

Pessimism is not an emotion, but more so a philosophy or way of thinking. Show pessimists a partial glass of water and their perspective will be that it is half empty. They tend to have negative expectations for themselves and others. Pessimists are more likely to ruminate, which is the process of focusing on something and mulling it over and over in one's mind, because they are more focused on the negative aspect of an event. There is a protective quality to having a pessimistic perspective; by ruminating on the negative dimensions of an experience they have little hope, which prevents disappointment.

Because they expect disappointment, pessimists tend to avoid situations that are at all risky, because they would spend too much time worrying about the problems and myriad possibilities, and that would create more stress. The problem is that avoidance is not a healthy coping strategy. Stressful situations remain negative and problematic while personal growth, and perspective taking solutions remain out of reach.

Age

Age can create a barrier to our ability to develop perspective. Our developmental progression from childhood into adolescence, to adulthood, and eventually into old age influences our ability to differentiate between others and ourselves, which is a prerequisite for perspective taking.

Young children are incapable of understanding the viewpoint of others. Perspective taking isn't even fully possible until children reach five years old when they start to become more logical and rational and can understand that others can have views different from their own. But it isn't until children are eight or nine years of age that they are capable of recognizing others' perspectives and able to fully understand what those differing perspectives might be.

It isn't until adolescence that children develop a broader view and can understand and predict the different perspectives of others. It can be a dangerous time because they are learning to understand different perspectives through modeling the behavior of others. Teens that do not have a good social support and role models are less likely to be successful in understanding other's perspectives, and may make impulsive and risky decisions.

At the other end of the age continuum, the elderly have been developing perspectives based on a lifetime of experiences. Those that have had greater difficulty in overcoming adversity and have suffered a decrease in their quality of life are less likely to have hope, feelings of positivity and feelings of being in control. If they have chronic health problems, financial concerns, or a limited support system, the loss of these resources will negatively impact on their confidence that they can cope with stress.

How to Use the Three Spheres of Support to Achieve Perspective

We cannot control adverse life events happening to us. Our perspective on the events will primarily determine our subsequent resilience. Having a healthy perspective can keep our distress from going into a chronic state and our physical health from being negatively affected. Being aware of how to find and promote broader perspective taking is located in the three spheres of support — Self, Society, and Spirituality.

Self

While our perceptions appear spontaneous, they probably never are. Reactions to adversity are mostly determined by the viewpoints we develop over time to past events and experiences. When we hear or see something, we respond by employing a cognitive process that tries to determine what meaning the new facts and ideas have to our lives. How we choose to respond to this information involves sorting through our "self" perspective, which includes our imagination, personal background, experiences, beliefs, ethics, sense of responsibility, and moral character. Simultaneously, we are factoring in the "other" perspective, which involves interpreting the often hidden meaning of other's behaviors. This complicated process of developing perspectives happens with lightning fast speed, each and every day, at all times of the day, and is of vital importance in overcoming adversity.

Sometimes following an experience with adversity, the perspective with which we view the world makes us feel uncertain and vulnerable because our painful memories of a similar circumstance. We needn't get stuck based on our past experiences. We all have the capacity to learn from the event, re-evaluate our values, and change our feelings. We can improve our goals and direction in life, and directly influence our personal growth. In other words, we can direct our perspective on the adversity. Some people execute this process very well. Others get stuck, feeling victimized, powerless and resentful. One of the reasons for success or failure in surviving and thriving an adversarial event is our own, unique psychological makeup.

Being aware of our psychological make-up will help us understand why we are getting stuck. With awareness, we are capable of expanding our perspectives on matters that otherwise might have resulted in emotions and behaviors that did not help us overcome adversity. We develop our perspectives, which impact on our ability to respond to setbacks, in many ways:

Psychological Theory

Probably no psychological theory explains how our reactions to adversity are influenced by our perceptions better than the cognitive-appraisal theory. It suggests that the way we respond to a situation is based on our subjective perception, rather than the situation itself. Our reactions follow three consecutive steps: event, thought, and emotion. How we unconsciously consider the event (the meaning we apply), which will influence the lens through which we see the event (our thoughts), and influence our emotion (our reaction).

Sometimes that lens through which we see an event has a smudge on it, like the boy in the example below who encounters a growling dog. If a young boy comes face to face with a dog that growls and bares its teeth (event), the child is likely to appraise the situation as harmful (thinking) and to experience feelings of trembling, racing heart, tension, heightened attention (emotion). Subsequent exposure to dogs is likely to be influenced by the boy's negative interpretation and emotional reaction to this particular dog-growling event.

According to the cognitive-appraisal theory, we all react differently to similar events because we apply our own unique meaning to it. We respond in different ways based on whether we feel we are prepared or ill prepared to cope with the stressful event. The boy described above created a viewpoint that was distorted, because we know that not all dogs are harmful. But because of his perception, he catastrophized the situation and generalized his belief to all dogs. Unless he challenges his thoughts, he will continue to have an inaccurate perspective on dogs.

Another child could encounter the same growling, teeth-baring dog (event) and give a different meaning to the dog's behavior. Perhaps this child views the dog as being fearful (thinking). This child could feel empathy for the dog and see the dog as needing reassurance (emotion). His positive interpretation will result in a very different emotional reaction and manner of coping with the event.

Neurological Function

The human brain brain only weighs about three pounds, but it functions as our command center, helping us interpret events and derive meaning from them. No single component of our brain controls our reaction to adversity. Rather, several interrelated systems work as a network for carrying information about stress to other parts of the brain. Sometimes our brain circuits, like the hippocampus, remember previous stressful events we have experienced. These memories can have a bearing on our perception of a new stressful event. This memory is helpful when we have previously suffered emotionally or physically in a situation, like burning ourselves on a hot stove. Remembering the risk of injury helps prevent subsequent burns.

Two systems in our brain that influence our response to adversity are the behavioral inhibition system (BIS), and the behavioral activation system (BAS). Interestingly, each is activated during adversity, but never at the same time. The BAS and BIS are the yin and yang, the salt and pepper, the sun and moon in our minds. The BIS regulates anxiety, fear, frustration and sadness experiences in the brain[4], which moves us away from the unpleasant adversarial event. The BAS regulates positive behavior, and moves us towards something desired, giving us a more hopeful perspective.

Without our awareness, when adversity strikes, our hippocampus, the BIS or BAS, and many other components of our brains are working with lightning speed to create a meaning to the event. Traumatic events have undesirable experiences attached to them, so our corresponding emotion is likely to be sadness or fear. When they occur, our brain is influencing us on whether we should move forward (BAS), or withdraw (BIS). But we're not all wired the same. Some of us have a higher BIS sensitivity, and will be more inclined to recall that negative memory, feel anxious, and want to hold back from acting until more information is available and it feels safe. Those of us with a lower BIS sensitivity might be less concerned about the risk of negative outcomes, comfortable with impulsivity, and be more willing to pursue a goal, even if risk is involved. Our perspective on the event and how to respond to it will be influenced by our tendency to be drawn in one direction versus the other.

Our brain is divided down the middle, with left and right hemispheres. Both function independently of, but communicate with, each other. We often hear the terms 'left-brain and right-brain responses' used to describe how a person tends to think. These responses also come into play when considering the role of the brain in developing perspective following adversity. When we face a difficulty, we naturally engage the left and right side of our brain to resolve the problem.

It is believed that one side is more dominant than the other, with us having a tendency towards processing information in either the left or right hemi-spheres of our brain. The left-brained person is inclined to be someone we view as logical; someone who processes information in an analytical, rational manner. This person thinks with facts, planning, and rules. A right-brained person is likely to be seen as more in touch with feelings and intuition, thoughtful, and to creatively think 'outside of the box.' Neither way of thinking is better or worse than the other. Yet it is to our benefit to recognize if we nat-urally lean towards being left or right brained because it comes in handy when adversity strikes and none of our solutions are working. At these moments, we might want to consciously kick into gear the other, less dominant, side of our brain. Doing so can jumpstart us when we are stuck, helping to develop new perspectives and identify new problem-solving solutions.

Memories from past adversities and our innate tendencies may help us, but at other times make us more prone to respond unproductively as we did in the past. It is nice to know that we aren't powerless to our biology. Just because the many components of our brain may be guiding us to respond in a certain manner to adversity does not mean that we cannot make useful changes. We can respect and honor that part of us that is innately 'wired' while striving for personal growth and not limit ourselves to our bio-psychological tendencies.

Specific Personality Characteristics
Our individual personality plays a significant role in how we respond to stress-ful events. Personality traits that promote positive, rather than negative feelings, may help us to endure distress, cope successfully with emotional pain, and help us find benefits from our experience.

As noted in chapter one, scientists believe that people usually fall into one of what is known as the Big Five major personality traits. These categories are openness, conscientiousness, extraversion, agreeableness and neuroticism. All except neuroticism serve as a support in developing resilience, although for different reasons.

Openess
People recognized to have an open personality like variety, and will be recep-tive and able to adjust to new experiences. Openness serves people well in times of adversity. They are likely to be thoughtful and careful about their

behavior, which enables them to broaden their perspective and find meaning and benefit from their experience.

Conscientiousness

Conscientious people have a low impulsivity rate. They are trustworthy because they are orderly, mindful of others around them, and are inclined to plan ahead. Their tendency to be self-disciplined and goal-directed provides them with the tenacity that helps in getting through challenging times. Through their willingness to put the time and energy into continually working on resolving their problems, they will likely broaden their perspectives, consider the information, and deliberate over the options available to them, before making a decision.

Extraversion

Extraverts are outgoing and enjoy social connections. They are quite adaptable to new situations, and are comfortable being in settings with others that offer new ideas. In difficult times this is a strength, as they can benefit from exposure to broader perspectives, even when under pressure.

Agreeableness

Individuals who are strong in the trait of agreeableness view situations in a positive manner, which is advantageous in difficult times. They can get along and work well with others because they regard humanity as trustworthy. Their ability to experience empathy helps them to establish a broad perspective in trying times, which helps them move through hardships.

Neuroticism

The one personality trait that is less likely to be able to meet the challenge of adversity is neuroticism. Neurotics tend to focus on the negative, and view new situations as unpleasant or threatening. Emotions such as anger, anxiety and depression, which are all poor reactions to experience when reacting to adversity, are easily provoked. Negative emotions tend to draw people's attention inward, reduce their perspective taking ability and inhibit their capacity to handle stress.

Optimism

The way we think about things shapes our perceptions, which in turn plays a critical role in how we tackle our problems. Our thinking involves cognitive skills such as knowing how to problem-solve, communicate, evaluate, reflect, develop opinions and make decisions. Our perspective on how we think about our difficulties is influenced by our tendency to be optimistic or pessimistic.

Optimists are people who have a sunny outlook. They expect things to go well and adjust to adversity by interpreting events with a positive perspective. The optimist views obstacles as temporary setbacks and problems as temporary events. The pessimist is more likely to see the negative event as a permanent part of life. Optimists are more likely to use humor and reframing of problems, than are pessimists, making them less susceptible to bad experiences in their lives.

Because of their perspective, optimists do not just survive but thrive following adversity. They look at what they have and use their problem-oriented efforts to focus on those who have provided them with support, rather than on those who have disappointed them. This strategy ensures they are not alone in their suffering. They will feel less stress when facing adversity in life and thrive when those who are more passive and focus on disappointments suffer.

Whereas optimists see possibilities, pessimists see troubles. But pessimists can modify their mindset. Like any new behavior or habit, it takes conscious effort to make the change. Allowing ourselves to be vulnerable, to take the risk of trusting that things will go well, will help us learn to transition from pessimist to optimist. Challenging our negative, self-limiting thinking and replacing it with more optimistic views will help us acquire new patterns of thinking. Being willing to define situations differently, to focus more on successes and less on the failures is a start down the path of optimism.

Positive Emotions

Our perceptions are greatly influenced by our emotions. We view experiences differently when we are feeling sad or frightened than when feeling confident and trusting. When upset, the right side of our brain, which is associated with emotions that provoke withdrawal, is activated. We are at risk of developing a narrower perspective, resulting in estrangement from our support systems.

Positive emotions, on the other hand, are associated with the left frontal region of the brain, which is related to closeness, or attachment. We tend to be happy, creative and confident that our problem can be solved. We want to be around other people, and other people want to be with us as well, because people are attracted to those who are positive, rather than sad. Our view will be broader and more flexible, providing us with a valuable support system to bring us necessary resources to help in the form of emotional and material assistance.

This knee-bone-connected-to-the-thigh-bone, or should I say, left-and-right-frontal-region-connected-to-the-emotions anatomy explanation of positive and sad emotions explains, to an extent, why some people are more likely to be open to new perspectives and experience personal growth when coping with adversity, while others continue to struggle and suffer.

Empathy

We experience empathy when we can understand what another person is thinking, feeling or doing from their perspective. It does not mean we agree with the other person or change our opinion, but it does mean that we attempt to see their ordeal as experienced by them. This provides us with insights into the meaning the experience has to the other person. When we do this, we are able to expand our perspective about them because we've been able to 'put ourselves in another person's shoes' and learn what their thoughts, feelings, concerns and motivations were at the time of the event.

Developing empathy and broadening our perspective about others helps us heal. We develop greater resilience because misunderstandings and defensiveness are often reduced. Our social ties are strengthened, helping us to not only cope better with the current adversity but also become more resilient in the future, should we experience additional hardship.

Empathy may be one of the ingredients that help people find personal growth following a hardship. It helps them to be more forgiving, view themselves and others without judgment, develop more social connections, and find spirituality in meaning and purpose in life.

Problem-Solving Coping Style

When faced with adversity, we have two primary coping options: avoidance or acceptance. Avoidance coping is an attempt to avoid the stressful feelings, thoughts, or memories. Examples of avoidance coping may include physical or emotional withdrawal, which will backfire because it can lead to social isolation. Or it may include ignoring the problem. These behaviors tend to be ineffective. Avoidance requires a lot of time and energy being directed into avoiding rather than finding solutions. It can create feelings of helpless, loss of control, and the problem growing in size.

Acceptance coping consists of acknowledging the stressor and focusing on what we can do to reduce the stress. Acceptance coping is an effective strategy because it helps us feel that we have some control over our situation. By focusing on what we can do to tackle a problem we have the perception of feeling more in control of the situation than helpless. It helps us to identify possible solutions and then implement them. Acceptance coping is an important promoter of emotional well-being, and may lower levels of depression, reduce distress, and contribute to what is called 'stress-related growth.'[5]

Our perspective on how to tackle adversity, be it avoidance or acceptance, will influence how effectively we manage it. Acceptance coping gives us the opportunity to face problems, find solutions, and move forward.

Benefit Finding

The way in which we perceive events in our lives will influence how we cope with them. Significantly stressful events can threaten our sense of self-esteem, leaving us feeling overwhelmed and out of control.

But if we find something positive in the adversity, often referred to as 'benefit finding,' our suffering can be reduced, and we will become better able to cope with the stressful situation. Finding meaning from the adversity is a benefit that enables us to lower the power of the painful situation. It provides a healthy buffer between the suffering that accompanies adversity and us. It also can change how we feel about others and ourselves by expanding our perspective. New perspectives help us to gain back a sense of control of our lives. They help restore our view of the world as being predictable and reduce our feelings of being vulnerable or victimized.

Our benefit will fall into one or more of the three spheres of coping with adversity; Self, Society or Spirituality. With the Self, our self-esteem rises. We feel more self-assured and in personal control of our lives. With Society, a benefit may result in our decision to redefine our life priorities, which includes choosing to spend more time with people who are important to us. With Spirituality, a benefit can come in receiving a broader sense of purpose and meaning from a higher power.

The perception of benefit is unique to the person experiencing the adverse event. Some may feel they have gained a greater sense of self-knowledge, such as understanding themselves better, or finding out that they are stronger than they realized. Others may find the benefit to be a catalyst for changing their priorities or goals. Thinking about how others have encountered similar painful experiences may trigger benefit finding. Wanting to help prevent similar tragedies from happening to others, and applying meaning to an otherwise unbearable loss does not replace suffering. But as Viktor Frankl, a neurologist, psychiatrist, and Nazi concentration camp survivor, wrote, "Suffering ceases to be suffering in some way at the moment it finds a meaning."[6]

Benefit finding has happened time and again in the creation of foundations, often by grieving parents. Candace Lightner founded Mothers Against Drunk Driving (MADD), following the death of her daughter, Cari, from a repeat drunk driving offender. Christopher Sloan worked with his local government to change Florida state laws regarding high-voltage pool lights following the accidental electrocution of his 7-year-old son, Sean. Donna Whitson, whose 9-year-old daughter Amber was abducted and murdered, established the People Against Sex Offenders, which, with the help of others, has become today's AMBER alert system (also known as America's Missing: Broadcast Emergency Response), notifying communities when a child is abducted or missing.

Perception of benefit is truly the gift that keeps giving. Research has found that people who believe that they gained a benefit, such as improved coping strategies from past stressful events, experience greater quality and longevity in their lives. They are able to view new stressors as less threatening, and are less impacted by future crises. Many experience a buffer against the risk to their physical health through an improved immune and neuroendocrine function, which influences mood and behavior, including appetite control and energy.

Previous Life Experience

Sometimes adversity occurs in our life, and we find ourselves reacting differently to it than we have to adversities in the past. Because of the knowledge we gathered from these previous events, our perspective has changed. We likely have developed wisdom from the past experiences, along with a deeper well of emotional strength and confidence.

As a result, we will view future adversities through a different viewpoint. We have learned lessons about life and developed insights about our coping skills. Our past experiences with troublesome points in our lives give us the gift of being more prepared to deal with future adversarial events.

Sense of Control

When struck by sudden, unexpected and overwhelming adversity, our psychological disequilibrium will likely register high on the emotional Richter scale. We become vulnerable to overwhelming anxiety and fears. We may lose trust in the fundamental goodness of the world. It is only natural that when such events occur, we will attempt to feel safe again and resume a sense of control by recreating order and meaning.

Born in Iran to an affluent and educated family, Azadeh Tabazadeh was a happy and optimistic child. From the age of seven, when her uncle gave her a chemistry set as a present, she dreamed of becoming a scientist. She spent hours memorizing the names of organic compounds, learning about chemical reactions and conducting chemical experiments.

Science was her savior when adversity struck in fifth grade. When the assistant principal, who was substituting for the absent teacher, instructed Ms. Tabazadeh to come to the blackboard, she suddenly realized she had the urge to go to the bathroom. The principal refused to excuse her. Unable to control herself, she was humiliated when "the next thing I know, urine is running down my bare legs and dripping over my black-soled uniform shoes." Shamed, with her classmates laughing, she ran home, threw away her soiled school uniform, and vowed never to return to school again. She walked to the nearby horse stable where she took lessons and mounted her favorite horse. With the reasoning of a young child, Ms. Tabazadeh decided to have the horse jump the arena fence so they could run away together.

She fell when her horse bucked instead of jumping the fence, losing consciousness and breaking her leg in three places. The recovery was long, and she had to miss many weeks of school. To prevent her from having to repeat fifth grade again, her teacher brought class assignments to her home daily. Knowing Ms. Tabazadeh's love of science, the teacher asked Ms. Tabazadeh to memorize the full structure of an animal cell so that she could write it on the blackboard when she returned to school. Ms. Tabazadeh was filled with dread at having to face the jeering of her peers, but at the beginning of class that first day back to school, her teacher instructed her to write the equation on the blackboard. She did so perfectly from memory. Her perspective changed at that point. Ms. Tabazadeh recalls that at that moment she no longer felt embarrassed and a victim, but instead felt empowered and intelligent. She focused on her strengths instead of past experiences over which she had no control.

Her love of science helped fuel her feelings of being in control when coping with adversity in fifth grade and again helped her as a young teenager during the Islamic Revolution. During this period of political and social upheaval, Ms. Tabazadeh observed women being treated with disrespect and animosity. Female judges were demoted to clerks, men were permitted to have multiple wives, and women lost custody of their children in the event of divorce. Strangers on the street slapped, pinched, pushed, taunted and threatened Ms. Tabazadeh. She and her friends were warned about acid being thrown "into your worthless faces," if they did not conform to wearing the sharia-prescribed full body covering, the hijab. She realized that the extremist governmental regime would neither permit her to get an education nor allow her to fulfill her lifelong dream of becoming a scientist.

Political leaders and society were not making sense, and visions of blood and death from riots on the streets were seared into her mind. To control her overwhelming confusion and sadness, Ms. Tabazadeh turned to science. "I loved science, and it was some kind of survival thing for me. In Iran, when the war was raging, I would read textbooks in English; chemistry textbooks or science textbooks. That was the way for me to go into another world."

Science mediated her ongoing life stresses by helping her feel in control, despite the external chaos and stress. "Everything (in science) makes sense. If you want to see why the sky is blue, there really is an explanation for it. It's kind of different than what you see about politics. People lie all the time and you can't trust anything. But when you have scientific facts, it is very truthful and trustworthy. It increases your knowledge. It's like science is a different world. In Iran you can be depressed but there's still another world with all these wonderful things that keep you learning and learning and learning."

Studying science gave her a greater sense of control, which helped broaden her perspective beyond that of the superstitious and fundamentalist Islamic Republic. "I think people who have perspective are more logical. They don't see the world as ending. You have to move on." To have not had this point of view may have resulted in her feeling that there was little she could do to rectify a bad situation, and she would not have responded in a purposeful and resilient manner. "In 1982", recalls Ms. Tabazadeh, "my brother, my cousin, and I, all teenagers at the time, fled Iran by crossing a vast barren desert to reach the borders of Pakistan and beyond. For thousands of miles, the scorching sun burned our faces as we traveled by foot, on crowded mopeds, and in the back of rusty pickup trucks, putting our lives in the hands of Pakistani smugglers. When we escaped Iran, there was always a chance for us to get caught, shot at or not make it. But the alternative of staying in Iran and living under what was going on at the time was not a better option."

She eventually found safety in the United States and a stabilizing sense of meaning in her studies. Ms. Tabazadeh's viewpoint was that through the books, there was a possibility of hope beyond the oppressiveness, which she had escaped. She went on to earn a doctoral degree in chemistry from University of California, Los Angeles (UCLA), worked at the National Aeronautics and Space Administration (NASA), was a visiting professor at Stanford University, published over sixty scientific articles, received a Presidential White House Science Award, and is the author of the book on her experience, *The Sky Detective*.

"I have survived the worst," recalls Dr. Tabazadeh. "It gives me a perspective. It makes me a lot stronger. So when something happens in life, I put it in perspective and become more resilient. It is because of my experiences. My life goes up and down, but I have been at the bottom of the well, so I know it is going to go up. I have a hopeful perspective."[7]

Dr. Tabazadeh's life story consists of focusing on what she could manage, rather than choosing a maladaptive path of giving in to feeling overwhelmed by the revolution and war, which could not be controlled. The empowerment she experienced by identifying what control she had in solving scientific equations and delving into scientific experiments helped broadened her perception of what she could accomplish. This enabled her to not only be better able to manage her adversity but to develop insights, drive, and a greater appreciation for how to control her destiny in the world.

Self-Confidence

Self-confidence is the foundation of our being able to improve our perspective on adversity. Much like the foundation of a building, if it is shaky, the structure may crumble. When our self-confidence is strong, we are comfortable taking in new ideas and experiences. If we have managed adversity successfully in the past, then we will have confidence in our ability to make decisions today, and view tomorrow with optimism. Self-confidence provides a barrier against stress and allows us to expand our perspective on how to best tackle an adverse situation.

Conversely, if we have a low level of self-confidence, our thoughts and decisions are likely to be peppered with feelings of anxiety, critical self-judgment, and pessimism. Negative thoughts that we will fail can flow through our mind, keeping us scared of failure and prevent us from being motivated to approach our problems or try new tasks. Stepping outside our comfort zone might seem daunting, and we will prefer to struggle on with what is known because it feels safe and familiar, even if it doesn't help us deal with our adversity.

Self-confidence is not an innate characteristic, but can be boosted by making intentional, healthy lifestyle changes. The adage, 'we are what we eat' has application to self-confidence. Diet influences our self-confidence and belief in ourselves that we can take risks. Foods high in sugar or caffeine can be detrimental because they are linked to lethargy, irritability or anxiety.

Carbohydrates, on the other hand, help the brain receive serotonin, a contributor to well-being and happiness.

Exercise helps our body and mind with benefits to our self-confidence as well. Exercise stirs the production of endorphins, which are chemicals in our brain that transmit signals from one neuron to another, and have been said to help turn a 'frown upside down.' The production of endorphins contributes towards our perspective that we have the potential to deal with problems that result from adversity because they give us a lower perception of stress, block pain and increase feelings of pleasure.

Humor

Your grade school teacher might have frowned when you showed off your humor as a student, but let's hope that you hung onto this valuable stress-defeating skill. Researchers, psychologists, and physicians all agree that humor is a healthy coping mechanism because it has the ability to change our perspective in a positive manner concerning our problems.

The view of humor as being an asset during times of adversity has endured the test of time. Sometimes, because humor makes us feel good, we can see hurtful experiences as less threatening and more manageable. This gives us a leg up in moving beyond the adversity.

Sigmund Freud, best known as the father of psychoanalysis, believed that humor was no laughing matter. Rather, he perceived laughter and humor to be a safe way to release feelings of anxiety, aggression, and fear. A group of people who have used humor very successfully for generations as a way to understand and cope with stress and negative conditions following persecution and exploitation is the Native Americans. Through humor, they can view their situation from different perspectives. They use humor to make fun of their oppressors, to reaffirm their bonds of connection, and to make light over hardships for which they have no control. Through humor, they are able to have the perception that they are not alone in their suffering and that others share their feelings. As a result, their sense of isolation is reduced, their sense of self-worth is increased, and they feel more connected to their support system, thereby reducing psychological distress.

The relatively new science of positive psychology similarly views humor as a safety release valve that enables us not to take ourselves too seriously, reduce stress and avoid the risk of becoming overwhelmed. It views humor as helping us gain perspective by detaching from our difficulties and looking at them in a different manner. In fact, positive psychology views humor as having such impact on our ability to think, feel, and behave, that the handbook, *Character Strengths and Virtues*, a classification and measurement of the most valued positive traits, included humor in the list of the 24 human strengths of character.

In 1964, Norman Cousins, a professor at UCLA's medical school was told that he had Ankylosing Spondylitis, a rare connective tissue disease and was advised by his physician that he had a one in 500 chance of survival, and to put his affairs in order. In response, he fired his doctor, arranged for massive injections of Vitamin C, and started watching movies that would make him laugh. He worked hard at laughing because he believed it would contribute directly to his ability to reduce his pain and extend his lifespan. Laughter helped him to overcome the pain and to sleep well at night. His sedimentation rate, an infection measure, significantly decreased following belly laughs. He lived an additional 26 years.

Research has shown that Norman Cousins was on to something, that sometimes laughter is indeed the best medicine. Studies have shown that laughing helps people recover faster from cardiovascular surgery, have an increase in dopamine and endorphins (happiness chemicals in our body that make people feel motivated and diminish feelings of pain), spend less time thinking about their aches and pains, and experience a greater life satisfaction.

Our brains are engineered to pump out positive emotions. A part of the brain called the amygdala, which is commonly associated with fear, also is linked to positive emotions, including humor. When we experience humor, our amygdala willingly responds by improving our mood. Our improved mood helps us overcome obstacles in our lives by providing a buffer against anxiety and stress, so we don't get stuck in feelings of disappointment and loss. Our positive emotions help us socially because when we have hope and optimism we have the energy to develop closer relationships with friends and family. The net result is that we feel more in control of ourselves, our perspective is broadened, and our resilience enhanced.

We have seen that many aspects of our Self, the part of us that makes us unique from everyone else, have the capacity to change. We can change our feelings, improve our focus, and directly influence our perspective. We may do this by employing humor, benefit finding, expanding our knowledge and learning new skills. We also accomplish this by developing empathy for ourselves or someone else. We have the ability to choose to examine how our previous life experiences are affecting the sense of control we feel we have over our lives today and make positive changes. Knowing that we are not locked into the limitations of our past experiences is empowering. Through our relationship with our Self, we can expand our perspective on matters that otherwise might have resulted in emotions and decisions that negatively impacted on our ability to respond to and overcome adversity.

Society

Regardless of how we receive it, social support is central to our successfully overcoming adversity. Social networks protect us against the full potential impact of physical and psychologically based health problems. The various ways in which we receive support contribute to making us feel safe and ready to develop fresh perspectives on issues and more equipped to respond in a useful way to our hardship. When this occurs, we build emotional hardiness despite the challenges we are facing.

Support

We seem to be hard-wired for being connected with other people. Ancient humans needed support from each other for hunting and to prevent being eaten by lions and crocodiles in the wild. Today we have grocery stores from which we can purchase our meat. More recently, our food can be ordered online and delivered directly to our homes. Yet the desire to be with other people in times of stress has not abated.

We still need support from those in our community, including friends, family, neighbors, colleagues and others, be it in the form of emotional or material items. We need emotional support to balance our negative thoughts, help us develop additional viewpoints, and offer much-needed resources. If we do not have access to material items, such as emergency shelter, finances, or medicine, our perspective on our situation can be impaired, and our emotional distress will likely increase. Being able to share our emotional challenges with others helps provide us with a feeling that we are not alone, and that there are others with whom we can experience interdependence and trust. An unreliable or lack of support, on the other hand, can negatively impact on our sense of self and incapacitate us.

Sometimes, when we are overwhelmed with a crisis and feeling vulnerable, the social network with which we are familiar is not there for us. In times like these, receiving the support from others may be as simple as having a stranger to talk with, someone who can understand us. This support can be what we need to help pull us through our darkest moments.

After the 2011 Japanese earthquake and tsunami, survivors were vulnerable and needed support from others. Many of the survivor's family members were missing or killed by the traumatic events. The country was so crippled by the disasters that rescue and relief teams could not reach many survivors, and for weeks many traumatized survivors had to rely on support from strangers. Instead of adopting the nation's unofficial mantra, *Shikata ga nai*, which means, "Nothing can be done about it," many survivors developed a stranger-to-stranger support system to help carry them through the toughest days of their crisis. The social support went two ways; helping as well as receiving emotional support and supplies from strangers. Studies found that this helped their overall sense of well-being and increased their resilience. One study of the Japanese earthquake survivors concluded that they broadened their perspectives about strangers, more readily accepted their losses, and adapted to the changes in their lives.

An example of another individual being supported by another person is Dwight Stones, of Orange County, California. Mr. Stones is recognized as one of the most incredible high jumpers in the history of the world. In his 16-year career, he was a two-time Olympic bronze medalist, won 19 national championships and remains history's all-time number one ranked high jumper. His accomplishments also include being the first athlete to both compete and announce at the same Olympics.

As a child, being on the receiving end of self-esteem crushing emotional abuse from his mother made Mr. Stones feel more like a loser than a winner. His parents were divorced, but court hearings and custody battles raged on for years. "I was raised by a very domineering mother. I would come home from visitation with my father and things my mother said to me really took their toll. She'd say things like, "You do this like your father", and "You're just like your father." Those words hurt me very deeply because she had made him to be the anti-Christ in my life. So when she said something like that, it was probably the deepest hurt she could make."

"I was the oldest of three kids. My sister took her own life in 1995. My mother pulled my 'genius IQ level' brother out of school in eighth grade, and he ended up in prison. My wife asked, "How did you escape from that abyss?" I said, "Simple. John Barnes. That's how I escaped from that abyss. I clung on to my coach.""

When Mr. Stones met Mr. Barnes, a high school track coach, he recalls being introverted and having a low sense of self-worth. Mr. Barnes guided the fourteen-year old high jumper out of the isolating experience of his bitter and unhappy childhood by providing hope for his future. His coach showed patience, commitment, caring, and kindness; characteristics Mr. Stones had never before received from either parent. "He would stay long after he should have gone home so he could work with me on the goals he had set." Unlike Mr. Stones' mother, who related to her son with harsh, belittling abuse, Mr. Stones' coach provided constructive criticism, aimed at helping Mr. Stones learn and grow. "When he dressed me down, I loved him more because it was appropriate."

Mr. Stones' coach did more than help him meet his goal of competing in the Olympics. He helped Mr. Stones change the way he saw himself and others. For the first time, he did not feel isolated and worthless. "I got other perspectives. I traveled all over the world and saw what a small pond my mother was living in and why she had the views that she had."

Having received the constructive surrogate parenting relationship he needed as a teenager, and benefiting so greatly from it, his perspective on life changed, and he came to believe he deserved positive experiences. When we feel loved or cared for by another person, such as Mr. Stones did towards his coach, we typically develop warm and positive feelings of gratitude. When people feel gratitude, they want to give back, either to the same person or 'pay it forward' to someone else. This is exactly what occurred with Mr. Stones. Mr. Stones learned to value giving as much as receiving. Now, decades later, he pays forward the supportive relationship he received from Coach Barnes by coaching hopeful young athletes who have dreams of their own, and who may be in need of a supportive relationship.[8]

Vulnerability

As young children, we develop the simplistic belief that we will be rewarded for good behavior and punished for bad behavior. When we see bad things happen to those who behave badly, we believe they are receiving what they deserve. This view makes us righteous and judgmental of others. This can result in people losing support from others and cause fractured relationships.

As we grow up, we realize the random nature of adversity. We learn that in fact, bad things can and do happen to good people. When adversity strikes us, we feel vulnerable to the often unpredictable and unavoidable calamities in life.

Receiving offers of emotional support and other resources, such as money, food, employment, etc., from friends, family and community organizations during these times can trigger a change in our perception of others. If people in our social network are there to support us, and we feel we deserved the tragedy, we will be appreciative of the nonjudgmental support. If we believe we did not do anything to bring the tragedy upon us, and people in the community comfort, encourage and look after us, we will also be very appreciative.

Going through such an experience changes us. We recognize how meaningful it is to have others around us bringing in much-needed assistance; be it emotional first aid, problem-solving, or helping connect us to a community resource. There is no escaping the negative experience, but the support network both eases our burden and broadens our former judgmental perspective that bad things can only happen to people deserving of bad things. We learn that it is these relationships that we need when struggling. Being comfortable with vulnerability also allows us to be more caring and empathic towards others. After all, we no longer view people as deserving or undeserving but as individuals who are suffering when adversity strikes and are in need of their community. This change in perspective opens us up to viewing others in a more positive light, with expanded and deeper relationships with others.

Roles
In times of emotional stress, our perspective tends to become narrower. The various roles we fill in life, such as a spouse, parent, neighbor, or employee, help us to function during difficult times because they provide structure and generate constant contact for us with other people. These other people give us feedback, both solicited and unsolicited, enabling us to obtain additional information, thereby broadening our perspective on how to manage in difficult times.

Roles keep us going when we might have otherwise felt too emotionally drained to keep going forward. On Valentine's Day, 2013, Colorado University student Sarah Gilchriese was sexually assaulted off campus. Her assailant was another student, whom she had thought to be a friend. She reported the assault, and the university suspended her assailant for eight months. However, it took the university's student discipline office four weeks to remove the offender from campus. During this time, her attacker was permitted back on campus, repeatedly establishing contact with and further traumatizing Ms. Gilchriese.

"Most people who get assaulted don't get out of bed. They are depressed and in fear of the entire world," says Ms. Gilchriese. She felt that she was not protected by the university as she should have been, and filed a complaint with the U.S. Department of Education's Office of Civil Rights, claiming that Colorado University violated Title IX, a federal education gender equality law prohibiting discrimination on the basis of sex.

Newspapers typically respect the privacy of sexual assault victims by not publishing their names. Ms. Gilchriese permitted hers to be used in an attempt to bring attention to the university's handling of her case. Assuming the dual roles as an advocate for gender equality in the university and sexual assault survivor gave her a sense of purpose.

She became active in the on-line community, going "public about it because no one knew that this huge university had mistreated a sexual assault case, let alone their student. Being assaulted is a very traumatic thing," explains Ms. Gilchriese. "Nothing can change what happened to me. Nothing can change the way the university handled it. But my actions and activism can change the way the university handles it for ongoing survivors."

Communicating with others online helped her connect with others in the community, whose encouragement and validation, in turn, contributed towards pushing her along when she didn't feel she had the strength. "The most difficult thing for me (going forward) is to trust people again. I didn't understand, and still don't understand, how one human being can hurt another, and consciously know they are hurting them and continue to hurt them."

The support she received in her role as an advocate for sexual assault survivors helped change her perspective by shielding her against anxiety, self-doubt and fear, as well as helped her learn to trust others again. It helped prevent her from self-solation and becoming depressed. It empowered her to step outside of her pain and think about the issues on a broader level. "The online community validated a lot of the fear I was having. The world 'assault' was not in my vocabulary before it happened to me. To think about where I was ... is so dramatically different than where I am now," Ms. Gilchriese reflects.[9]

Social Institutions
Society is comprised of community institutions, including educational, religious, medical, governmental, political and the family, each providing different yet significant help to us when in need. Teachers, counselors and coaches can offer mentoring, which help us find our footing during challenging times.

They help relieve stress by expanding our perspective about relationships and need for compliance, and teaching us social skills so that we might cope better. In addition to moral guidance, religious institutions provide economic support in the form of contributions, social services, and volunteers to those in need. Sometimes they also offer health care, items such as clothing and food for the needy, and even help build low-income housing. Local, state and federal governments provide community support for different at-risk groups including the aged and people with disabilities and help financially in disasters.

One of the most significant social institutions, and one that is common to everyone is the family. It is within the family that members can help each other see a problem from a different perspective, or understand another's viewpoint. Caring families can help members understand the connection between events and become aware of the bigger picture. By doing so, members can find different meanings and optimism, which helps them have more hope when everything else may feel out of control.

The importance of the extended family for support is evident in the African American families. Historically, it is within their extended families that the deeply rooted past is culturally defined and handed down from generation to generation in the form of storytelling. These stories are more than mere stories and should not be underestimated. These are emotional oral records of past generations living under the effects of the domestic slave trade. They provide a historical and cultural perspective of intergenerational efforts in overcoming barriers due to racial discrimination, poverty, unemployment and other forms of adversity. When children who have been told these stories find themselves struggling with difficulty, they can turn to their family history of suffering. They will be able to see from an extended family perspective the importance of strength and courage when surrounded by foreboding times. They will be assisted in making difficult decisions because the connection to the behaviors, attitudes and beliefs drawn from their history helps provide a buffer against feeling alone in their pain. They will believe that they can cope better with adversity today and tomorrow because of the suffering experienced in past generations.

Spirituality
Spirituality is a highly subjective, personal experience in which we find meaning or belief in something that is greater than ourselves. It is sometimes described as the process of being aware of and accepting our inner truths so as

to be authentic, grounded and whole. Spirituality is different from religion. One can be spiritual with or without being religious, and outside of organized religion. Religion has spirituality as its basis but also has a formal set of beliefs, practices and rituals to which followers are expected to adhere.

Spirituality can help us expand our perspectives by providing meaning to our suffering. Sometimes, a traumatic experience serves as a stimulus for seeking a spiritual connection so as to reduce stress and obtain a greater sense of internal peace. Vann Henderson, of London, was just turning 18 years old and enjoying his first semester in college when he was involved in a severe automobile accident. "The police report said I hit ice. I was in a coma … with a head injury on the right side of my brain. " During his recovery, Mr. Henderson found that "everything was mechanical and slower. I went through everything; self-pity, sorrow, why me?"

A former champion high school pole-vaulter, Mr. Henderson had to go back to basics, learning to walk again. He spent three months in the hospital and a rehabilitation facility, where he applied the discipline he had learned from former sports training to his physical therapy before turning to spirituality.

"I've always kept my spirituality. It's never been a feeling of aloneness inside of me. Connected to something higher than me, I yearn for that." One day after finishing some stretching exercises, he states he "sat down to pray. But this prayer was different. It was of the deepest gratitude I could possibly describe. I closed my eyes and said, thank you so much, for the love of God and gratitude."

"Suddenly my eyes opened. And it was as though all the space in the room began to enclose on me … like being loved to death. When I felt this love enclose me, I could do nothing but cry. It was so overwhelming. It wasn't scary. The thing that was powerful about that was not the experience itself but the connection that was already there. It was feeling close to and accepting the source. Call it gratitude or appreciation, you feel connected with everything. Seeing the joy and the wonder of the world. I have observed that if you see love everywhere, the universe cannot wait to return it."

With the help of his spirituality, Mr. Henderson's perspective changed. "I now can relate to people (and help) someone going through a depression, self-pity, sorrow. I have more gifts to give through this experience. I didn't know what I really had until I didn't have it any longer. It feels like I can give anyone wings."

The spiritual reawakening, he says, "let me realize that nothing, absolutely nothing, is happening to us. Everything that we are experiencing, on one level, we bring to ourselves. And that is something that happened to me, something that I got to experience. It became so easy to control it, to persevere." Mr. Henderson's passion for others to experience his insights and happiness is so great that he states, "I would wish everyone in the world an automobile accident."[10]

Through his spiritual connection, Mr. Henderson used his experience to not only accept his suffering but to also appreciate the value of suffering as a springboard to personal growth. His spirituality broadened his perspective by enabling him to reframe a major crisis in his life and to find strengths and a deeper sense of meaning and purpose.

Religion

When we feel unprepared for the uncertainties that befall us when adversity strikes, we may struggle with self-doubt, depression, loneliness and bitterness. We will seek help for these challenges, hoping to again find our happiness. Ironically, it is through adversity that our perspective can broaden, allowing us to learn the most valuable lessons about ourselves, improve our lives, and recover our happiness. Faith that there is something greater than us lends itself to this healing and personal growth and is the basis of spirituality. While spirituality can be experienced on its own, it also is found in all major organized religions.

Religious literature is filled with examples in ancient history of how, following a significant struggle in their lives that has resulted in hardships or loss, people's perspectives changed. Often, these changes were in ways that brought renewed hope and encouragement and contributed to personal growth.

An example is a story in Genesis of Adam and Eve, God's first children who lived in a perfect state in the Garden of Eden. When they went against God's commandment and ate the forbidden fruit from the Tree of Knowledge of Good and Evil, they faced punishing adversity. God made them mortal, which meant they would now suffer sickness, pain, and eventual death.

But Eve's perspective allowed her to be aware of the opportunity for personal growth as a result of their adversity. Eve said, "Were it not for our transgression we never should have had seed children, and never should have known good and evil, and the joy of our redemption, and the eternal life which God giveth unto all the obedient." ("Pearl of Great Price," Book of Moses, 5:11)

Formal religions can help us move from anguish to a brighter place by reframing unfair and traumatic events, offering us spiritual identification with biblical characters, and providing us with different perspectives. They help us move from a place of dwelling on our despair to a place of solace and support in our most stressful moments. Like Eve, we can find a broader sense of opportunity, purpose and hope.

Christianity

Christianity's perspective is that adversity is an attention grabber; an opportunity to turn suffering into a stronger relationship with God. Before experiencing hardships, people may have allowed their focus to be downward, toward material possessions. When difficult times arise, and those previously valued possessions fail to provide the needed guidance, comfort or encouragement, they look for, they shift their focus upward toward Heaven. In doing so, Christians gain strength through their faith because they know they are not alone and that no problem is too big for God's wisdom. An example from the Bible conveys this support; "For I am the Lord, your God, who takes hold of your right hand and says to you, do not fear; I will help you." (Isaiah 41:13)

Through pain and suffering, Christian's lives can be strengthened because it is an opportunity to determine if they are living their lives as they should, and honoring God's word. Religion offers a critical yet positive moment in people's lives during which they can develop different meanings to their emotionally upsetting experiences. For example, they may decide that their pain is coming from having sinned or violated principals essential to their faith. Such interpretations can motivate them to reinvest in their relationship with God and re-examine their priorities. They can evaluate the path they are taking, and ensure that they are investing their time in healthy relationships, both with those around them and with God.

Christianity's perspective on the strength that its followers develop from the pain they experience is that it should be used to support others who are suffering. They are reminded that when in despair God did not forsake them. As God was there for them in our time of need, they can help others find hope, endurance and strength. Ultimately, faith rests on the idea that God helps Christians move on and gain newer perspectives on their lives.

Hinduism

Unlike many other religions, in which adversity may fall upon people because of their actions or actions of others, Hinduism views adversity in a broader context. Suffering is perceived as punishment for offenses committed previously, either earlier in this lifetime or a past life. If pain befalls them, it must be assumed that it is because bad karma from a past life was not entirely eradicated. So there is little they can do to correct theirs, or anyone else's, adversity. No one causes another person's difficulty. All that they can do is accept their ill fate as due punishment from a previous life.

In other words, the Hindu perspective is that people get what they deserve, but they can use their suffering as opportunities to learn about themselves so that they can modify their thoughts and attitudes. Value is placed on learning about oneself, through thoughtfulness and personal experience so as to grow beyond today's pain. Spiritual activities such as meditation, yoga, and mindfulness (focused thinking) help bring the body and mind together and serve to overcome negative thinking and debilitating fears. Insight is achieved, compassion increased, whereby they can better control their responses and reactions. Their perspective is enhanced, allowing them to see things more clearly and calmly.

Buddhism
Much like Hinduism, the Eastern-originated religion of Buddhism does not conform to the traditional Abrahamic religions concerning having a God. It is internally driven and holds Buddhists accountable for living a compassionate and peaceful existence. Their perspective on adversity is that sometimes, bad things happen because of karma.

While karma may be the cause, members can impact on the effect. Buddhism's perspective on emotions is that they should not harbor negative feelings. Buddhists are encouraged to recognize the toxic effect that negative emotions can have. For example, self-pity or pessimism will twist one's emotions and will take control of the situation. Greed and hate can arise from becoming attached to worldly things. Instead, Buddhism encourages follows to be peaceful and use inner reflection to empower appropriate responses to themselves and others, until the evil from the karmic event passes. Similar to Hindus, use of spiritual activities such as meditation, yoga, and mindfulness can broaden their ability to cope with threats to their happiness and build resilience.

Islam
The Islamic view of adversity is that it is a fact of life, is unavoidable, and is God's plan. God will test the genuineness of followers through adversity. "Do the people think that they will be left because they say, "We believe," and they will not be tested?" (Qur'an 29:2 Al Ankabut) The purpose of testing follow-

ers through suffering is to achieve the greater goal of Muslims renewing their faith in God, heeding the fact that there is only one God, and accepting that He has absolute authority in their lives. "Who responds to the distressed one when he calls Him and He removes the evil and makes you inheritors (of) the earth? Is there any god with Allah? Little (is) what you remember." (Qur'an 27:62 An Naml)

The Qur'an states that Muslims, who remain devoted to God will be able to endure the hardships of adversity and emerge morally stronger as a result of it. Staying close to God will facilitate personal rediscovery of one's inner strength. Psychological and spiritual growth can occur if followers repent, pray and perform good deeds.

Judaism

Judaism views adversity as a recurring challenge in its 3,500-year long history. The chosen people wandered the desert for 40 years, faced extermination of six million in Nazi Germany, and continue to struggle for everyday survival with suicide bombers and hostile neighbors. The theme of triumphing over adversity repeats itself continuously and is even taught annually around the family dining room table during the Passover Seder holiday. The Jewish perspective on adversity is that resilience is a life-long learning process, during which people should never give up. Jews grow up learning that in life struggles will be faced, mistakes made, frustrations overcome, weaknesses mastered, obstacles defeated, and success eventually achieved.

God is viewed as being forgiving of mistakes, even though followers must still deal with the consequences of their actions. Jews feel confident not being perfect and using trial and error to resolve problems. Questioning and doubting of God is tolerated, which also likely instills the confidence in members that they can test while not risk losing, their faith. Arguing with God about belief in one's religion is practice for learning how to resolve struggles with one's belief other life matters.

The majority of Jews are not affiliated with synagogues, yet their identity with Judaism provides a resilient factor in their perspective about resilience. Jews are encouraged to help others who are suffering. The Talmud, which speaks of Tikkun Olam, or 'to repair the world,' sets a value of helping others who face adversity. Helping others, in turn, results in helping themselves, because they learn more about adapting to stressful situations and solving problems.

Conclusion

Being able to view our adversity from different perspectives offers tremendous value in developing resilience. When we can see connections between events, and how actions influence behaviors, we begin to be able to experience shifts in our understanding of difficult situations. Much like the clarity obtained from flipping on the light switch in a darkened room, this process of collecting this information provides a powerful amount of clarity in how we see a situation.

All too often we approach the world forgetting that we are interacting with a unique view that has developed from past experiences, values, and beliefs. Sometimes we may resist in wanting to hear what others think and feel. To be open to new information means that we may have to reevaluate and even change a belief we previously held. Or we may find the information confuses us, and leaves us with mixed emotions. It can be a difficult process to go through. Our spirituality and support system helps create a positive perspective within us and break down barriers. It helps keep us grounded so that we can be motivated to receive and incorporate this information, while reducing our feelings of vulnerability. This can result in our being able to view people in a more positive light as opposed to labeling them in a negative manner.

We cannot undo the pain caused by the adversity. But our positive feelings towards others can grow when we broaden our perspective and learn more about the world outside of us. When we are able to better understand others, our trust, understanding, empathy and social bonds grows. We are then more capable of interpreting and making sense of the actions of others, which in turn helps us to be more prepared to handle the many accompanying challenges.

Suggested Exercises
for Using the Three Spheres of Support
to Enhance Your Perspective-Taking Abilities

Solving adversity is easier to do if we consider different points of view. Perspective taking isn't easy to master, but well worth the effort, since we cannot read other's minds, nor they ours. To help us learn how to view perspectives from three points of view; from ourselves, from the other person, and from that of a third party (like a fly on the wall), practice exercises are provided below. The perspective building activities are grouped in the three spheres of support: Self, Society, and Spirituality.

Self

1. *Rewrite Ends of Your Sentences*

   Your negative thoughts interfere with your ability to move successfully beyond adversity. They keep you focused on problems rather than solutions. Negative thoughts keep you trapped in the black hole of pessimism, where we are likely to develop unhelpful or incorrect perspectives that are negatively charged.

   Changing your thoughts can change your perspective. Instead of allowing yourself to have negative thoughts, such as, "I'm a loser. I did such a poor presentation. I lost the promotion I had hoped to get," reframe it with, "I may not get promoted, but now I know I have an opportunity to work on and improve my speech delivery techniques. This will help me in either this job, for future promotions or in other jobs, should I decide to look elsewhere for employment."

   Reframing keeps you from becoming a victim. It is empowering because it helps you cultivate confident feelings and connect with others. The pessimistic self-talk is replaced with new encouraging words, which will replace your negative thoughts. Your focus will become more positive, your perspectives broadened, and your resiliency enhanced.

2. *Journaling*

   Many times, you have a problem and it takes up residency in your head, like an unwanted trespassing visitor. You end up ruminating about it, which often doesn't solve the problem. Rather, you just end up feeling more isolated and frustrated.

   Nothing helps you make sense of such a problem as well as transferring it from your head and on to paper. No matter how many times you have ruminated about a problem in your mind, there is a clarify that comes from writing down your thoughts and feelings about the arduous life experience. It gives you an opportunity to organize your beliefs and self-reflect on what you feel needs to be done to overcome the obstacles.

This isn't a graded paper. It is just an exercise that allows you to organize your thoughts so you can reflect on where you have been and where you are going. Reading it over will facilitate personal growth as you learn more about yourself. You might discover different ideas that had not previously been considered.

3. *Write Your Obituary*

It may sound morbid, but go ahead and write your obituary. Write it as though you had died today. Do you like what you see? Is that how you want your life to be remembered? Are you happy, or is something missing?

Reviewing what you wrote will give you a new perspective on your life. Reflect on how, if you do not like the direction in which you are going, you can 'rewrite' your life so that you to more become more self-accepting and focused on moving forward.

4. *Review Your Script*

Sometimes you may have these voices in your head that get in your way. These are not the voices of psychosis, but rather, voices that are judgmental and critical of you. It gets to be that way because you have linked a memory with your emotion and perception. It becomes your truth, even if the facts are exaggerated or wrong, distorting our perspective. You can call it noise, or 'self-talk'; but it becomes a script that you hear over and over again. It reappears when an event similar to the one that created the scenario occurs.

An example of a story is that of a woman who views herself as unlovable and undeserving. How did this become her truth? When she was four years old, her parents divorced. Before the divorce, her parents argued violently. She often heard her name spoken in those arguments. Young children are too young to understand adult matters, and she wrongly assumed she was responsible for the breakup of her parent's marriage. She saw her parents struggle financially and emotionally following the divorce, and they often did not have the energy to attend to her emotional needs. As a sad and lonely four-year-old, she came to believe that she did not deserve love.

You can see that this script is plain out wrong. But it is her truth and she has carried it into adulthood, impairing her ability to live a full and happy life. To a larger or lesser degree, we all have our scripts. They hinder our ability to cope in times of adversity.

Think about the scripts that are blocking your ability to achieve your goals. If you changed your viewpoint on these scripts, how would your life be different? Challenge them by broadening your perspectives. Face your fears and consider other ways to address the situation you now face. Challenge them with positive, gentle, compassionate words. Reframe mistakes or disappointments; they needn't be because of what your life-long script has had you believe. Be open to making mistakes. You will find yourself developing new perspectives about yourself and others, which will aid you in conflict resolution.

5. *Catch Yourself Changing Perspectives*

    Personal growth in developing new perspectives can feel slower than watching a group of snails crawl through a mud puddle in your backyard. Valuable changes can take place in the process of personal growth, but you may fail to recognize them as being important. What you have to remember is that successful changing of perspectives is accomplished through the small changes in thinking, feeling or behaving. Each change is an accomplishment and should be recognized and memorialized, lest you forget.

    Write down each time you find yourself considering a change in your perspective, or learn that the motivation for the other person's behavior was different from what you had previously thought. For example, if you tend to be negative or judgmental but find yourself listening to someone with an open mind, document this positive change in perspective development. You will be expanding your current beliefs, and begin thinking in a different, more accurate manner.

6. *Make a Gratitude List*

    Gratitude is a mind shift in the way we think about things. It is the process of noticing and acknowledging that we have been the beneficiary of receiving something positive. You can have gratitude for common day experiences, such as being able to see the sunset, or for something you receive, such as a favor from a friend. Dr. Robert Emmons, considered the world's leading authority on gratitude, found that gratitude contributes to being happy, having stronger relationships and helps you bounce back faster from adversity.

You are likely appreciative of all the small and large things that are already present in your life. But written gratitude lists help remind you to keep focused on appreciating the blessings in your life rather than taking the good things for granted. Developing a gratitude list helps broaden your perspective on the positive things in your life, and helps you build up the muscle of appreciation.

The exercise consists of committing to writing something every day for which you have gratitude. Writing by hand slows down and separates the process from the many other hours spent pounding away on the computer. Hand-connected-to-pen-connected-to-paper brings you closer to the feeling of gratitude.

There are two caveats: each entry has to be unique and detailed. In other words, if you are appreciative of your friend coming and caring for your baby yesterday when you were sick, it cannot be used again if the helpful gesture was repeated the following day. Second, the event should be described in detail as opposed to an abbreviated note.

Gratitude will help put things in perspective when adversity strikes. The more you train yourself to look for gratitude, the more the attitude of gratitude will grow. You will be in the habit of looking for things to be thankful for, and will view problems with the question of, 'What is the gift in here for me? How can I learn from this?'

Finally, the list will help you when you are stressed. Taking out the list and reading it will help put things in perspective for you by arresting negative thoughts that make you feel angry or powerless. Instead, it will help you feel in control of your future and make your situation feel more manageable.

7. *Forest vs. Trees Perspective*

   In a crisis, how often do you have difficulty seeing the forest for the trees? Do you tend to focus on one single tree — one viewpoint — in times of adversity? If so, while that is entirely understandable, doing so narrows your perspective.

   But if you change your perspective and look at the entire forest, you will see the bigger picture. It helps detach you from a self-oriented to a more expansive perspective. You will benefit because you become aware of information, resources, and other views that you previously overlooked.

   Sometimes spending time alone can enable you to set aside some of your emotions so that you can reflect on your situation with a healthy, more rational outlook. Allow yourself some time each day to be without electronic distractions or other people. It needn't be a long period of time. When you remove distractions and allow yourself the opportunity to concentrate, you can discover a deeper layer of thinking that lends itself to finding fresh and creative strategies for working through your problems.

8. *Focus On What You Can Control*

   Long-term stress, the type that accompanies adversity, can have detrimental effects on your health, and prevent you from achieving your goals and objectives. You can reduce your level of stress by changing your perspective.

   Focus on what you can control, rather than focusing too much attention, time, and energy trying to manage things out of your control. It's hard to accept this, but in the long run, you will feel less like a victim, will have more confidence in yourself, and can regain control over your life.

   To achieve this goal, start by keeping a list of the things within your control. You will be surprised to see how the list grows as your awareness of all that you still have control over is greater than originally realized.

9. *Optimism*

   Optimism helps you stay capable and confident during challenging times, so consciously choosing to have an optimistic, rather than pessimistic perspective, will help you manage adversity better.

You can make optimism a new habit by keeping a list of negative thoughts as they develop, and asking yourself if they are valid. In particular, ask yourself how pervasive the issue is, if it is temporary or permanent, and are other aspects of your life still manageable? Follow this by responding optimistically and ask yourself what the 'gift,' or learning experience is? By focusing on the positive rather than on the bad things, you will be better able to find good outcomes.

10. *Change Your Vantage Point*

Increase your awareness of how your perspective may be limited by considering things from a different point of view. Compare your perspective with that of a toddler's. Discover how a child might see your home differently than you by getting down on the floor and crawling around on your hands and knees. Crawl up the stairs and notice how big they are to someone who is so little. Notice how nearly everything you want is out of reach. You will learn to appreciate the different realities two people can have even when sharing the same setting.

Society

1. *Ask Others to Share Their Perspectives With You*

If you have difficulty viewing different perspectives on a matter, ask someone you know about their perspective on this issue. Do you find them to have a broader view, more options, or more flexibility in overcoming an obstacle? If so, ask them how they came to that conclusion and consider incorporating what you have learned into your view of a situation.

2. *Empathic Listening*

Empathic listening is a mixture of listening to the other person while trying to see the world through their perspective. It builds mutual understanding and trust, reduces tension, helps us learn additional information, and makes the setting feel safe to all parties to be able to express themselves.

You can practice developing this skill with someone with whom you feel comfortable. Have the other person share their view on a topic. He talks, you listen. Listen without interrupting or giving advice or expressing criticism. Work at staying present, listening without thinking about how you want to respond. Listen to the other person's words, emotions, and facial expression. Perhaps you will be learning something. You do not have to forsake your perspective to be able to appreciate his viewpoint. When the person is done, encourage him to continue, if he wants to add anything else. Then, summarize what you heard the other person say, and his feelings. You will be able to receive confirmation as to whether you were listening, heard him correctly, and respected his perspective.

When you have completed this, switch sides, and have the other person listen to your point of view. How does it feel to have someone listen to your perspective? Do you notice any change in his perspective after you have had the opportunity to share?

3. *Partner Perception Check*

Ask someone you trust to partner with you to correct inaccurate perspectives that are causing you to experience negative feelings.

Partner A: Share a troubling event and describe your negative feelings and thoughts about it.

Partner B: After hearing about the event, ask your partner if there are any facts to support his viewpoint. Listen for accuracy in your partner's description and possible distortions in thinking.

Partner B: Now ask your partner if any other possible viewpoints could have existed that would have impacted on his negative reaction.

Partner A: Reflect on what you have discussed. Are there changes in how you think and feel about the event, now that you have a broader perspective? If the same event were to occur again, would your thoughts and emotional reactions be different?

4. *Parental Conversations*

Children typically view an incident from their viewpoint. It is a learning process to understand that others have different motivations, needs, thoughts or feelings. Parents can teach children an awareness of other people's perspectives by talking about them. When upset with someone else, ask the child what they believe to be the other person's intention. Did the other person mean to do harm, or was it an accident? Were there other factors to consider? Modeling the value of a broader view on life helps children learn not to jump to conclusions.

Spirituality

1. *Spiritual Reflection*

   Contemplative practices such as spiritual reflection help you become more aware of your life, and your connection to the world around you. When conducted in a quiet and peaceful way, it helps you connect all aspects of yourself: your body, mind, and spirituality. The result is a greater peace of mind and reduction in stress. Positive feelings and a sense of empowerment, which provide the path to considering different perspectives, will follow. You will find yourself capable of shifting from a place of powerlessness stemming from the challenges to discovering a sense of meaning and purpose, thereby increasing the resiliency in your life.

2. *Meditation*

   Find time each day to sit quietly, focus on your breathing, and calm your mind. It can open your mind to alternative points of view and see things with a new perspective. Choose the time of day and how long you want to commit to this exercise. The amount of time spent is not as important as creating a new habit of incorporating meditation into your lifestyle.

3. *Nature*

   Being able to step outside of yourself and view the larger picture is a perspective changing opportunity. Visit a place where you can sit outdoors, undisturbed. Spend an hour alone, just being in nature, without distractions of music or talking. Relax. Observe. Be.

4. *Serve Others*

   When coping with adversity, people often turn the full range of their time and attention on to themselves. Ironically, helping others less fortunate can help you cope better with your problems. This occurs because doing for others releases the good chemicals in the brain that make you feel good. Feeling good reduces your stress, allowing space for positive emotions to grow. Helping others and thinking of their challenges, and what they need to do to resolve their problems shifts your view of the world from 'me' to 'we'. You're able to see things from another vantage point, increasing your perspective of the world.

Chapter 4

Perseverance

"No one succeeds without effort ... Those who
succeed owe their success to perseverance."

— Bhagavan Sri Ramana Maharshi, Indian sage, and jivanmukta

Why is it, that when two people share similar attributes, assets, resources, social skills, strategies, emotional intelligence, and personality traits, one perseveres in times of adversity while the other does not? What exactly are the strengths and resources that enable some people not just to survive, but thrive, when exposed to stressful circumstances?

For example, why does one talented person invest time and energy writing a manuscript but become discouraged and give up searching for a publisher after five, or six, or even a dozen rejections? Theodor Seuss Geisel persevered, even though 23 publishers rejected his first book. Best known for his pen name, Dr. Seuss, he went on to write a total of 46 children's books. Agatha Christie waited 5 years before finding a publisher that would agree to accept her first book. Her perseverance paid off, with book sales topping two billion dollars.

Many others in history have exhibited a relentless drive that enabled them to endure difficult times. Howard Schultz, the founder of Starbucks, talked to

200 investors before he had sufficient financial backing to start his company. Inventor James Dyson spent five years developing well over five thousand prototypes before he succeeded in perfecting the Dual Cyclone bagless vacuum cleaner. He reportedly then faced rejection by manufacturers and distributors of the vacuum cleaner because it would eliminate the need for replacement bags (a financially rewarding market). Rather than accept failure, he undertook the daunting task of developing his own manufacturing company, and in time his vacuum cleaner became the market leader. Wanting to inspire others by his perseverance, Dyson co-wrote a book about his experience, *Against the Odds*.

There are individual differences in the ways in which people think about and approach adversity. But research scientists have found that one quality, perseverance, helps people keep their heads up and eyes focused on the goal, helping them maintain their determination despite early failures.

Individuals who persevere don't withdraw from challenges. They ignore the message that "good things will come to those who wait." Instead, those who persevere push forward and take on challenging endeavors, even when they stumble and encounter disappointment time and time again. Rather than quitting, they get up, wipe off the dust, assess what they have learned from these mistakes, and rethink how they will improve the likelihood of reaching their goals.

Perseverance has always helped people overcome adversity. It has contributed to the formation of societies and countries. Perseverance has helped us move from the wheel to the plow, eyeglasses to contacts, and light bulbs to power plants. Perseverance has resulted in breakthroughs in all categories of achievement, and impacted on modern life as we know it today.

What is Perseverance?

In times of adversity, people are faced with numerous decisions, problems, and challenges. Perseverance is critical at these times. It denotes a "can-do" attitude, the refusal to surrender, and instead, to persist even when making mistakes, experiencing failures and ongoing problems. When some people are viewed as lucky, it is likely that in truth, their hard work and steadfast dedication fuels them along to remain motivated in achieving the goal they want.

We grow up hearing stories about how, through perseverance, people ultimately break down barriers that develop along the way and triumph over their problems. Be it in business or health matters, in romantic relationships or academics, the dogged determination of perseverance influences all courses of action in our lives.

We've all succeeded in persevering. Remember the process you engaged in when learning to play an instrument, speak a new language, or drive a stick shift? We didn't quit after our first attempt. Instead, when we encountered unexpected challenges, we applied persistence, resolution, backbone and determination. We had a "stick-to-itiveness" and rather than be defeated, we eventually found success. We were successful because we put the needed amount of effort into the activity and committed the amount of time that would be required when we had inevitable setbacks or failure. Had we not been perseverant, we would have become discouraged from the stress resulting from the problems along the way and given up.

Being able to look at a situation and believe that we can have a meaningful influence on it occurs because we have a combination of unique qualities and resources. This includes the interplay between our self-efficacy, grit, social intelligence, self-control, brain chemistry, personality, adjustability, agreeableness, and malleability.

Self-Efficacy

Self-efficacy leads to resilience. Originally coined by psychologist Albert Bandura, self-efficacy is the belief that we have the skills to accomplish a goal, even if we experience disappointment along the way. If we believe we have the attitude, ability, and intellectual skills to experience success, we will be more likely to persevere when struggling with adversity. This belief in ourselves means we will welcome taking on difficult tasks that can help us overcome adversity, motivated in part because we attribute success as being within our control. Unlike people with a low self-efficacy, we will put more effort into it because we believe that if we do not have all the skills required to tackle a situation that we can learn along the way, improve our skills, and achieve success. We stand a greater chance of success in completing the task because we are able to visualize ourselves succeeding.

We develop a strong sense of efficacy by applying effort and experiencing accomplishments. Think back to when you learned to ride a bicycle. It took considerable effort to master the skills required to stay upright, while simultaneously balancing, steering, pedaling, and keeping an eye out for pedestrians, dogs, and thorny bushes. The lessons learned in falling, applying Band-Aids, and maybe shedding a tear or two taught us that sticking it out would help us eventually emerge victors. We built confidence in ourselves in these previous experiences and learned that we could have some control over our current situation as well as other problems in the future.

The same motivation that drove the commitment to mastering the skill of bike riding is a trait found in perseverant people. They are not passive when they experience difficulties. Instead, the more they believe in themselves, and the more they can visualize success, the harder they will work to achieve it. They can recall previous struggles and how rewarding it was to push through uncertainties and problems.

A few years ago, Alan Levy was facing a mid-life crisis. Too young to retire, but feeling like he was unappreciated, unsupported, and disrespected at work, he quit his job. Change is never easy, but Mr. Levy decided to seek employment in another industry, in which he had formerly worked, ten years prior. When he discovered that he was no longer a good match for that youth driven, constantly changing industry, he found himself home, unemployed again, and miserable.

"I was struggling. I was at a crossroads and didn't know what to do with the rest of my life," he reflects. "I could very easily have fallen into a depression. Not having a purpose, I lost my self-esteem, and I lost myself." He looked for employment, but had difficulty because, "I had a fear of rejection that no one was going to hire me."

Reflecting on his fear of rejection, and how it was immobilizing him, he recalled a painful time in his past when he had been fearful of being rejected, and drew from that experience. Mr. Levy is homosexual. He recalls that, "When I was in my 20's I was homophobic because I was afraid of rejection from my family and my parents. From the 1980's to the 1990's I led a double life. It was like a ten-ton weight on my shoulders. One day, despite my major fear of my parents and family rejecting me, I met with them and said, 'I can't take it anymore. This is who I am,' and hoped that they would love me as I am. They accepted it and said they want me be happy."

While he now feels "that fear of rejection (for being gay) is a distant memory," he recognizes the positive impact it had on his life. "It lifted that weight off of my shoulder and made me who I am today. I used to worry that people were judging me. Coming out to my parents helped me learn that I am OK as a person," recalls Mr. Levy. "Dealing with the career change and period of unemployment would have been much harder had I not had that experience of coming out to my family. I don't know what place I'd be in today. It absolutely helped me take the career rejections a little less harshly."

Mr. Levy felt more capable of mastering challenges because his view of himself and his capabilities had changed forever. Now realizing that he had the capacity to master problems, he was less likely to shy away from, and avoid them. This increased his commitment to working on the arduous task of selecting a career path and securing a job. He recovered faster from his difficulties because he saw himself as the primary influencer of his own success. "I overcame that fear," he happily reports. "I knew I could do it and I proved it. I realized that only I can take myself out of that (place of depression and unemployment), and that I had the choice to make the change. I decided I am going to revitalize myself, I am going to start fresh, and I am going to be consistent. And it has paid off. The other day someone came up to me and said, 'Alan, you've changed. I see the passion in you that I did not see not see at the old company. I see how different you are working and how happy you are.' I guess it just took me a while to overcome that fear and realize I had learned so much," said Mr. Levy.[1]

Rather than becoming overwhelmed by a new problem, people with a high level of self-efficacy look at situations as a challenging task. In times of adversity they are curious and eager to master the hardship and believe that they have the skill set to address it.

This confidence does not always bring about success when dealing with their challenges. However, if they fail, they will be less likely to experience as much stress, self-blame, and depression, as those with lower levels of efficacy. People with low self-efficacy are more likely to avoid taking risks because they do not have confidence in their skills. Rather than focusing on their strengths, they put their time and energy into tallying up what they perceive to be their personal shortcomings, the various obstacles they might encounter, and all the undesirable consequences that might come as a result of taking on a challenge. When they do take on a challenge, their extreme anxiety undermines efforts to master the inevitable difficult tasks they encounter, placing them at higher risk of dropping out.

The good news is that efficacy can be developed. Experiencing success with small tasks will increase our likelihood of succeeding with more challenging tasks in the future. Vicariously watching others thrive helps us believe that we, too, can succeed when facing problems. Visualizing success, and being able to see ourselves as accomplishing our goal will help build self-efficacy. Preparing ahead for the inevitable problems, and having a plan for addressing them, will also contribute to building self-efficacy.

Chapters one and two of this book address the enormous role that belief in ourselves plays in overcoming our challenges. The importance of self-belief is seen in current research. In her book *Mindset,* Dweck identified two different types of mindsets, fixed and growth, and found that what people achieve is based on what they believe about themselves. Those with a fixed mindset believe it's all in the genes. They think their skills are mostly fixed and predetermined, that they're born with basic qualities and abilities like brains and talent, or they're not. They can't be changed or developed. Therefore, any success we can achieve can be obtained without effort, and any limitations we have are permanent. People with a fixed mindset have little incentive to pursue goals in which they do not feel competent and confident. Because they prefer to surround themselves with safe and familiar goals, rather than goals that involve learning and growing, their motivation to persevere is undermined.

A growth mindset, on the other hand, occurs when people embrace the belief that their intelligence and talents can be developed and strengthened through training, hard work and practice. They're willing to try new things, even if they're experiencing some failure. Rather than abandoning ship when the going gets tough, they see obstacles and failure as a normal part of life. They value feedback, recognizing that others have also had struggles and failures along the way, and can help them learn new skills. It's those with a growth mindset, those who believe that they can learn, change, and grow, that gives them a feeling of control over their destiny and are more likely to find resilience.

The role of perseverance has been researched in many settings, including student academic performance. It has been found that students with a growth mindset demonstrate a higher level of perseverance in attending class, completing assignments, learning from failure, and sticking to tasks until completed.[2] They devote more effort in overcoming their challenges than are those with a fixed mindset and will more likely persevere and attain their goals.

Tenacity/Persistence/Grit

Some people may refer to perseverance as tenacity, persistence or grit. There are similarities and overlap in these terms. Each addresses the ability to work hard, manage challenges and aim for goals. Differences between these three terms are slight. Tenacity is about being very determined, and sticking with something even during the difficult times. Persistence is also about remaining in pursuit of a goal. Grit is probably the closest to perseverance, providing energy and helping us achieve our long-term goals.

Gritty people are known for staying the course when striving for a goal rather than being deterred by distractions. Research done by psychologist Angela Duckworth discovered grit, the ability to set and keep goals, to be important in achieving success. Lack of grittiness is one explanation for why one in five cadets cannot persevere in their education and training at the United States Military Academy at West Point and drops out before graduation. Dr. Duckworth found that possession of grit plays a role in students' willingness to persevere in hopes of winning the Scripps National Spelling Bee. But perhaps her research is best known for its discovery about academic success and grittiness. Duckworth identified a relationship between grittiness and high reading and math achievement in elementary school students. She also found grittiness to be a greater indicator of likelihood to graduate high school than grade point average and IQ.[3]

Academic goals are often set years in the future. If our goal is to become a veterinarian, chemical engineer, or lawyer, there are many obstacles and distractions we encounter along the way, requiring the ability to delay gratification and maintain self-discipline. These are skills that comprise perseverance. Grit, persistence, and tenacity are valuable components of perseverance, providing us with the ability to persist in reaching our goal, and not become overwhelmed by unexpected stress, failure and plateaus.

Social Intelligence

Psychologists identify different ways we learn and solve problems. Our ability to overcome adversity is largely dependent on how we think about ourselves and the world, and different ways we incorporate this information for ourselves. For example, understanding ourselves factors in to how successful we are at avoiding past mistakes, as well as moving forward towards revised and more productive new goals.

Many people are familiar with the term emotional intelligence (EI), a concept brought to the attention of many by Daniel Goleman in his book, *Emotional Intelligence.* Emotional intelligence is about managing our own feelings and emotions, being empathic to others, and having the social skills to handle other's emotions. Social intelligence, a concept discussed widely by developmental psychologist Dr. Howard Gardner, is about our social competence, and how well we understand and can relate to others and build relationships with them. Like emotional intelligence, social intelligence has nothing to do with how smart we are.

Social intelligence will get us where our book smarts won't because it includes the ability to relate to individuals or groups in different social, economic, political and cultural contexts. We need to have a willingness to approach people and unfamiliar situations when struggling to overcome our adversity. By being open to new ideas from other people we can collect helpful information. In turn, we will be better able to manage our stress, make wiser decisions, and persevere in overcoming adversity.

Charles Darwin, the father of evolutionary biology, recognized the importance of empathy, labeling it a "powerful aid to survival in nature's toolkit." When dealing with adversity our ability to connect with others is often vital for our survival, and fortunately, our brain is built for helping us succeed in connecting and empathizing with others. In the 1990s it was discovered that mirror neurons, a special class of brain cells that fire up when interacting with another person, play a role in communication by helping us relate to the behavior of others. This fascinating finding that our neurons connect with others' neurons may be behind the saying, "Neurons that fire together, wire together." After all, if we are able to understand and experience the emotions others are feeling, be it anger, confusion, happiness or sadness, then it is likely that we are hard-wired to empathize with others.

This sociability plays a role in the survival of the rhesus macaques, a group of monkeys that live on the remote island of Cayo Santiago in the Caribbean. When entering adolescence, the male monkeys strike out in search of a new troop. This is a treacherous time for the monkeys, with up to 20 percent of them killed when they approach an unfamiliar troop. Researchers discovered that the most social monkeys, who are able to approach, befriend and challenge monkeys in the new troop are also the ones most likely to survive.[4]

Like the Caribbean monkeys, connecting with others will help us persevere when faced with difficult situations. When we validate other's feelings, are open-minded about learning about them, are genuinely empathic towards others who are different in some manner of belief, appearance, behavior, or thinking, we can establish rapport. When we become more aware of nonverbal emotional cues others are providing and are cooperative and respectful of their boundaries, our social intelligence increases and we are better able to understand them. We will be more likely able to share our views in a way that enables others to help us. Even if exhausted and struggling to find the bandwidth to keep pushing forward, social intelligence will help us bounce back with the resilience to try again.

Self-Control

Self-control is the yellow brick road that leads us to perseverance. It is an excellent indicator of impulse control and being able to delay gratification. Being able to forgo short-term pleasures, distractions, and indulgences, for the purpose of keeping our eye on the prize, will help us in the challenges of overcoming adversity.

Self-control has been studied extensively over the decades. We know that a lack of it causes stress and a host of impulsive, shortsighted behaviors. When we lose the ability to stick to our goals we make short-term decisions that create long-term problems. Such problems can lead to difficulties with relatively small consequences, such as overeating and under-exercising, to life changing effects such as ruptured personal and professional relationships, academic failure, addictive and illegal behavior. Self-control is at the root of our being able to persevere in times of adversity, yet people tend to not appreciate its value, nor do they recognize it in themselves. When over a million people worldwide were asked to identify their virtues, self-control came in dead last, lagging far behind honesty, kindness, humor, creativity, and bravery.[5]

Exercising self-control is a conscious choice we make. It requires self-awareness because when we acknowledge what we are doing, the likelihood that we will influence our behavior increases by leaps and bounds. Just ask anyone who wants to lose weight to spend the next week documenting every morsel that goes in his or her mouth. Simple awareness of their behavior will result in a reduction of calorie intake and a likelihood of weight loss, even before starting on their diet!

It requires energy to exercise self-control. Sometimes in our struggle we may find our energy is zapped, but we still need to persevere. It is analogous to muscle fatigue. The marathon runner hits that 20-mile wall. His legs cramp and feel like wooden pegs. But self-control prevents him from giving up and quitting the race. That marathon runner is able to push to the 26-mile finish line because he has an expectation of how he wants to be. He knows he can change his behavior. He invested in reliable running shoes, spent time practicing running this long race, and he developed healthy habits, including eating nutritious food that would energize him for long durations and getting a proper amount of sleep. He devised visualizations, solved problems in his head, or listened to music, as a way of distracting himself from the grueling asphalt streets he was running. We aren't born with self-control. But like the runner, we can learn to make self-control more automatic and impulsivity less attractive by creating behaviors that will enhance the likelihood of remaining true to our values and goals.

Neuroscience (Brain Chemistry)

We are wired to persevere. In our brain, we have neurotransmitters, whose job is to shuttle information from one brain cell to another. The king neurotransmitter is that "feel-good" chemical, dopamine, which is associated with providing motivation, learning, and curiosity that helps us want to achieve a goal.

Dopamine's chemical signal travels a path in our brain, across the spaces between cells, interacting with different docking station molecules called receptors. These receptors carry the dopamine signal from one cell to another. This remarkable neurotransmitter was originally biologically designed to help with our survival. Forty thousand years ago, dopamine helped our ancestors with their survival by providing a desire for exploration and information. If they didn't have dopamine, they'd have been lethargic and would not have accomplished tasks necessary for their survival, such as hunting for meals, and building shelters. We have evolved over the centuries. Today we are more likely to be chased by a bill collector than a saber tooth tiger. We now have grocery stores and comfortable beds and don't need this surge of chemicals to kick us into gear so that we focus on our survival. As a result, our primal instincts are not triggering the production and release of dopamine for day-to-day survival.

However, we need the release of dopamine because it makes us want something. Much like it worked for our prehistoric ancestors, dopamine encourages our motivation to explore and learn. The motivation of wanting something helps us be more flexible and open to new thoughts and behaviors and provides us with the drive and incentive to want to seek answers. None of us delight in uncertainty. Uncertainty tends to trigger stress in us, but dopamine helps us feel comfortable with ambiguity, and less likely to quit before reaching our goal. It contributes to our memory, our thoughts, and our behavior. It is easy to see why the evolutionary process has not deleted dopamine from our brains. This drive to explore provides us with essential perseverance skills when we are struggling to overcome adversity.

It appears that we are supposed to be using our dopamine because scientists have found it to be a "use it or lose it" feel-good neurotransmitter. People who have lower levels of dopamine in their brains are more tired, and are less able to focus and concentrate. Christopher Bergland, a three-time champion of the Triple Ironman, says, "If you do not accomplish something every day your dopamine reserves will diminish. Humans are designed to work hard and to be rewarded for their efforts biologically. Being uninspired and lacking self-motivation is a downward spiral that can snowball out of control. It's so easy to become bitter, cynical and hopeless when your dopamine reserves are low."[6]

The good news is that we can train our brains to provide us with more dopamine. Neurologist Judy Willis, an authority on brain research, suggests we provide ourselves with positive feedback along the way when struggling to overcome a challenge. Years ago, this author worked with surgical nurses at George Washington University Medical Center in Washington D.C. Many were emotionally drained and physically fatigued from spending long hours dealing with documentation, changing technology, caring for very complicated, sick patients, and communicating with these patient's family members. Positioned at the receiving end of orders from physicians and stress from patients, the nurses were committed to providing a high level of care yet feeling, in some cases, burned out. Learning self-care techniques, such as pausing each hour to reflect on small accomplishments and give themselves a pat on the back, rather than waiting for appreciation from others, and learning to practice meditation and relaxation techniques, reduced their anxiety and increased their motivation. Understanding how to appreciate incremental success along the way to attaining long-term goals resulted in a reduction in anxiety and a greater sense of career satisfaction. In essence, the nurses learned the skills to help their dopamine to flow more frequently.

Another way we can have a positive influence on our dopamine is to be attentive to our nutrition. Many foods play a role in helping balance our dopamine levels. They include eggs, fish, chicken, kale, apples, bananas, strawberries, wheat germ, edamame, oatmeal, seaweed, and wheat germ.

Personality and Achievement

Psychologists have found that personality traits are anchored in biology, remain relatively stable throughout our lives, and tend to fit into one of five core character traits. As discussed earlier in chapters one and three, these traits are openness, conscientiousness, extroversion, agreeableness, and neuroticism.

While some days we may exhibit one character trait more than another, on the average, we will fit into one of these five traits. These five traits, which influence the likelihood of being able to persevere when facing challenges in our lives, are addressed below.

Openness

People who are characterized as having openness as a personality trait tend to be curious. Curiosity is linked to a variety of behaviors that support perseverance, including a search for new information and experiences. These individuals place value in trying new ideas, thinking unconventionally, and continuously learning. Openness is also tied to being able to tolerate uncertainty, and feel more confident about how to manage unexpected feelings or thoughts, which makes moving into unfamiliar environments less intimidating when overcoming adversity.[7]

Conscientiousness

People who are conscientious are achievement oriented. They tend to be highly self-disciplined and will doggedly pursue possible resolutions. Rather than being spontaneous or impulsive, which could result in poor decision-making, they will be organized and develop behaviors designed to reach their goals. They persevere when they encounter obstacles, working continuously to create new ways to reach these goals, and are more likely to achieve success.

Extraversion

It seems that many of us like to surround ourselves with extraverts. And why not? They're friendly, cheerful and have positive energy. They are social and can develop relationships rather effortlessly. They also tend to be assertive, which helps them push forward and persevere. While these traits would make it appear that extraverts are built to overcome adversity, research findings reveal that we shouldn't be discouraged if our personality type leans more to being the opposite, an introvert. In her book, *Quiet: The Power of Introverts in a World That Can't Stop Talking*, Susan Cain writes that while it is true that introverts approach problems more quietly and slowly, they do so with careful, concentrated attention. They tend to be more reflective, listen well to others, and have a good social intelligence and empathy for others. Extraverts, on the other hand, tend to have a higher activity level but aren't always as focused as the introvert. Extraverts are more likely to get distracted, losing sight of the goal. It's not their fault. "Extraverts have lower levels of cortisol arousal and therefore tend to seek out external stimulation to reach an optimal level of arousal. Introverts, however, have higher levels of cortical arousal, so too much stimulation can be draining," Cain points out.[8]

Agreeableness

Agreeable personalities are well suited for perseverance because of their ability to be honest and direct, while also being cooperative, accepting, and caring. Their openness makes them receptive to changing their views when presented with new ideas from others, and able to learn from their mistakes, which helps in tackling problems.

People who are disagreeable, on the other hand, tend to be critical, unfriendly and uncooperative. This reduces their ability to benefit from additional information, less likely to enhance their understanding of a problem, and therefore less likely to develop new skills needed for overcoming adversity.

Neuroticism

Neurotic people are not stable under pressure. When they view a situation to be a problem, they will be more reactive than other personality types. They tend to be more susceptible to negative emotions, including pessimism, fear, and anger, with less control over their impulses, and less adaptable to adversity.

Malleability

To persevere, we must accept that change is possible. If we view situations as fixed and unchangeable, we are likely to feel discouraged and stuck. We won't see the value in putting forth the energy to make changes that could enhance our ability to overcome the adversity. We won't see the opportunities that arise along the way that could help us.

Being malleable means we accept that our viewpoints can be influenced, and that we have the ability to learn from new information presented to us. Novel experiences influence our perspectives, which in turn impacts on our awareness of available options. This malleability helps us to reframe the event in such a manner as to find new ways to persevere.

Why is Perseverance so Important?

Adversity often begins with one painful event, but is ongoing, changes, and impacts on many aspects of our lives. Having the resilience to persevere helps create the right actions to deal with these difficult circumstances.

Many people give up when they become overwhelmed by their distress. Giving up is easy. It is the path of least resistance. To persevere is to learn from our failures, push past obstacles and continue trying to reach our goals. Following are some of the most significant ways perseverance helps us become more resilient in difficult times.

Prevents Procrastination

None of us are strangers to procrastination. We've all had the experience of putting off something important that needs to be done, even though doing so was not in our interest. Sometimes procrastination is a protective mechanism. When solving a problem means we would have to step outside our comfort zone, it can create anxiety. Perhaps we are afraid of making a mistake. Or we are afraid of what a change might mean to us. We might not realize it, but if we don't focus on dealing with the issue being avoided, it will continue to exist, remain a source of stress, and even grow. New and seemingly unrelated problems will pop up as fast as weeds in a flowerbed following a summer rain. We'll see our mental health take a beating and our emotional stress grow as our self-confidence shrinks. We'll make poor life decisions that include not taking care of ourselves, and withdrawing from relationships. In doing so, we will become more vulnerable to suffering poor physical health because we are more apt to select unhealthy lifestyle choices such as increased cigarette smoking, poor diet or lack of exercise. Procrastination will become our lifestyle, and impact on reaching out for medical care for conditions such as hypertension or cardiovascular disease, further hindering our ability to cope.

Perseverance helps us embrace the challenging thoughts or behaviors and become more emotionally invested in working toward our goal. Our motivation will increase, while tendencies to procrastinate diminish, as we push forward on tasks required for overcoming our adversity.

Prevents Frustration, Blame and Anger

Anger is a healthy emotion and serves the purpose of alarming us that a threat is present. Most of the time we can manage our anger as well as the perceived threat. But often, when trying to cope with adversity, we are also struggling with the loss of structure and predictability in our lives, leaving us frustrated and blaming others. Frustration can build, and if we let it get out of control, our anger can go against our best interests and create physical and emotional problems for us.

If we suppress our anger rather than express our feelings directly to those who have hurt us, we risk becoming cynical, passive-aggressive, or openly hostile. Or we can end up expressing our anger at someone else, retaliating, or ruminating about our hurt. Either way, being stuck in anger can make us sick. We may develop dizziness, nausea, muscle tension, and problems with concentration and memory. Relationships might be negatively impacted, and long-term depression may result.

Frustration, blame, and anger create barriers to taking ownership of the situation we are facing, making it difficult to push forward and develop resiliency. When persevering towards a goal, it is helpful if we take those angry impulses and instead look for opportunities for learning how to work with our strengths and persevere, rather than allow frustration, anger, and blame to direct our future.

Prevents Feeling Out of Control

Feeling that we understand what is going on in our lives and having the ability to predict the future brings a sense of control over our lives. We all need this, and our bodies are hard-wired to assist us with this process. When we experience intense emotional or physical stress, our body responds like a well-rehearsed military brigade readying for combat, with a chain of automatic physiological reactions. The autonomic nervous system puts our body on alert with a fight-or-flight response. A tiny region in the brain called the hypothalamus is stimulated and sets off an alarm, causing the adrenal glands to release a surge of the stress hormones adrenaline and cortisol, into our bloodstream. Our body is readying us to respond to the event, with adrenaline causing our hearts to beat faster, and our energy, breathing and pain threshold to rise. Our awareness increases, with our dilated pupils ready to hone in on any detail that could pose a risk. The thyroid gland stimulates our metabolism so that blood is redirected to our larger muscles. Our body is now prepared, both physically and psychologically, to run or fight in response to danger.

Being an automated response, and not a conscious decision of choice, sometimes the fight-or-flight response isn't what we really want or need. It is shallow, defensive and superficial. The lens through which we see the world may get distorted and give us false positives. We risk reacting with exaggerated fear and moving into attack mode, scanning the environment, looking for the enemy. As our perspective is crisis oriented, our motivation will be to survive the short-term, rather than persevere towards developing long-term goals.

Bringing how we feel in our gut up to our conscious viewing level helps us avoid getting stuck in an inner world of turmoil. Viewing ourselves as having personal responsibility in overcoming adversity, regardless of how the event occurred, helps us move beyond our fight-or-flight reactions and instead to cognitively focus on the next step we need to take. Doing so enables us to engage our rational mind, be open to broadening our perspectives, be more flexible, and find different ways to reach our goal.

Following completion of law school, Jerry Bame was as interested in becoming a successful business litigator as he was in enhancing his personal growth. "For years I have worked on myself," he recalls. Enrolling in various personal growth-training programs helped him learn about the influence of his beliefs on emotions and behaviors, and how to stay true to himself.

"I have learned that life is a matter of choice, and have carried those lessons all through my life," reflects Mr. Bame. When he discovered that he had no control over his work schedule as a litigator, he transitioned to business trans-actional law. Years later he expanded his work to include executive coaching to other lawyers, where he emphasizes the importance of holding oneself person-ally accountable. "I tell my coaching clients that their life is a matter of choice."

Mr. Bame understands that owning personal responsibility helps us experi-ence the locus of control for our lives as being internal rather than external and that we, rather than other people or external circumstances, control our lives. Awareness of this is what helped Mr. Bame guide his professional career and his executive coaching clients, and is helping Mr. Bame cope with his own personal adversity today.

Four months ago, Mr. Bame's life changed forever when, following a routine blood test, he was diagnosed with acute myeloid leukemia (AML), an aggres-sive cancer. "The doctor said that if I were to go through the standard type of treatment, my life could be measured in a matter of months. There is no cure for me. The most I can hope for is to be maintained," states Mr. Bame.

"So I've taken that part of my philosophy," he says, which includes reducing feelings of anxiety and apathy, managing stress, and focusing on social support networks, "into my illness." Participating in a drug study that is searching for a cure requires him to fly from Southern California to Seattle, Washington to receive aggressive medical treatment every five weeks. When home, he receives daily chemotherapy. It has given him hope for longevity.

"I'm trying to teach myself that every day I go into the clinic for these infusions is a matter of choice. I don't have to go in there if I don't want. On the other hand, I can go in there if I want. If I decide to go in there, I can look at it in one of two ways. I can bitch and complain about it, or I can say how wonderful it is that I am getting drugs that will hopefully help me. So I make the choice of going into the clinic. I make the choice of being happy about it," he observes.

"In the clinic there are about fifteen people being infused. They're all complaining, moaning, and grumpy. All the nurses come over and talk to me because they are happy when they leave me. They don't talk to the other patients until they have to do something with them. I'm trying to follow through on this philosophy that I've taught others and learned from these classes I've taken; that in a lot of situations we have no ultimate decision. What is going to happen is going to happen. But we do have the ability to choose how we are going to react to these things," he reflects.

Assuming personal responsibility is helping Mr. Bame view his medical situation as being within his control. In doing so, it feeds his stamina and the ability to persevere during these oppressive times. "I will probably have to be on chemo for the rest of my life," he notes. But instead of being resentful and victimized, "I look at my current illness as what I call my 'great adventure.' I don't look at myself as being ill, even though I am very ill. I've had crazy adventures in my life but this is the craziest. Every time I go into the clinic or go up to Seattle I marvel at what miracles life and medicine have to offer. I cherish those miracles and relish them."[9]

Research has concluded that people who view themselves as having a higher sense of control are able to remove some of the uncertainties occurring in adversity. This helps them experience less despair and apathy and even live longer. Research studies have shown increased rates of survival linking the perception of having control with cardiovascular disease and diseases such as amyotrophic lateral sclerosis (ALS) and kidney disease. "How you construe your circumstances and challenges determine whether you take action or give up, or feel stressed or motivated, " states Margie Lachman, Ph.D., a psychologist who has extensively studied the relationship between feeling in control and lifespan.[10]

What Perseverance is Not

Endurance

Endurance is about having stamina when coping with a difficult experience. It implies acceptance of a burden. Perseverance consists of endurance, but it goes beyond this by also developing a plan that will lead to the desired goal, in spite of fears, limiting beliefs, difficulties, or distractions.

Intelligence

Our intelligence quotient (IQ) is important in helping us work through problems in a rational and purposeful way. Intelligence can make the process easier because using logical and abstract thinking for problem solving can reduce the potential of encountering obstacles before they occur.

But intelligence is different from perseverance. It won't necessarily be intellect that drives a person to success, but rather, the capacity to persist in working hard despite the obstacles and challenges. Passion for reaching a goal, rather than intelligence, will enable people to successfully persevere.

Luck

Luck carries little weight in our efforts to overcome adversity. It can help, of course. Sometimes having the right timing, or being in the right place, can be a central ingredient. But success in reaching our goals requires purposeful effort and planning. To overcome hurdles along the way to reaching our goals, we have to learn from our mistakes and problems and make good choices. Luck involves none of this. One thing is for sure, however: the more we persevere, the luckier we tend to be.

Perfectionism

Perfectionists have exceedingly high self-imposed performance standards. Unfortunately, they also worry about not being good enough. They have an inner critical voice that judges them as failing if they don't measure up. This excessive focus on avoiding failure creates a lifestyle tarnished with a toxic chronic anxiety. They remain anxious when experiencing a roadblock. They don't realize that they can learn from their failure, acquire new skills, try again and move forward. Instead of persevering, they withdraw from what they were trying to accomplish.

Talent

Talent is an innate quality. It does not have the drive and determination found in perseverance. A talented individual who has been born with a natural gift, such as an athlete, singer, or chess player, will not achieve his or her highest potential without practice, determination, and persistently working to overcome obstacles along the way. Research originally performed by psychologist Anders Ericsson, and written about in detail in Malcolm Gladwell's book, *Outliers*, and Geoff Colvin's book, *Talent Is Overrated*, has concluded that 10,000 hours of deliberate, dedicated practice can make an expert of us. It is the behavior of hard work, including determination and commitment to overcoming obstacles, that enables the talented person to persevere and achieve success.

Barriers to Perseverance

Avoidance

Avoidance occurs when we ignore a problem because of our negative thoughts and feelings. We are aware of the existence of the problem, but choose to do nothing. The reasons for preferring to avoid something range from perfectionism, to low tolerance of emotional or physical pain, or procrastination. Usually, avoidance of a problem prevents the opportunity for resolution, and it gets worse or leads to additional struggles.

Rumination

When we are emotionally upset, distortions in our reasoning can occur. Attempts to understand what happened will often result in our ruminating; repeatedly dwelling on the causes and consequences of our problems. People who ruminate have difficulty with problem solving because they mull the difficulty over and over again in their head, spending an inordinate amount of time on "backward thinking." This can lead to depression and anxiety, both detrimental to developing plans for problem solving. Perseverance, on the other hand, is "forward thinking," and involves planning and focusing on the solutions.

Substance Abuse

Perseverance requires focus, commitment, and energy. Both prescribed and illegal mood-altering substances can derail us from being able to experience these qualities. Chemical use and abuse can interfere with our ability to process information and alter portions of the brain that we need to draw on in trying times.

The brain is organized into different regions. Functions performed by the cerebral cortex, the outer gray matter covering the brain, are concerned with higher mental activity such as mood, memory, and reasoning. Drugs that suppress cellular activity in this area of the brain can result in impaired problem-solving capabilities.

Another part of the brain, the frontal cortex, or forebrain, is responsible for being able to think, plan, and make decisions. It is here that we have the ability for abstract thought and planning and to associate memories with thoughts. When this is impaired, we lose our ability to control our cognitive processes, resulting in impaired decision-making abilities.

The limbic system is the region of the brain best known as the reward center of the brain. It is responsible for creating feelings, motivation, and pleasure. Some drugs are so powerful that they disrupt the connection people experience between reality, feelings and motivation. When this occurs, people can find drugs to be more rewarding than food and sex, negatively influencing their ability to problem-solve and pursue goals.

Unhealthy Defense Mechanisms

All of us have learned various coping strategies over the years as a way of dealing with our emotions. When we are faced with out of the ordinary or intolerable stress, we may find our emotions to be overwhelming. Some coping mechanisms we turn to are helpful, while others can trip us up, impairing our ability to persevere.

Unhealthy coping can result in unhealthy responses. They may lead to our withdrawal from valuable social ties, thereby reducing our opportunity to obtain support, further escalating our stress. Withdrawing, such as zoning out in front of the television or computer, excessive sleeping, over eating, procrastinating, avoiding personal relationships and activities, consuming too much alcohol, or drug abuse, is unhealthy. Over-activity is also unhealthy, such as keeping oneself overloaded with activity as a way of avoiding problematic feelings, situations or individuals.

Adversity causes us to experience anxiety, conflict, frustration and failure. We need to figure out how to regulate our emotions so that we do not distort reality or avoid issues that require our attention when overcoming our hardship.

When we attempt to avoid painful and unacceptable thoughts, we often employ unhealthy coping techniques. We are not always consciously aware we are engaging in these behaviors, which the field of psychology identifies as defense mechanisms. Although they can provide relief in the short term, they are ineffective in the long run, because while we have distanced ourselves from the emotional pain, we haven't learned how to deal with stress or adverse situations. Six commonly employed defense mechanisms are discussed below.

1. Compartmentalization

This defense mechanism is like having two rooms, with all of the feelings being put in one room and the facts placed in a separate room. For example, one may put the pain of having lost a loved one in the back of his or her mind in order to enjoy celebrating the holidays with relatives. While this can be a healthy coping technique if used in the short term, problems arise when these feelings are pushed back. If not dealt with, the painful and unresolved feelings will come out again, when unexpected, or when another conflict strikes. The person will then have to deal with two issues; the former unresolved matter as well as the new problem, making it more burdensome and challenging to continue working toward a goal.

2. Denial

Denial is the process of not admitting the existence of a painful event by reacting as if it did not happen. In the short-term, denial can be helpful in that it provides time to adjust to a new challenge. But if the issue is avoided for too long a period of time then it can be detrimental because the situation is not dealt with and resolved. Time passes and opportunities to absorb new information needed for responding appropriately to the situation are missed.

3. Displacement

Taking the stress out on someone other than the source of one's anger is an unhealthy way of warding off unpleasant feelings. It is seen in situations where an individual is angry with his or her boss and engages in road rage on the way home from work. Typically, this person is using a substitute target for his or her anger. Failure to recognize and accept the actual cause of one's feelings prevents the possibility of working towards a satisfactory resolution.

4. Intellectualization

When individuals are unable to handle their feelings related to a situation, they may control or avoid them by ignoring their feelings altogether and focusing instead on facts and logic. The facts surrounding the situation are not denied, just the emotions.

5. Rationalization

When we come up with various explanations for a behavior, we are said to be explaining it away, or rationalizing. An example is a person saying that he failed the final exam, but it didn't matter because the class wasn't important to him. The rationalization usually isn't valid, because rather than based on logic, the intention is deception of self or someone else. The need to bring about change is reduced when rationalizing, thereby impairing one's motivation to persevere.

6. Repression

Repression is our effort to keep uncomfortable or unacceptable thoughts from entering our mind. The problem is that while we might try to fool our brain, our body is not so easily deceived. These 'forgotten memories' will push through, often causing anxious thoughts and unhealthy urges as well as psychosomatic illnesses.

False Hope

False hope is destructive because it is not reality-based. It can relieve stress, but in doing so, we are not likely to improve our situation. It will prevent us from focusing on creating a realistic plan, and can reduce our motivation to seek change. Hope must contain the true (if painful) reality of the risks and the difficult challenges that lie ahead.

Childhood Events

Chronic Stress in Childhood

Acute stress is a part of our routine, every day existence. When repeatedly subjected to emotional stress or physical pain for an extended period, it becomes a chronic stressor and affects us in ways that makes perseverance challenging. Stress hormones are released, causing wear and tear on our emotions. We can develop maladaptive coping styles including insomnia or sleeping too much. Maladaptive coping can also cause us to have a decreased attention span, energy, or ability to problem-solve. Our body systems can also begin to deregulate, with chronic stress being linked to many medical problems, including high cholesterol and blood pressure, diabetes, and heart disease.

Stress resulting from chronic physical pain derails us from successfully developing problem-solving solutions for adversity. This is because our bodies are hardwired to use pain as a way of grabbing our attention, making the resolution of pain the first order of importance. While this is vital, it is possible at times that the pain can serve a psychological purpose in masking unacceptable feelings such as anger or anxiety, leaving them excluded, unaddressed, and unresolved.

Adversity in Childhood

Our brain circuitry is influenced by our exposure to caretakers as we develop. Experiences that impair the ability to feel safe, secure, and supported in childhood, such as being raised in poverty or by indifferent, hostile, or depressed parents, impact on a child's ability to persevere in later years. Growing up with "toxic" stress situations, such as chaos, deprivation, domestic violence, or maltreatment, places children at greater risk for psychiatric disorders, especially depression.

Negative early childhood experiences may color their view of themselves and the world. Support and feedback helps children learn how to filter their thoughts and impulses and adjust to changing situations. Children in these situations may not be able to have access to a social network that can offer them support or feedback. Without it, they have fewer coping skills in knowing how to change priorities and problem solve, inhibiting their ability to persevere in difficult times.

Fortunately, because of the brain's plasticity and ability to change, exposure to other influences, such as therapy or nurturing adults, can help modify the brain circuitry, helping these individuals recover.

Damaged Executive Functions

The executive functions, located in our brain, take administrative control of our ability to organize (plan, problem solve, think abstractly, use memory), and regulate various cognitive functions including language, emotions, and other cognitive functions. Damage can occur as a result of childhood trauma, dementia, depression, and drug addiction, to name a few causes. Unfortunately, damage to the executive system is associated with reduced interest in seeking goals and an inability to learn from past actions. It can even result in the lack of acknowledgement that a problem exists. One cannot persevere in planning for an improved future in the absence of a recognized problem.

How to Use the Three Spheres of Support to Achieve Perseverance

To be perseverant, we need more than positive words of encouragement to 'keep going' or 'stay focused.' Rather, we need to identify which behaviors will help us find the passion for embracing the unknown, pushing through possible defeat, and keeping in pursuit of our goals. Our three spheres of support —

Self, Society, and Spirituality — all play significant roles in persevering in our efforts to overcome adversity.

Self

The 19th century scientist, Louis Pasteur, exclaimed, "Fortune favors the prepared mind." Dr. Pasteur recognized that preparation helped him persevere and achieve his objectives and goals when discovering the rabies vaccination and developing the pasteurization of wine and milk. Preparation helps us to persevere in difficult circumstances as well, be they scientific, business or personal.

Preparation provides us with the ability to move beyond chance, and to have more control over our destiny, instead of letting things happen to us. Fortune will more likely favor us when we take the time to understand our temperaments, the value of setting goals, establish healthy coping skills, develop good habits, view life with optimism, learn to be kind to ourselves, and consider the importance of physical activity and nutrition.

Temperament

Temperament is how we are inclined to react, and it varies with each of us. It is often called our personality, makeup, spirit, or constitution. We're aware of the temperaments in others when we notice their moodiness, adaptability, attention span, sensitivity, and perseverance. We are aware of our own temperament when we see patterns of how we react to adverse situations. Rooted in our biology and influenced by life experiences, our temperament evolves through the blend of nature and nurture. It is when we can understand the strengths and weaknesses of our personality makeup that we can knowingly react to situations in a productive manner.

For example, a temperament that is flexible is most adaptable in challenging times. It will help us react in a favorable way to our emotional reactions, afford us with being more open to others, and more able to manage unexpected struggles. But this does not mean that a more highly emotional person who acts impulsively, or the person who ranks high on criticism and judgment but low on self-confidence, cannot successfully persevere. Or that the easygoing individual who avoids conflict and situations that create anger and challenges, is doomed.

The exciting news is that we have the ability to modify our temperament. Both people with highly emotional and easygoing temperaments can work thorough the challenges they encounter. Highly emotional_people can realize the importance of being aware of their feelings, and channel their emotional energy on to the path that will help them establish the right goals. They can figure out how to accept help from others and not get distracted by over attention to details. They can reduce their risk of getting stuck in over analyzing everything, and requiring perfection before getting started. Learning to focus on one step at a time can reduce the hazard of getting overwhelmed by the magnitude of what needs to be done, and not get disheartened when things go wrong. This will help provide confidence in coping with these challenges. Individuals with a conflict avoidant temperament can learn to become more comfortable with experiencing disagreement in their lives. Rather than being threatened by differing options, they can focus on remaining committed and focused when dealing with obstacles.

Goal Setting

When we have goals, we challenge ourselves to put both effort and action into doing the work to persevere and attain them. We can help ourselves by creating clear and specific, rather than vague and general goals. When we are actively involved in pursuing goals we will feel more responsible for their success, and put in more effort. The more effort we exert, the more invested we become, and the greater the likelihood that others will notice. This enhances our connection with others, putting us in a position to receive emotional support.

Our social network can help provide positive feedback, support, information, or help us with building necessary skills. This resource of support helps increase our self-confidence and improve our resiliency. Having others in our network to discuss problems that arise can change our perspective from seeing something as a problem, to viewing it as a challenge. This helps us increase our ability to accomplish the task and create even more incentive for us to identify a goal, plan on how to attain it, and continually evaluate along the way whether the goal is being reached.

Healthy Coping Skills

Healthy coping skills are life skills. They help us regulate our emotions when dealing with life's challenging moments. They increase our distress tolerance and open up more opportunities to achieve success. When we employ life skills, they help provide us with self-confidence and self-esteem. We feel empowered to problem-solve in times of crisis. We will be better able to manage disappointment, anger, fear, loss and grief. There are unlimited strategies for integrating healthy ways of approaching difficult life situations. Below are a few coping skills that can be incorporated by each of us.

Relaxation Techniques

Relaxation techniques such as deep breathing, yoga, and meditation, can reduce the effect of stress on our body and mind by slowing our heart rate and breathing, lowering our blood pressure, fatigue, anger and frustration, and improving our concentration and mood. The Internet has a variety of exercises for yoga, and many local communities offer classes.

For the religious and nonreligious alike, meditation provides an opportunity to experience relaxation and mindfulness. Stress is reduced when we focus on our breathing as opposed to worrying about what we need to be doing in the future or what we should or should not have done in the past. When we are able to reduce our stress we benefit with clearer thinking, control over our emotions, and we are more capable of making high-level decisions necessary for resolving adversity in our lives.

Focus on Positives

Negative thinking can become an easy, but bad habit. Negative thoughts, including focusing on difficulties and previous disappointments can lead us to create additional negativity. Concentrating on negatives sets us up for failure because that is the direction in which we are looking. If we instead focus on the positives, we will find our mood improves and stress decreases. We will have more hopefulness for the future, be able to push forward, and persevere in difficult times.

Moods are infectious, so it is helpful to surround ourselves with the company of positive people. Others who believe in us, provide encouragement, and avoid focusing on problems help us experience a positive mindset. Removing from our inner 'self-talk' any words that reinforce our feeling powerless and like a victim, such as 'cannot' and 'difficult' are important steps as well. It frees us to put our focus on positive thinking.

Sometimes learning to reframe our view of a situation is sufficient in helping us remain positive. It helps us reappraise the situation, allowing us to modify how we think about a potentially emotionally upsetting event, and to see our strengths rather than weaknesses. The change for us will be increased feelings of confidence that we can persevere in times of adversity.

Journaling

For generations, people have been writing down their thoughts and feelings in a diary. Today more people than ever are engaging in a similar process: a little more structured, a lot more researched, and repackaged as "journaling." Diaries differ from journaling in that diaries could serve the sole purpose of venting emotions, whereas the purpose of the journal is for writers to reduce stress by examining their uncomfortable thoughts and feelings, develop insights, and track their experience of personal growth over time.

In the age of the computer, journaling has us pushing the keyboard aside and taking pen to paper to write our journal entries so as to become more intimately connected with our thoughts and feelings. Research has found that not only does regular journaling help writers come to terms with some of the stressors in their lives and improve their sense of well-being, but it can boost immune functioning in patients with asthma, arthritis, and HIV/AIDS.[11]

Exercise

Get moving. After checking with your doctor first, consider starting an exercise program. Even walking daily will reduce symptoms of stress, anxiety, and depression, help increase your sleep, and boost your self-confidence. While walking, you might discover an unintended benefit such as enjoying an observation in nature, or exchanging pleasantries with a passerby.

Practice Gratitude

Gratitude is like driving a car. How often have we heard the phrase, "Keep your eyes on the road?" If we fail to do so, we will swerve off the road, have a collision, and never reach our destination. If we think about things for which we are resentful, we will "drive" in this direction, and our negative thoughts will cause us to 'collide' with unhealthy decisions. Instead, if we "drive" towards that in our lives for which we are appreciative, our spirits will be lifted and we will be motivated to keep going in a positive direction.

Develop Good Habits

Good habits are a panacea for overcoming adversity. Good habits remove luck from our lives, replacing it with well-deserved success. We develop healthy habits by being able to continuously learn from our mistakes, reducing the chances that we will make similar mistakes in the future. Good habits beget more good habits, keeping us on track to attain our goal.

Good habits require perseverance, and are what set apart the most successful from others in any given field. Extensive research on the development of expertise in many fields of athletics, arts, and academia indicate that developing the habit of committing oneself to repetitive practice along with consistent measurement of one's improvement along the way will influence how they think, feel and act.

Sometimes we develop habits that are detrimental to overcoming our adversity. It may be a result of repeatedly practicing a behavior that is harmful to us. Over time it becomes so ingrained it is a bad habit, consisting of attitudes, beliefs, and behaviors that create roadblocks to our success. While good habits, when practiced over and over become automatic, so do the bad habits we develop over the years. Learning to be aware of which behaviors are detrimental to overcoming adversity is a first step to changing them. When we assume personal responsibility for rejecting the bad habits, we are telling ourselves that we want to change and we believe we have the power to make this happen.

Bad habit breaking is more difficult than habit forming because the habits — even bad habits — can become a comfortable and well-ingrained way of coping with situations. According to Michael Merzenich, author of *The Brain That Changes Itself*, eventually with concerted effort, we will be able to create new habits. But the process is slow. Changing our neural pathways takes, on the average, around three months.

Such change requires discipline, honesty, and a plan. There will be some internal struggle as we make these changes, but being consistent and putting in the work, even if not motivated, will help us regulate ourselves as we attempt to change a bad habit. If we think before we act, keep our priorities in focus, and visualize how the change in pattern will improve our lives we will be able to persevere.

The more success we have with a new habit, the more enthusiastic we will become and the more we will reinforce the positive behavior. As these good habit muscles slowly strengthen, the bad habit will become increasingly less meaningful, and our resiliency will grow.

Optimism

Dr. Martin Seligman, the leader of the positive psychology movement and author of many books on optimism, has performed extensive research to understand why people opt to either persevere or give up when facing adversity. He found the key factor to be perception.

Optimists perceive that life is good and that even if things go wrong, that good things will happen to them in the future. This attitude impacts on how they interpret stressful life events. While acknowledging the negative information, they will also optimize the positive aspects of situations. This helps them feel more in control of their lives, and will likely engage in activities that enhance their sense of control. When faced with adversity, optimists will be creative in determining how to use both positive and negative information for their benefit, will be flexible, and not give up as quickly.

This broad perceptual approach to expecting positive events to occur in their lives is different from the experience of a pessimist. Pessimists view the future negatively and will expect the worst. They see constraints rather than opportunities. They are the "Debbie Downer," and the "glass half empty" people who view new information or options that arise from a negative viewpoint.

The benefits of optimism have been well documented in medical and psychology literature. Because optimists have positive expectations, they are better at managing stress. They are rewarded richly in nearly every category of life. Optimists have been found to have better coping skills, more satisfaction in relationships, better adjustment to life transitions, less depression and anxiety, stronger immune systems, reduced likelihood of getting a heart attack or cancer, and even tend to live longer.

Pessimism, located at the opposite end of the continuum, is a protective mechanism, with low expectations being used to prevent one from experiencing disappointment or hurt. Fortunately, pessimists can learn to become optimists and benefit from the vast array of mental and physical benefits. We can combat pessimism by coming up with different explanations for problems that occur and checking out our negative assumptions to determine which ones are unfounded and are weighing us down. Surrounding ourselves with positive people will challenge our pessimism, as optimism is contagious. Believing that we are going to succeed, despite the odds, despite our past failures, and despite limited resources, contributes to optimism. The higher our optimism, the more likely we will persevere in finding the resilience to overcome our adversity.

Ms. Ratschave, if nothing else, is the consummate optimist. She is intelligent and academically accomplished, with a master's degree in general experimental psychology, and nearing completion on a second master's degree in marriage and family therapy. But intelligence alone has not been enough to prevent her from spending most of her lifetime struggling to overcome an escalating problem with addictive behavior.

"I started cutting (a term used for making small cuts to one's body) when I was 11 years old," recalls Ms. Ratschave. "We had moved out to California, and my mother wasn't too happy about it. So she moved back to Wisconsin with the kids, but there was a lot of tension in the house. I decided it would be easier to deal with physical pain than the emotional pain. So I started cutting."

"I didn't respect myself. From the second to seventh grade I was bullied by a lot of kids in my class. Then my mom made a comment about my weight, so when I was around 12 or 13, I started researching calories. When I was a sophomore in high school I weighed 122 pounds, and by the time I was a junior in high school I weighed 92 pounds because I had become anorexic and perfectionistic. I thought if I had the perfect body and the perfect grades my mother would love and accept me more," she recalls.

"When my parents divorced in 2005 I moved out to California and started getting more heavily into alcohol," adds Ms. Ratschave. I used to get my validation through guys, having sex two to three times a day. I thought if he had sex with me he loved me, but that's not the case at all. I didn't know how to love myself. In 2008 I was raped because of the alcohol."

"Then I met a 'friend' who introduced me to heroin," Ms. Ratschave continues. "I started smoking it, then used it intravenously. I moved in with friends who (helped me find) cocaine and ecstasy. By the time 2010 and 2011 came around, I blacked out on crystal meth because I was up for four days straight. That was when I started a 12-Step program. But I didn't stay clean and sober. I went back to using heroin."

"In 2013," she adds, "I had a really bad relapse when I was prescribed Norco. I then started shooting up oxycodone. I overdosed twice, got admitted to the hospital under a 51-50 (a legal term in California to involuntarily confine patients for 72 hours in a psychiatric hospital who appear to have a mental disorder that places them at risk to themselves or someone else), got into a car accident, and had my license suspended for six months."

"I've been clean and sober almost a year this time," she states. What's different this time is that Ms. Ratschave now believes that the way to manage her life is to exercise self-control and own full responsibility for her behaviors. "I'm always going to be an addict, but I can be an addict in recovery. It is a growing process. I'm learning to live life a different way; how to respect myself while respecting the other person, how to set boundaries, and how to communicate better. I learned to look at my part, my value system, and how to manage my behaviors and self-control in Narcotics Anonymous. It's not easy. My eating disorder and drugs kind of play off of each other. I'm either active in my eating disorder or active in my drug addiction. It's a constant battle within my head, still," she admits.

She is now optimistic and forward thinking, choosing to focus not on what people in her past did that was detrimental to her, or the hurt she has brought on herself, but rather on what hope and change she can bring to other addicts needing help.

"They say in the program you have to create a life that's worth living," observes Ms. Ratschave. "I want to open my own treatment program that treats eating disorders and addiction combined because a lot of programs say they treat both but don't know how. Since I struggle with both those problems, I have a unique perspective on it. And I want to have my own equine therapy program. I want to give back to others. If you have those experiences, it gives you the hope that you can change. I think that's what keeps me going; I want to give that hope away to other people."[12]

Self-Kindness

Sometimes we make mistakes that prevent us from being able to persevere. Being kind to ourselves means accepting ourselves for who we are, and not beating ourselves up for being human. Recognizing why this happened will enable us to learn from our experience and make better choices next time. Sometimes, we simply did not have enough information. Perhaps the needed information wasn't available at that time or perhaps we needed to identify other ways to seek it out.

Other times it is a matter of understanding what is happening in our bodies. That phrase, 'running on empty,' applies to us when we feel emotionally and physically drained. Dealing with a major conflict in our lives impacts on our body. We are flooded with many tasks, thoughts, and emotions, while our resources and time might be limited. Our ego strengths (our ability to maintain emotional stability when also coping with stress) become depleted, and we lose our internal strength required for self-control. Like an electrical socket in the process of short-circuiting from overload, the stage is set for our body to respond as well. Our heart rate and blood pressure can rise while our serotonin, a neurotransmitter that helps us feel valuable, drops, causing depression, anxiety, and insomnia. Our thinking loses its clarity and our willpower becomes fatigued from overuse. We lose the ability to respond in the way that we would normally prefer and are more likely to react in a way that is outside of our value system or against our interests.

Being kind to ourselves also means being honest with ourselves, looking at the situation realistically, and understanding what we really want. It is helpful for us to spend a few moments from time to time, reflecting on what we want to create. It is tough to persevere towards goals that belong to another person, or those that we feel 'should' want. Rather, being kind to ourselves is about listening and being connected to our authentic self.

Humor is a gift of kindness for those struggling to persevere. Psychology, dating as far back as Sigmund Freud, has seen benefits from being able to laugh at ourselves in times of adversity. It helps to broaden our perspective and not be as inner-focused but also to be able to consider our situation from the view-points of other people. Adversity is burdensome, and not taking ourselves so seriously from time to time provides a release from the chronic tension. An occasional dose of humor can help distract us from our day-to-day problems, and make the adversity feel more manageable. This broadening of perspective provided from laughter is an opportunity to look at ourselves without judgment and make changes in the way we think, feel, or act that will help us increase our ability to persevere.

Physical Activity and Nutrition

Perseverance requires maintaining a healthy lifestyle. This is because stress resulting from adversity can have a detrimental impact on our thoughts, emotions, and on our body. Anyone dealing with personal challenge knows that they need to channel all their energy into moving past obstacles in search of their goals, and physical activity is a catalyst in making this happen.

Physical activity increases the blood supply to the brain, promoting the growth of new brain cells. When this happens our brain grows in cognitive ability, including memory and learning, enabling us to keep up our drive and determination, and work at our optimum capacity. When physically active we are also able to enjoy an improved immune response and normalize our glucose (an energy source required by all cells and organs in the body), insulin (a hormone that allows the body to use the glucose), and leptin levels (hormones that control hunger and feelings of satiety), which help reduce our risk factors for obesity, cardiovascular disease, diabetes, and colon cancer.

When physically active we receive mental health benefits as well. Our creative problem-solving skills increase, while negative thinking and rumination decrease. Physical activity bumps up the production of endorphins, our feel-good neurotransmitters. Endorphins are our body's natural morphine-like painkiller, reducing our perception of physical pain, alleviating our anxiety, and providing us with a good feeling. Marathon runners benefit from the release of endorphins when they get their "runner's high." Fortunately we can increase our physical activity to the point of inducing endorphin release without having to commit to a grueling 26.1 mile marathon competition.

Good nutrition and physical activity work hand in hand together. We often hear about the attention professional athletes give to nutrition in an attempt to enhance their performances. They recognize that nutrients, vitamins, and minerals found in food and supplements protect cells from getting damaged, and that healthy eating helps maintain their energy at a constant level through-out the day. Anyone overcoming adversity requires a nutritional boost similar to someone preparing for an Olympic event; both situations require optimal decision-making and stress reduction for goals to be achieved.

Society

It's difficult to imagine living without our social support. When experiencing adversity, our strong social ties provide us with what has been called a protec-tive "stress-buffering effect," and it's no surprise why.

Adversity is rarely immobile. Obstacles and challenges can emerge and change when we are trying to move forward, exhausting our problem-solving ability, and impairing our ability to persevere. Our social network is often the first responder when we are struggling. All forms of social support help us develop a positive perspective of ourselves when we are unsure and worried. Meaningful relationships that support our goals when we lack confidence in our competence and need encouragement are found in our family, community, and culture. The more integrated we are with others, the greater our ability to cope with hardship.

Source of Stability

How wonderful it is to have a support system to talk and vent with when we don't feel we have control over circumstances in our lives. This helps our self-esteem, making us feel less helpless and unable to cope. Social relationships can remind us that some things in our lives are stable and predictable, and provide us with the reassurance that we have value regardless of what is occurring in our lives. They can contribute to our resilience by reminding us of our strengths, by pointing out when we have succeeded with obstacles in the past and expanded our perspectives. They can provide us with substantial resources such as information, safety, and security. When everything else in our lives seems unpredictable, they offer a cultural and spiritual or religious identification.

Studies on survivors of natural disasters such as earthquakes, tsunamis, as well as human-induced tragedies, including terrorist attacks and war, have found that close social resources have a positive impact in helping people respond to and overcome adversity.

Influence From Family

In 2009 an earthquake measuring 6.1 on the Richter scale completely devastated the small town of Cinchona in Costa Rica. Landslides, highway failures, crumbled homes, damaged bridges, and loss of the hydroelectric power station, made rescuing the injured and displaced inhabitants of this mountainous community difficult. Relatives of survivors played a critical role in buffering the harmful impact of the traumatic event by helping them reduce the consequences of all that they lost, providing information, social, emotional and financial support, and helping them believe that they could cope. A study of the earthquake survivors three years later found that only those "who lacked family support were traumatized in the long run."[13]

The definition of a family is broad. It can be defined as immediate family, extended family, or even family created through marriage. The more connected we are to other family members, the more likely that assistance will be available in a disaster. Those without family ties, such as immigrants, estranged from family members, or coming from a small family, will be more vulnerable. Having a smaller family network means access to more limited resources, which may exacerbate the obstacles they face, especially if community social support institutions are fractured during adversity.

Cultural differences in families play a relevant role in helping when disasters strike. For example, the Hispanic culture tends to demonstrate a strong norm of supporting extended family members. Interestingly, researchers found that when the devastating Category 5 hurricanes Hugo and Andrew made landfall, Hispanic families were among those most likely to evacuate.[14] It is suspected that the strong family ties provided a protective role by helping with evacuation and material assistance for people coping with the crisis.

Socioeconomic Differences

Social support is different for the haves and have-nots. Those who are in a lower social standing in society tend to experience less availability of supportive relationships. Individuals who live in poverty do not have access to the same resources as do the more affluent. Resources tend to be scarcer, and stress will be experienced deeply. In 2005, the infrastructure of the community could not withstand the unprecedented devastation wrought by Hurricane Katrina on New Orleans. Nearly half a million people were displaced due to the wind, rain, and storm-surge destruction, which caused the levee to fail. The residents of the Lower Ninth Ward, which is largely comprised of poor African Americans, had less support available to them from their personal network. They had fewer resources, such as transportation, fewer relationships with people outside of their community, no hotel reservations out of town, and paradoxically, wanted to remain in town to receive government checks. Anyone they would turn to for support was struggling with the same disaster.[15] The residents of more affluent communities had more resources, including their own transportation, a more extensive network of people to tap during the crisis that could support them, and ability to pay rent for hotels and apartments, permitting them to have access to more options, enhancing their resilience.

Offers of help can reach beyond that of extended kinship. A social network that includes neighbors, friends, colleagues, teachers, professional resources, church, mental health professionals, and local government or others, can also help reduce the negative aspects of adversity and increase one's ability to persevere.

The power of a supportive network is most impressive when we stop to realize that it can bring people with a low-self efficacy up to the same level of coping abilities of those who have high self-efficacy. This has been found to hold true in many studies of older adults and those with multiple chronic medical conditions. Those who did not have the personal resources to cope well with health problems including cancer or rheumatoid arthritis were able to make a much better adjustment if supported by their social network.

Had it not been for her social support system, Jill Yanke may not have persevered. Mrs. Yanke and her husband, Dave, live in Wisconsin with their nine children, ranging in age from four to 21 years old. Eight are biological. Their adopted son, Bryson, was adopted when he was four and a half years old.

Mr. and Mrs. Yanke were well aware of Bryson's special needs before his adoption. He, as does one of their biological children, has Down syndrome. Children born with Down syndrome have an extra copy of chromosome 21 and accompanying learning and physical problems. Bryson also has been diagnosed as having Reactive Attachment Disorder (RAD). RAD is a psychiatric diagnosis for severe disruptions in bonding with a parent or caretaker that occurs early in a child's life. This early trauma results in children not knowing how to accept love. They will be disobedient, defiant, socially inappropriate, and act younger than their age. Aware of his diagnosis, the Yankees willingly and without hesitation welcomed Bryson to their family.

Mrs. Yanke identifies her greatest challenge to be that of working with Bryson's attachment therapy. "We started working with an attachment therapist even before he came home because we knew that love wasn't enough." To some, the problems Mrs. Yanke encountered would have been viewed as insurmountable.

Developing a trusting therapeutic relationship with mental health providers was problematic. Few lived in their geographical area. They had to terminate with one therapist, with whom they communicated long distance via email "when we weren't getting responses to emails, which were our primary mode of support, and the last email took seven weeks to get a response."

"During the most intensive treatment, on several occasions, it was recommended that we consider stopping the therapy because it wasn't effective for him." Within the first day of treatment with one therapist, "it appeared my son had a psychotic break," recalls Mrs. Yanke. "He was grabbing paint from the craft area and trying to run around the house. He was taking things he knew he shouldn't have, and locking himself in bedrooms and bathrooms."

Finances also proved a hurdle to overcome in seeking therapeutic help for their son. "A therapist said he could cure Bryson of the attachment disorder in six to twelve months. But even at their hardship pricing of $300 an hour it wasn't in our budget to do weekly sessions for that period of time." After five and a half years of struggling, "we did a GoFundMe (an internet-based crowdfunding for donations) to help cover the treatment with the therapist," states Mrs. Yanke.

Dealing with a challenging child can create feelings of being overwhelmed, socially isolated, and strain one's marriage. "Every moment of every day I couldn't think of myself," recalls Mrs. Yanke. "I couldn't go to the bathroom by myself. I couldn't do anything. There were times, honestly, when I'd be driving down a two-lane road, and I'd see a semi (truck) coming, and I'd think, 'Just veer my way. Just put me out of my misery.' It's not that I have a death wish. It's not that I was ever going to commit suicide. But life was so hard that if it had ended, I would have been OK."

Social support was Mrs. Yanke's lifeline.

Support came in the form of her husband. "There were lots of times when Dave and I would need to have some time for ourselves, but we couldn't go out when Bryson was awake," she says. "So it wasn't uncommon that we would wait until 8:30 or 9 pm when our little people were settled. Then we would go out to our favorite frozen custard place for an hour and talk, or not talk. It was our time to reconnect. We had to find moments like that because we couldn't find someone who could handle Bryson much of the time. We had to be on the same page, and we had to strive for that, and that kept our marriage strong. Like I told our kids, our marriage is a sacrament."

Support came in the form of her friends and neighbors. "When we opened ourselves up to being humble and saying we needed help, people helped. They would bring me a pot of soup, saying, 'I made this and thought of you guys and wanted to help tonight.' This was at a time when I couldn't even be in the kitchen because if I had unlocked the cabinets, which were all locked, Bryson would start emptying them. Or he'd start eating out of the sour cream container if the refrigerator was unlocked, or dumping the milk or doing whatever he pleased. I was counting on my 11-year-old daughter, or Dave, to do most of the cooking for a while," says Mrs. Yanke.

"Our whole house was locked. We had deadbolts on all the doors. We went through three padlocks on the patio because he was breaking them. We had a global radio telemetry system tracking him because he would take off. So for a good part of the summer, I couldn't be outside with him unless Dave was home. There is just so much challenge; his behavior really impacted the way we did everything."

"It helped to know that there are others behind me, and I am not alone," she says. "When I shared my story (through the GoFundMe) it felt like our circle grew. We have an amazing support system. There was a time a few years ago when we were dealing with some challenging things outside our immediate family. We talked about the fact that we could move anywhere because we homeschool the children and Dave was working from home at the time. I started looking at options of places to move. But then we decided we could never replace the support system we have here. We have such an amazing group of friends.

Support came in the form of her church. "I had to say, 'OK, God, I know that I'm not alone. I know you will give me all the tools I need because I cannot do it by myself. I need to totally lean on you, and you put other people in our path who can help us.'"

With Bryson transitioning from homeschooling to attending public school this year, Mrs. Yanke has found spiritual support by attending church. "When Bryson started going to school I started taking my kids to Mass on weekdays. To me, that is very helpful and assists me in focusing on what is important in life. We continue to do that every week. It fills us up so we can be available to face the challenges."

And support came in the form of the mental health professionals. "Bryson still has a long way to go. But our therapist said that as of last Wednesday he was healed from the Reactive Attachment Disorder. It will likely take him a year to catch up developmentally to whatever he would be chronologically, given his disabilities. With just our natural parenting that should happen."

"I am so thankful we have been through this. I'm thankful that we are now on the easier side of the slope. We've still got a ways to go," says Mrs. Yanke. "But through this experience, we have taken the skills we have learned during this intense time with Bryson and applied them to our other children and even to other relationships in general. We've learned new tools, grown in patience, and developed an insight into seeing Bryson and others in a different way. I feel like it has helped us learn to parent and relate to our children stronger and more positively."

There is no question that Mrs. Yanke persevered time and again over the course of many years in her struggle to care for her child. She stayed motivated even when isolation and finances proved to be a barrier. She strengthened her self-efficacy by building on what she learned along the way. She remained motivated rather than passive and benefitted by being curious, continuously learning, and researching treatment options. She showed strength in being able to delay self-gratification and stay focused on her goal of healing for Bryson. Despite each setback, she assumed responsibility for working through disappointments and failures and persevered rather than give up. Wisely, she was able to reduce her frustration and refuel her energy tank, by allowing herself to be vulnerable rather than perfect, by humbling herself and asking for help from a broad and meaningful support system.[16]

Spirituality

Spirituality can help provide us with the motivation and ability to persevere when challenged by obstacles. When faced with a traumatic event, being able to look beyond ourselves to a higher power can give us something hopeful on which to focus. When the devastating terrorist attacks occurred on September

11, 2001, United States residents found themselves pushed to the limit of their personal resources. A study found that turning to spirituality was second only to talking with others in providing people with explanations, a sense of control, and a way to reduce stress.[17]

For those of us who, as a result of adversity, are trying to understand questions about meaning and purpose in life, belief in a higher power can provide comfort by helping us integrate the experience into our life story. This contributes to our ability to persevere as we re-evaluate what we are doing, change priorities, and use the event as an opportunity to make positive life changes that lead us towards our goal.

Rather than feeling helpless and hopeless, spirituality helps us expand our perspective and find wisdom and growth in the hurtful experiences resulting from adversity. It helps us develop broader conclusions and insights, reminding us that we have value for who we are rather than what has occurred to us, and re-instills the belief that we can have an influence over our lives.

Spirituality, both secular and non-secular, also helps us persevere by providing a protective effect against poor health. Dr. Harold G. Koenig, a psychiatrist on the faculty of Duke University, concluded from his review of medical research that spirituality and religious practices are strongly related to improved well-being. Stress and a sense of loss of control that would have an undesirable impact on mental health, immune function (infection and possibly cancer) and the cardiovascular function are reduced. Unhealthy coping behaviors, such as the use of addictive drugs, cigarette smoking, risky sexual practices, and excessive alcohol, are replaced with positive coping behaviors when a person attends religious services, engages in prayer, or believes in a higher power. Hypertension drops, disease progression for HIV-1 is slowed, and coronary artery bypass surgery patients experience fewer complications.[18]

Religion
Spirituality and religion are often used interchangeably, but they are different. Spirituality refers to a personal connection with a higher power. It is possible to consider oneself spiritual but be secular without any religious affiliation. Spirituality can be attained individually through various means, including meditation or connectedness with nature, music or art.

For others, spirituality is rooted within a structured religious framework consisting of behaviors (such as attending services, reading the Bible, praying), beliefs (that there is a superhuman controlling power that does not give up), organization (having a place of worship in which one can observe and pray, and being surrounded by others who share similar goals of obtaining spiritual growth), attitudes (being taught that one needs self-control for perseverance, to practice patience, development of good habits, and an understanding of the importance of goals), and experiences (worshiping in specific buildings, rituals, being able to ask for help without it feeling like a sign of weakness, and availability of support groups).

The many components of religion saved Danny Duchene when he believed he was unsalvageable. For by the time he was 19 years old, Mr. Duchene was in prison facing the death penalty for committing a crime resulting in the murder of two men. Plea-bargaining reduced his sentence to 50 years to life, but he knew to expect to spend the rest of his life in prison.

Mr. Duchene's life started spiraling out of control when he was 16 years old, and both parents were arrested. He recalls, "I responded very badly to that. Over the next couple of years getting drunk became my daily goal of life, from morning to night. I was out of control and expelled from school. Alcohol led to drugs, and I graduated towards crime as a way of supporting myself and hiding my hurt on the inside about what was happening with my parents."

Upon entering prison, "I felt complete defeat. I felt completely broken," he recalls. "When I was at my lowest and could not think less of myself, other people would come into the prison and talk about God and unconditional forgiveness." But Mr. Duchene could not relate. "I had to get over the guilt and sense of shame. How could God have anything to do with me, after what I had done, and what I had become? How could anything good happen?"

"After all the hurt and harm I had caused, it took me a while to believe that God didn't give up on me. I was at a complete low, psychologically and emotionally, as well as my belief about God and my future. It was completely over. I thought that I had gone too far and couldn't come back."

Eventually, he realized that "through the example of other people, I saw that God cared for me. Without them, I wouldn't have known how to get out of that hole," he admits. Feeling safe to talk with the religious visitors about his feelings and fears enabled Mr. Duchene to "open my heart, let down my guilt and feelings of shame, and to want this new start, this new life. Even though I would be spending the rest of my life in prison, I wanted God to take hold of me and change my heart and make me a better person."

These growing feelings of closeness with God and fellowship with others provided a bond that helped him persevere in pursuit of personal acceptance. Mr. Duchene's risk of isolation was reduced, while he learned to care for others. "Over the years it helped keep my heart soft and helped keep me from quitting. I began to internalize that love from others and I began to see myself that way, more and more. I came to believe that God loved me unconditionally and I became a person who could love others unconditionally."

Religions hold guiding values or beliefs, which can inspire people to persevere and work towards goals rather than become discouraged during times of adversity. "I developed different values," states Mr. Duchene. "I now view people, including myself, as not all good or bad. That helps me to just be a better-integrated person and see other people that way. I think that those values of unconditional love are a huge part of why I am a pastor now. Those habits that I got at the age of 19 in the county jail turned my heart to God. I began to read. I read every book I could get my hands on about being a better person. I earned a two-year degree, then a four-year degree, Bible college certificates, and six vocational trades. I became the person who wanted to take the next best class. My path of life included getting involved with the right Bible service in the prison as well as recovery meetings, especially Celebrate Recovery," a Christian-based forward-looking recovery program that focuses on personal accountability and making wise choices.

"While I was still very young in my 20's", he recalls, "I felt called from God personally. I found conviction in my heart, and confirmation from people around me. I began to pastor while I was inside (the prison). I began to do the work without titles and structure of buildings. Then, in 2003, Saddleback Church of California got involved with a church that I was a part of inside the prison. The leaders, including Pastor Rick Warren, came to the prison. We had singing and Baptisms in the yard. That was the day that we publically started a church at that facility."

"I never thought I would be released when I was sentenced to two consecutive life terms. But after 30 years in the prison, the laws changed. Because church in the prison had become a pathway of life, the authorities were able to say that this is the course of my life, and that I am ready to go home. Now," states Mr. Duchene, "I am a pastor for Celebrate Recovery inside prisons. I get to help with local church members who are struggling with addiction as well as their families who may be struggling with areas of the criminal justice system, and help get Celebrate Recovery into prison systems throughout the country."

"I sit here humbly and think of the people who have invested in me over the years, and how that helped me to persevere and help me change, keep a soft heart, and not be hardened against the world, and to really feel loved and to be able to share that love with others."

Religion in general, and Celebrate Recovery in particular, was hugely instrumental in Mr. Duchene's ability to persevere, and not only survive, but thrive, in prison. "It kept my mind on the right than on depressive, angry or self-centered things. For the 32 years I was in prison I was either in church service, in the visiting room, at a good job that was usually educationally oriented, doing college classes, or in my cell doing self-study just about every day of the week. Because of that, I can't tell you how many times troubles happened inside the prison while I was elsewhere, doing the right thing with the right people. If you were to ask the prison wardens, they would say, 'they're studying and talking out problems, rather than creating problems,'" states Mr. Duchene.

Conclusion

Attempting to overcome adversity is a daunting task. When we strive to develop resilience we find ourselves encountering unfamiliar feelings, thoughts and experiences. With time, we recognize that talent and passion are not enough to keep us from running into brick walls. We cannot take the easy route of procrastination, feeling victimized, or hoping for a streak of luck. When the obstacles are numerous and intimidating, it is perseverance that helps us discover other ways to push forward.

Components of perseverance, including self-efficacy, self-control, and personal responsibility, convince us that there is a correlation between pushing forward and possible success. Knowing this helps us prepare for the struggle. Our feelings of frustration are reduced because we understand the value of learning from our mistakes and the importance of goal setting.

To not persevere is to experience complacency. This is a dangerous place because we must be open to learning and trying new tasks if we are to develop resiliency. We may fail in one attempt but succeed the next time. When we believe in our ability to take on struggles, we develop the inner strength needed to acquire new skills and are able to experience relief at making a decision to try to change.

Knowing we are not alone helps us persevere. When we have demands that we are unable to address on our own, we have the comfort of knowing we can turn to others in our social network for support. Our family, friends, colleagues or others in the community can provide us with the tools, including emotional, informational, or concrete support, to keep going forward despite our disappointments. The strength we derive from our spirituality can reduce our frustration, cynicism, and despair, thereby increasing our coping strengths. The response of our societal resources has the ability to ameliorate some of the more negative and destructive psychological and physiological effects of our stress.

Perseverance can take time to develop, but with focus and planning it rewards us by enabling us to change directions and never quit trying. Greater than talent and intelligence, perseverance is a learnable skill and available to all, at any point in our lives. Perseverance will always be there for people who have indefatigable determination geared toward overcoming their adversity.

Suggested Exercises
for Using the Three Spheres of Support
to Enhance Your Perseverance

Self

1. *Raise Your Dopamine Level*
   Raising your dopamine level will help provide you with the motivation to persevere. It will discourage feelings of self-doubt and tendencies to procrastinate. Following are several things you can do to elevate your dopamine level.

a. Visualize Success

It is difficult to persevere when you view a goal as a chore to be endured, or are uncertain about your capabilities. Visualization prepares our brain for an experience. In an experiment in the 1960s, one group of high school basketball players was instructed to practice shooting free throws each morning. A second group was to engage in just visualizing themselves making free throws. Both groups improved their free throw shooting, even though the second group did so without touching a basketball![19]

Taking the time to visualize can increase your success because it helps you clarify what you want, and gives you an opportunity to reflect on the experience and correct mistakes. Visualize what you will be seeing, hearing, feeling, and doing as you undertake a goal you have set for yourself.

Select a goal you would like to achieve, and spend 10 minutes each day visualizing yourself going through the steps to reach the goal. You will feel better about working toward the goal, which can trigger your neurotransmitter, dopamine. Dopamine helps motivate you to be more focused on working toward your goals, and even more pleased when you achieve them.

b. Reframing

Looking at this situation in a different way will allow you to change your perspective about a challenge and increase your ability to persevere. You may need to de-emphasize one aspect or remove assumptions you have that are interfering with the facts. By looking at the same situation in a different light you can begin to feel good, or more hopeful about it. Once again, your dopamine level will increase with practice, and you will experience more energy to tackle the matter at hand.

c. Motivation

Drive and willpower are a large part of perseverance. Start your day by listening to music. End your day by practicing an instrument. Dopamine levels will rise in response to music. You will be happier and more motivated to exert the effort needed to achieve your goal.

d. Mindfulness

Mindfulness is not prayer, and it is not intended to solve problems. It is the ability to train our brain to be fully present so that we are not overwhelmed by our stresses. There are many ways to practice mindfulness, but a good one is to focus on your breathing. The goal is to focus your attention on the sensation of your breath coming in, how it moves through your body, and how you exhale. With practice, mindfulness can help you feel comfortable and less anxious with uncertainty in your life.

Focusing on your breathing, and letting go of thinking about the past or what will happen in the future, will help reduce your stress and make it easier to avoid distractions that impair your ability to pursue goals. Harmful habits can be replaced with beneficial ones, such as being better able to select words, actions, and thoughts that best serve your personal wellbeing.

e. Break Long-Term Goals Into Short-Term Goals

There is a riddle that goes like this: Q: "How do you eat an entire elephant?" A: "One bite at a time." If depressed and lethargic, or if you find that you have been procrastinating, taking on a monumental long term goal can feel as overwhelming as being expected to eat an intact elephant. In such situations, you'll feel frustrated and likely give up trying. It is possible your dopamine levels are in the dump, but they can be jump-started once you learn to celebrate each of the smaller goals you successfully accomplish along the way. By breaking down a large goal into several smaller goals and recognizing each achievement that provides you with interim success with a pat on the back before continuing on to the next small task, you will avoid becoming discouraged and remain dedicated to reaching your ultimate goal.

f. Nutrition

Select nutritious foods that will enhance your dopamine. Fruit and vegetables elevate dopamine. Caffeine and alcohol create dopamine bursts, but they'll die out quickly. Foods high in sugar, cholesterol and fat tend to lower dopamine. Make a point of having healthy foods to snack on readily available in your refrigerator. A dietician can help you identify a healthy diet.

g. Laugh

Watch a favorite sitcom or read a funny story. You will trigger the production of dopamine. We need dopamine to feel motivated to make changes in our lives. Better yet, engage in one of these activities with someone from your social network. Laughter is a bonding experience and will enhance your relationship.

2. *Read About Others Who Have Persevered*

    Remaining steadfast on a journey tasked with overcoming adversity can be lonely. Reading stories about famous people who have had difficulties but persevered can provide the motivation we need to not give up. An example of someone who refused to be discouraged by repeated failure was Abraham Lincoln. Prior to being elected as President of the United States in 1860, he failed twice in business (1831, 1833), was defeated twice for state legislature (1832, 1834), was denied acceptance into law school (1832), his fiancée died (1835), had a nervous breakdown and was in bed for six months (1836), was defeated in a run for speaker of the state legislature (1838), was defeated once for elector (1840), defeated twice for Congress (1843, 1848), defeated twice for Senate (1855, 1858), and defeated once for vice-president (1858).[20] Ironically, despite so much failure, he is remembered in history only for his success.

3. *Get in Touch With Your Feelings*

    Awareness of both our conscious and unconscious feelings is imperative in finding resilience. You may establish a goal but find yourself unable to persevere, quitting before you experience success. Perhaps you underestimated how far-reaching the goal was, had too many interruptions or didn't have clarity on what you needed to accomplish it.

    To enhance your chances of success, you need to understand your feelings. Before beginning to work on your goal, take a few minutes to imagine how you will feel when it is finished. Visualize yourself going through the steps, and how each stage of the task will provide you with a sense of accomplishment. Before you start, brainstorm the potential problems that may arise, and not only identify how you will resolve the difficulties but also how it may negatively influence your view of yourself. Write this down on paper. Examine any self-criticism, and counter it with a kind, non-critical comment about yourself.

4. *Parenting:*

a. Encourage a Growth Mindset

Help your children view negative feedback as something from which they can benefit. It is important for them to know that they need not be perfect, and that learning from a failure and being able to keep moving forward is what will help them feel best about themselves. Remind them that mistakes are a necessary part of learning.

b. Avoid Becoming a Helicopter Parent

Your children should not be rescued from making all mistakes. Important life skills are learned when they experience failure and challenges. Depriving children of these experiences results in children having a lower self-esteem, increased anxiety, and a sense of entitlement. They will grow up feeling less than competent to deal with obstacles in adulthood.

c. Reframe Problems

Teach children how to reframe problems so that they can interpret challenging situations to be more 'user-friendly.' You can point out to them what they have achieved. Using logic and facts, they can learn how to view situations as energizing rather than debilitating and establish alternative approaches to achieving goals.

d. Social Connections

Help increase children's motivation to face challenges by providing them with a solid foundation. Ensure they are experiencing social connectedness and a sense of belonging at school, as opposed to bullying. Encourage them to engage in academic, social and athletic activities that provide them with a sense of competence.

e. Learn to Take Care of Matters Today

Parents can use every day experiences to help children recognize that they have the ability to persevere, and that doing so makes them happier in the long run. For example, children can be reminded that even though they do not like bothering to pick their bikes off the lawn and put them away before dinner, they are benefitted because the bikes are then not at risk of being rusted, damaged or stolen. I call this explanation 'the back story' to why we think or act as we do. Too often we expect others to simply know why. But I have also found that because people (myself included) are poor mind readers, sharing the 'back story' helps with comprehension and compliance.

f. Role Model

Parents can use themselves as role models to teach perseverance. Parent in a way that models high values, and encourages learning solid values. Share examples when learning something new did not go well for you. Explain how, even though you have made mistakes and suffered frustration when learning something new, that by not giving up you succeeded in solving a problem or acquiring a new skill. Describe how you learned from your mistakes, how it helped you in the future, and how good you felt about having the willpower to not give up on your goal.

Society

1. *Establish a Safe Environment*

    Schools can help children learn the value of perseverance by creating an environment in which they feel the freedom to be who they are. Knowing that belonging does not require having a specific group of friends, club membership, or attire helps students feel comfortable with trusting and liking themselves, and boosts self-confidence.

2. *Surround Yourself with Friends who Foster Growth*

    You are influenced by the company you keep. Avoid those who are dishonest, drain you of your energy, and treat you poorly. You will pick up their negative energy. Instead, associate with people who are supportive, nurturing and encouraging. If they set goals for themselves and try to overcome obstacles, you will find their positive energy to be contagious. You will find yourself to be empowered: calmer, healing faster, learning, growing, and better able to persevere.

Make a list of the most supportive and successful people in your life. Schedule them into your calendar so that you are spending time with one of them at least weekly.

3. *Identify Barriers to Perseverance at Work*
    Businesses can instill perseverance in their workers by looking at the connection between working conditions and employee satisfaction. A focus on health, wellness, people development, values and workplace culture, will help employees to want to perform to the best of their ability, in spite of any hardships they encounter.

Spirituality

1. *Identify Spiritual Leaders with Struggles*
    Think about a spiritual leader, present or past, who had to endure and persevere in his or her life. Write down your thoughts about this person and the struggles he or she faced. Now reflect back on your current life struggle. Does this reflection help you find a deeper commitment to persevering? Does your adversity seem less difficult knowing that you are not alone in life struggles?

2. *Draw a Support System*
    If you choose to continue working towards your goals, you have a chance of overcoming your adversity. Draw a detailed picture of what you look like when persevering. Be sure to add expressions and pay attention to size. Now add into this picture others in your social network who are supportive of you that do not want you to quit in your efforts to move forward. Think about how different the picture looks and feels to you when you are taking on difficult challenges alone versus with the support of others.

3. *Find Acceptance*

   Sometimes adversity will not go away. Changing your perspective on your situation and approach it in a different manner can help. Turning to a higher power and looking for a purpose in your experience will help you feel protected and strengthened during these difficult times. Spend time each day reflecting on how wisdom garnered from your adversity can help you grow in humility, gratitude, and the choice to not become overwhelmed or give up.

4. *Positivity Craft*

   Crafts can serve as visual reinforcement for children that they can tap into their own strength in difficult times. Below are instructions for making a wire hanger mobile that will help provide them with confidence when they feel discouraged. Parents may enjoy this project as well!

   • Cut any five shapes out of cardboard for your mobile.

   • On the first piece of cardboard write the words, "I will continue to ... (add a positive attribute that you want to continue to do"). On the second one write, "With hard work and belief I can ...", on the third, fourth, and fifth shapes write, "My higher power (or God) supports me in doing (add your statement) so that I can ..." Continue writing as many as you want. Select topics that will remind you of your strength, or connect you to your spirituality.

   • The last piece of cardboard will only have the word, "Persevere" written on it. Make this last shape the belle of the ball. Add glitter, lots of colorful drawings, shells, or anything else the child would like to glue on to this special shape.

   • Cut five pieces of string (or yarn or ribbon or anything else you find to be of creative interest) in slightly different sizes. For instance, if one is a foot long, then cut the second string two inches shorter than the first, and the third two inches shorter than the second, and so on.

   • Punch a hole in the top of each of the cardboard shapes and thread the string through each shape. Apply the longest string to the shape with the word Perseverance.

- Glue the ends of the string to the hanger. Spread them out so they are balanced, with Perseverance being placed in the center of the mobile.
- You can add more cardboard shapes by cutting more string or ribbon. Simply suspend them in a way so as to create balance.
- Hang your mobile on the wall or from the ceiling.

5.   *View Perseverance Via Planting*

Place seeds or small plants in a garden prepared with soil that is rich in vitamins and minerals that will help them grow strong. When done, water it well. Think about how these plants will have to have deep roots to be able to survive the wind, rain, and harsh sun. Consider how you will not only water the plants regularly, but will rely on your faith for them to survive.

When tending to the plants, reflect on what you are doing to nourish yourself so that you, too, can develop strong, hardy roots and grow, despite the obstacles.

Chapter 5

Hope

"To live without hope is to cease to live."
— Fyodor Dostoevsky, Russian novelist

Hope. We all want, even crave it. Sometimes, the struggle we face in times of adversity is so burdensome there is little else for us to cling to aside from hope. Holding on to hope can be a lifeline to which we desperately grip, as we endure our day-to-day challenges. In the end, it is hope that has the capacity to move us from doing little more than surviving, to thriving. Unfortunately, many of us do not know what hope is, and therefore won't be able to find it.

Hope has a long history of being misunderstood. Although hope is an ancient concept, society has been debating the meaning and value of hope for many centuries. Greek mythology's story about Pandora's box depicted a healing spirit named Hope, who could heal people suffering from illnesses and disasters. On the other hand, Norse mythology viewed hope as irrelevant, favoring courage in the form of physical prowess and military might during times of adversity. Benjamin Franklin said, "He that lives on hope will die fasting," whereas Martin Luther, who stated, "Everything that is done in the world is done by hope," viewed hope as associated with positivity.

Times have changed, and today hope has been said to be as "indispensable as oxygen" when coping with adversity. Without hope, many of us would be overwhelmed by and prevented from overcoming our adversity. Hope gives us the confidence to face reality and keep going, despite the hardships, when attempting to achieve what at times feels impossible. Theologians, philosophers, physicians, psychologists, and sociologists have collectively embraced the belief that "hope is central to life." Hope keeps us going when without it, we might have nothing in life at all.

What is Hope?

It is a challenge to define or measure hope, because hope is a combination of how we think, feel and act. Positive psychologist Charles Snyder, a prolific writer on the subject of hope, published six books and 262 articles on the topic. Dr. Snyder defined hopeful people as those who have an attitude of pursuing a goal in the face of difficulty, can imagine multiple ways to get to those goals, and have the motivation to persevere, even when unexpected obstacles get in the way.[1]

Every time we encounter an obstacle, we must question ourselves whether to persist or give up. Being able to envision and develop different routes around unexpected obstacles that get thrown in front of us in life allow us to keep moving forward towards our goal. Being creative about overcoming obstacles helps us develop a hopeful approach to problem-solving, and influences our ability to change, recover, and heal.

Without goals, we could not hope. Goals help us to focus more on what is real and possible in our future, rather than merely probable. Goals are the targets of change at which we point our bow and arrow. In order to develop hopeful thinking, we have to create a plan. This can't be just any plan, however. It must be based on a realistic understanding of the situation, in line with our values, and carry meaning. By creating such a plan we will find the courage to refuse to accept our current painful situation. We will find it possible to stay the course of pursuing our goals despite the challenges and unknowns.

Hope is more than a mental and emotional event. In his book, *The Anatomy of Hope*, Jerome Groopman, M.D., professor of medicine at Harvard Medical School, writes that "Hope is so vital to our survival that some scientists believe our brains are hardwired to be optimistic."

How does this occur? When people have belief and expectation, which are the key components of hope, their emotions spark changes in the nervous system. The brain begins to increase the body's production of endorphins, which have a structure similar to the pain-killing effects of morphine and other opiate painkillers. These endorphins carry messages from the nervous system through the bloodstream to the endocrine and immune systems. In doing so, the brain is functioning as an extremely powerful entity by providing the body's own natural painkiller and helping reduce a person's pain.

This chemical change occurs because of what is known as the placebo effect. If we believe in the treatment and want it to work, we will experience a positive outcome. The concept was probably born long, long ago, in the 1500s, when doctors would sometimes prescribe prescriptions to patients they believed to be hypochondriacs. Remarkably, many of these patients reported positive results. Since then, many studies, some dating back as far as half a century ago, have studied the placebo effect, finding success with treating a variety of ailments.

We are familiar with the term placebos when referring to "sugar pills." The most typical example of using a placebo is in medical clinical trials where the participants are divided into two groups. One group receives the active ingredients in the prescription pill and the other a fake pill that looks real but only includes only inactive substances that are contained in the prescription pill. Or it may be an injection containing only sugar and water. No one knows which group received the real medication and who received the inactive substance. If the patients who are given the placebo believe it is real, and expect benefits from it, their hopeful and positive outlook will often result in their body chemistry briefly reacting as though they received the real medication.

Placebos are also used in fake surgeries, including damaged knees and broken backs. Over the course of our lifetime, our knees take a lot of abuse from us. They get overworked in athletics, sustain injuries in falls, and are the source of chronic pain. Arthroscopic surgery is typically the treatment of choice. Remarkably, a Baylor College of Medicine study found that of patients receiving knee surgery, those who received placebo arthroscopic surgery reported the same decrease in pain and the same return to activities, as did those who underwent the real procedure. Placebo surgeries are used in vertebroplasty, a procedure for fixing broken backs, with similar success. These patients were not tricked. Ethically, all patients have to sign a consent form informing them that there is a possibility of receiving a placebo.

The list of physical and psychological changes experienced when receiving only a placebo extends well beyond knees and backs. Researchers have found many participants in placebo groups to have changes in heart rate, blood pressure, pain perception, fatigue, and even brain activity. In some cases it can help conditions including coughs, headaches, diabetes, insomnia and nausea relief. Hope is measured not only physically, but psychologically as well, providing benefit for several ailments including anxiety, depression, and even some psychoses.

Little wonder that it has been suggested the term 'placebo' instead be called 'hope.' This is echoed in an interview on National Public Radio's Talk of the Nation with Dr. Ted Kaptchuk, director of Harvard University's Program in Placebo Studies and the Therapeutic Encounter. "Ultimately, we think the placebo is about the power of the imagination, trust, and hope in the medical encounter," commented Dr. Kaptchuk.[2] The unmistakable takeaway is that hope provides resilience in helping our mind and body respond positively to adversity. Hope is measured not only physically, but psychologically as well.

Social scientists have developed scales to measure hope, which helps us understand how having or not having hope impacts on people experiencing hardships. The importance of hope in our lives cannot be overstated. As will be detailed later in this chapter, hopefulness increases our ability to experience academic achievement, athletic success, problem resolutions, self-esteem, and health in the entire range of our lives. In other words, hope influences our ability to feel happy in every sphere of our existence.

The power of hope has not been lost on politicians. Many Americans voted for Barack Obama in the 2008 United States presidential election because they were swept up by his successful presidential campaign message of *Hope and Change*. He convinced struggling, uncertain and worried Americans that their lives could change in a positive direction if he was elected president. The hope and change movement resonated again in 2016, with voters seeing presidential candidates Bernie Sanders and Donald Trump as the embodiment of hope.

Hope is not experienced in a similar manner in all cultures. Different histories, languages, codes of conduct, patterns of interaction, and political and social concerns influence the importance placed on the concept of hope. For example, Western cultures place value on hope that is related to autonomy and personal satisfaction, while Eastern cultures focus more on harmony and collective cooperation.

Why is Hope so Important?

Hope is, hands down, one of the most powerful components for overcoming adversity available to every living person on this planet, regardless of race, socioeconomic status, health, gender, or age. Hope is an essential, dynamic life force that enables us to visualize a better future. It is what makes the difference between feeling overrun with negative emotions and wanting to give up, and feeling motivated to persevere towards a brighter future. Through hope, we identify ways to overcome challenges, plan alternate routes when obstacles arise and continue to strive towards reaching a solution to our adversity.

Without hope, we would not be committed in our attempts to move forward. We would be discouraged and unable to develop clarity on how to reach our goals. Instead, hope offers us the opportunity to imagine a positive outcome and greater happiness.

Abraham Lincoln once said, "Most folks are about as happy as they make their mind to be." Hopeful people tend to be happy people because they set their mind to it. Hopeful people react to difficult and challenging life experiences in a manner that makes them more resilient. When they hit an obstruction, they don't give in to negative emotions that have the ability to stifle their willpower to keep moving forward. Nor do they burden themselves with negative thoughts that would demoralize them, lower their sense of self-worth, and reduce any chances of striving for a desired goal. Instead, they are interested in learning from their experience, making adjustments, and trying again.

When adversity strikes, hopeful people set goals for themselves as they have likely done in the past when recovering from physical injuries, studying for exams, or dealing with previous experiences of loss. They look at problem-solving in a positive manner. When their hoped for goals are blocked, they continue to look for different ways to reach success.

Simply put, hopeful people expect to succeed in their efforts. The result is empowering. Their hopefulness provides not just one, but alternative goals when adversity takes away so much. Their goals are clear and measurable, and can be broken down into segments or steps. This clarity helps them to be more successful in achieving their goals, as vague goals instill little motivation. Hope is the driving force that keeps them moving on a positive path toward achieving these goals, bringing them closer to a solution to adversity.

Mental Health

Previously, the field of psychology helped people through use of a disease model, concentrating on people's problems, psychopathology, and unhappy past events, and repairing damage that was causing their troubled feelings. But the last couple of decades have experienced a shift in focus. Now, extensive research is conducted around the globe in the field of positive psychology, in an attempt to not just fix what is broken, but to strengthen what is already good. Research into understanding the role our emotions play on how well we cope with stress helps us better understand what factors contribute to a happy and meaningful life. If we have difficulty managing feelings of anger, anxiety, and fear, we will likely have greater difficulty coping with disappointments, losses, and significant challenges, and will experience hopelessness.

The inverse is also true. If we can maintain a positive outlook, we will be more resilient. Our thinking will be more rational, less emotional, and more flexible. Our problem-solving skills will increase. Previously overwhelming situations can now be less challenging because we will feel hopeful about having the skills to break tasks down into smaller and more manageable portions, making problems resolvable.

As our sense of competence grows, so does our self-esteem. When we feel good about and like ourselves we are less judgmental of others and ourselves. We will be stronger in not being susceptible to negativity from others because we believe in ourselves and are hopeful in finding a positive resolution. We will be more likely to want to surround ourselves with positive people who offer us helpful suggestions. If our adversity is a result of being hurt by another person, this emotional support will help us bridge that gap we have in trusting others. As our hurt begins to heal, we will feel more hopeful about our relationships with others.

Believing that we can create changes to our situation and influence our future grows our sense of hope. With hope we become emotionally stronger, and find ourselves experiencing more clarity and motivation, even pushing past obstacles and accomplishing more than what we had previously thought possible. We will view ourselves as competent to manage the problems that lie in our path.

Physical Health

Research has found a direct correlation between the ability to hope and people who suffer from physical pain and chronic conditions, such as severe burns, arthritis, spinal cord injury, fibromyalgia, (a disorder characterized by often debilitating pain), and blindness. Even when there is no cure, hoping for different possibilities can help people develop a greater sense of inner peace because they are no longer focusing exclusively on their losses. Instead, they are more forward focused and planning alternative goals for themselves. This higher level of hope helps reduce their anxiety, remain energized, experience less pain, and tolerate pain much longer than low-hopers.

No group of physicians is more familiar with the importance of hope in patient survival than oncologists. Ninety percent of surveyed oncologists rated hope as the most important psychological factor associated with increased survival rates among cancer patients.[3] Studies have similarly shown that hopelessness negatively impacts patients' recovery. Elderly patients who self-identified as hopeless were found to have a lower quality of life, lower self-esteem, and sadly, were nearly three times as likely to die than the self-identified hopeful patients. On the other hand, patients with breast cancer who had high hope were found to experience a better immunity than those with less hope.

Academic Success

Hope has been found to be a measure of predicting academic success for students ranging from elementary school to college. Students with hope do better at maintaining healthy lifestyles, problem-solving behaviors, and experiencing positive psychological well-being. Studies on college students have found that those who were more successful were those who, when overwhelmed, were able to identify what they wanted, and establish effective alternative avenues to stay on task or redirect themselves around unexpected barriers. In other words, they had a 'can-do' approach and focused more on hope than on failure. Students who focused on failure when they got overwhelmed felt anxious and unempowered, lost focus when encountering obstacles, tended to reactive passively, and were less successful academically.[4]

While academic ability is important in achieving success in college, students would be ill advised to rely on the gray matter alone to secure their diploma. Remarkably, research has found hopefulness to be a more reliable predictor of grades in college than scores from the Scholastic Aptitude Test, and a greater indicator of success in the first year of law school than either undergraduate grades or LSAT scores, the entry exam for law students.[5]

Similarly, many employers, in an effort to identify what characteristics are important in hiring, have shifted in their focus from a weighted emphasis on academic standing to looking for other, less tangible, qualities in job applicants. Shelley Jones, former Human Resource Director for a Fortune 50 company, looked at the applicant's ability to work well with people, manage their emotions, be goal-driven, and successful at problem solving, all qualities that contribute to high levels of hopefulness. Recalling conversations she would have with hiring managers, she remembers their saying, "We gotta hire him. He's from the top of his class from Stanford, or Harvard." Mrs. Jones, recognizing it takes more than raw IQ to lead a team, would respond by saying, "That has as much to do with his future success as his shoe size."[6]

Athletic Success

Anyone betting on an athletic event would do well to factor in the level of hopefulness experienced by participating athletes. Studies have shown that hopefulness is a greater indicator of successful athletic performance than the amount of practice, natural athletic talent, their mood, self-esteem, or confidence. A study of female track athletes found that "hope experienced just before a race enhances the predictions regarding achievement."[7] This likely occurs because the athlete develops a mental plan, remains focused on the desired goal, and avoids being distracted by extraneous interferences. As we witness time and again in the Olympics and Super Bowl, unanticipated obstacles, such as encountering a more skilled opponent, or an unexpected injury, do not derail hopeful athletes. Instead, they quickly adjust and create new plans with their focus remaining on reaching the original goal.

Employment

Job burnout is experienced when people dealing with continuous work-related stressors find themselves becoming unmotivated, cynical, and unenthusiastic about work. Burned out individuals struggle because they have little hope about any positive changes occurring in their current situation. The ramifications for low levels of hope at work are more than just not liking getting up in the morning and going to the job. They tend to experience goal blockage, frustration, and negative affect. They find their sleep cycle disrupted, feel disconnected with others, and depressed. This hopelessness, if not resolved, can cause medical problems, including an increased risk of gastrointestinal disorders and cardiovascular disease.

Post-Traumatic Growth

Without hope, people might find themselves stuck and overwhelmed by their adversity. To be hopeful does not mean they do not experience distress, pessimism, and helplessness. They may at times even find themselves experiencing despair because hope is not a constant. Doubt always exists, because they never lose sight of reality.

For this reason, hope remains a fragile and fluid experience. It is typical for people to repeatedly cycle between hope and despair, despair and hope, and hope and despair. The key is that hopeful people are always aware that they have a choice of either throwing in the towel or hoping. They choose hope because it serves as a buffer against despair along the way. From this, people find that their conditions are not hopeless and that solutions to problems can exist. And amazingly, the hopeful find that good can sometimes come from the suffering. Psychologists refer to these positive changes as "post-traumatic growth" or "benefit finding."

Benefit finding is a paradox. It occurs when we begin to look beyond an event that caused us an incredible amount of pain and can find some constructive meaning and a sense of purpose. Benefit finding gives us a sense of control over our circumstances and an opportunity to learn hopefulness. Our relationship with ourselves changes, with a feeling of increased wisdom, resilience and personal growth.

Misty Wilson was in her early 30s, married, and owner of a successful business in tony Newport Beach, California. With flowing blond hair and living adjacent to the beach, she seemed to be a symbol from the easy-going surf, sand, and paneled woodies era. But Ms. Wilson had a secret. No one knew she was an alcoholic. She hid it from her employees, her friends, and even her husband. When she recognized it was a problem, she became sober and hid that as well. She didn't discuss it with anyone. Nor did she share or interact at Alcoholics Anonymous meetings she attended.

Ms. Wilson did not realize that she had been using the alcohol to bury her emotions deep inside. Dependent on unhealthy coping mechanisms of denial and avoidance, she had never learned how to deal with unpleasant feelings, how to heal past hurts and to grow emotionally. Unknowingly, she had only succeeded in temporarily suppressing her emotions; they hadn't gone away. They were still there, just sitting on a shelf waiting to be dusted off and dealt with.

Not knowing how to manage her feelings, and without the alcohol to mask them proved to be disruptive. "It started affecting my marriage," recalls Ms. Wilson. Within the year, her husband asked for a divorce. "Once my marriage ended I didn't understand what was going on. I was lost. That was a really big struggle. The only thing that really helped me was to keep talking. And I kept talking and talking and getting out everything I was feeling," states Ms. Wilson.

Previously dependent on her husband to make decisions for her, she started learning new coping behaviors and taking ownership of her life. "I just started doing things that were positive. I started going to Alcoholics Anonymous meetings and working with my sponsor, and the steps. I began making my friendships grow back into regular, good relationships, letting people do things for me, and doing things for other people. I was doing things I enjoy again, like getting into yoga. I started dancing again, I started traveling, and I basically just started watering the part of me that died when I got married."

The changes occurred slowly, but as her confidence has grown, and new skills have been developed, Ms. Wilson has discovered a part of herself that had never before been revealed. For the first time in her life, she feels strength coming from within and no longer feels pessimistic and powerless.

"I think that once I started growing, I started feeling better, a little bit at a time. I still don't feel like I am where I want to be, but I feel a lot better now. Every day I wake up, say a prayer, and go on my morning walk. I tell myself all the things that I am grateful for, and I just try to stay grateful. Looking ahead at what I can accomplish rather than things in the past over which I have no control has given me a lot of hope. I have a lot of hope that I'm going to get through this," reflects Ms. Wilson.

"I definitely changed my view of myself. I now can rely on my own decisions. I like myself. I have a lot of self-confidence. Anything I want to do, I think I can do it. I really hid behind my ex-husband and his opinions," acknowledges Ms. Wilson. "I put him in front. I basically attached myself to his life and I let go of my life."

Ms. Wilson has found the good — the benefit — in her suffering.

"Now I'm creating a whole new life, and can do whatever I want," says Ms. Wilson. "So it is like writing a new story. I'm definitely feeling more empowered. I'm still working on being kinder to myself, but I'm much better at this than I used to be. I still have good and bad days, but I don't blame myself for everything. Now I see my part in things. I clean up my end of things when

I see something that needs to be addressed, but I don't take the blame for every problem anymore."

"I've been in recovery for two years, tomorrow. I'm still in a lot of pain and hurt from my marriage ending, but I'm still happier than I've ever been. Although I'm grieving a lot, I found myself again. So I'm feeling happier and more confident than I've ever been personally with myself. I feel like I've never been who I'm supposed to be. I'm really sorry for my loss, but I'm really happy at the other end at the same time," she reflects.[8]

Following the ensuing months in her struggle to cope with her life crisis, Ms. Wilson's hopeful approach enabled her to not only experience benefit finding that made her more resilient, but also change the way she views herself and others.

She has changed her priorities from trying to please others to taking care of herself and owning her feelings. She finds this new belief in herself to be empowering. Her life is richer, personal relationships deeper, and more spiritual. While still struggling with processing the ending of her marriage, she exhibits hopeful thinking; is now able to develop plans for achieving goals, and envisions a positive future for herself.

What Hope is Not

As the word hope is used often and sometimes incorrectly in our daily lives, it is helpful to provide clarification as to what comprises the concept of hope. Removing the confusion can enable us to heal more quickly. Below is a list of several terms of which hope is not.

A Fix
The thought of hope alone does not resolve problems. Hope should stimulate action.

Cliché
Hope is rooted in reality, not clichés such as "don't worry, things work out in the end," or "think positively."

Control
Hope contains elements of uncertainty. Hope often comes about as a response to a crisis, loss or hardship. It is not possible to have all the answers or know what the end accomplishment will look like. We must be flexible so that when

something that is hoped for is not obtainable, we do not give up. Instead of focusing on the failure we substitute a new goal.

Defense Mechanisms

Psychological defense mechanisms are self-protective mechanisms we use when feeling anxious or guilty. They tend to distort or deny reality so that it doesn't feel so painful. Hope differs because it requires acknowledgment of reality. Two commonly experienced defense mechanisms are:

1. **Denial.** Denial is a psychological defense mechanism that protects an individual from accepting information that is too painful to integrate. To deny the pain is to ignore it. Hope consists of acknowledging the pain, the risks and obstacles standing in the way of resolving the pain, and development of plans on how to resolve the painful situation.
2. **Repression.** Repression is an unconscious mechanism used to 'forget' something painful. To repress a thought is to push away unacceptable or upsetting thoughts one doesn't feel able to cope with at the time. This is not entirely successful, as the uncomfortable thoughts never fully vanish. Memories of traumatic events that are repressed are only temporarily hidden from thought and may reappear, causing additional anxiety and problems to occur. Hopefulness provides a way to face, address and resolve, rather than hide, these thoughts.

Dreams or Wishing

Wishing doesn't have a plan. Dreams are not necessarily realistic. They are more about visualizations of happy endings, like unicorns, marrying a prince, and winning the lottery. Hope is more than simply wanting something. Hope must be reasonable and there must be a concrete plan for reaching the goal. Plans associated with hope can contain elements of uncertainty, but their foundation is based on realism.

Intelligence-Based

Hopeful thinking is a state of mind, not brainpower. Hope is associated with divergent thinking, which is not exclusive to those with a high IQ. Divergent thinking is a thought process in which we create new and "out of the box" ideas by brainstorming and considering various resolutions. In times of adversity, divergent thinkers use their imaginations to develop new strategies that will successfully lead to obtaining a goal.

Joy

Hope and joy are often used interchangeably, yet are different. Hope is the belief that when we are in a painful situation, that pursuing a goal is the right thing to do, even if success is not guaranteed. Joy is the experience we have when things are going well.

Obstacle-Free

Hopefulness is born out of problematic times in our lives when we need to make changes that can feel daring and risky. It is scary knowing that despite the uncertainty and unknowns, these changes will impact on our lives. We often have to develop new coping skills and explore using previously untapped resources within our self and society. Obstacles will arise along the way when unforeseen barriers are encountered. Hopefulness is never obstacle-free.

One Exclusive Path

Hope does not have tunnel vision when striving for a goal. Life is too complicated, is never static, and solutions to a problem today may be irrelevant tomorrow. Hope allows us to be flexible in modifying our goals, so that we can pursue those that are important to us at the present moment.

Optimism

Although both are future oriented, hope is distinguishable from optimism. Optimism is the passive belief that we will be okay. It doesn't have a plan for achieving the goal. Hope involves the active belief that we can make things better by establishing goals, creating plans, and considering potential obstacles to achieve them. By not considering the risk of potential obstacles, optimism might minimize the possibility of glitches, thereby creating problems later on. For example, consider the situation in which an elderly man with an unstable medical condition decides to go on a lengthy cruise. If he is optimistic, he is likely to brush away any concerns and assume that everything will be just fine, not take into consideration the increased medical risk of being at sea, far from his physicians, or the cost of an air evacuation resulting from poor planning that can arise from optimism. Hope, on the other hand, would involve developing realistic plans for being able to achieve the goal of safely if sailing on a cruise. This might include having a strategy comprised of having a conversation with his physician about risk factors before booking the cruise, selecting an itinerary that included visiting many ports of call so he could disembark and get medical help if needed, and determining the cost of cancellation fees.

Passivity

Hope is active. It involves decision-making, willpower, searching, trying, and making adjustments if original plans do not work. To be passive is to stay stationary and wait, whereas hope is a forward thinking thought process and active behavior.

Prayer

Praying without doing anything will not bring about any results. For prayer to work, believers ask a higher power to provide advice on how to improve their situation. Receiving divine guidance is only the first part of hopefulness. We must use that information or inspiration to motivate us to creatively develop an action that will bring about the desired change.

Presumption

To make assumptions that something is true, or will happen, can lead to a failure to plan. It fails to take into consideration that we may need to take action to modify our plans so that we can achieve our goals.

Reality Escape

Hope does not involve our avoidance of truth or reality. Nor does it provide a way for us to ignore our problems. Hope has an unwavering commitment to truth and reality, recognizing the risks and threats while seeking the best path around these obstacles.

Reminiscence

Reminiscence is backward looking, whereas hopefulness is future oriented. In a study of depressed older men and women, some were to focus on hope and others on reminiscence. The hope group was instructed to plant a bush, go to the mall, etc. The reminiscence group was to recall memories from their past. At the conclusion of the study, the hope group's depression measured almost three times less than the reminiscence group. Additionally, they became more pro-social, baking and bringing food to their group, and thanked the leader afterward for what they had accomplished.

Risk-Taking

Hopefulness involves motivation to reach a goal in the future. Risk-taking is more associated with seeking immediate rewards. With risk-taking there is a greater chance of harming oneself because the consequences for the behaviors are often overlooked or minimized.

Self-Efficacy

Like hope, self-efficacy refers to an individuals' perception about their ability to accomplish a goal and make a positive impact on their life. The difference is that self-efficacy places more importance on the expectations than the outcome. Hope emphasizes the will of the person and the way the goal is sought, as well as the goal.

Barriers to Hope

If we don't have hope, we cannot consider alternative ways to combat a terrible circumstance in our lives. We shut down and pull within ourselves where we feel safe, and life is more predictable. We might wait for something to happen, but we expect that the fix will come from someone else. We have no role in the solution but are passive and solely reliant on someone else to make our needs to come true. Hopelessness keeps us stuck and unable to make progress. Following is a list of barriers that can inhibit our ability to achieve hopefulness.

Acceptance

Acceptance is resignation. It is the belief that there is little we can do and that this is the way it will be.

Additional Stressors

Stress is a negative force that drains our energy. It opens us up more to being paralyzed by fear and uncertainty, and viewing defeat as an option. Examples of common stressors are physical pain, exhaustion, anxiety, and loss of a support system.

Apathy

Apathy is a way for people to protect themselves from feeling vulnerable to anxiety and fear. It often results from the painful memories collected from a previous failure in reaching a goal. When people lose hope in believing that their plans will work to reach the goal, or think that the goal is too much effort or unattainable, they can lose faith in their ability to experience success. They become apathetic, shut down emotionally, and quit trying.

Cynicism

Cynicism is a protective coping mechanism designed to keep us from getting hurt. Cynics distrust other people's ideas, are negative, do not view themselves as being able to bring about positive change, and avoid risk. Hope involves changing one's behavior. Cynics have difficulty changing their behavior because they tend to rationalize their problems and blame others for their unhappiness. This lack of personal responsibility conflicts with the personal motivation needed for hopefulness.

Expecting a Solution

Hope is about having the perception that we can make an improvement in our lives, even when there is no guarantee.

Expecting Plans to go Smoothly

Hope is about getting around obstacles and unanticipated challenges. Otherwise, we would not need hope, just a plan.

False Hope

Hope is based on reaching appropriate goals. False hope is based on idealistic views and unrealistic goals, and can cause people to fail. People exhibiting false hope may be over-confident and assume the changes to be easy and achievable in an unreasonably short period of time because they did not factor in the stress, risks, coping skills or tangible resources required. The emotional toll for failing to understand the situation correctly and the consequences for not meeting the desired goal is high, often resulting in squashed feelings of hopefulness.

Fear of Failure

Fear is always a part of hope. To take a risk at making a change one has to recognize that failure, and the feelings of disappointment that accompany it, are always a risk. Hope helps us go beyond focusing on the things that can go wrong, and instead helps us try to control our future.

Hopelessness or Depression

It takes a lot of energy to move away from our current situation to move towards a more positive future. The depressed individual will feel hopeless and helpless, with lowered expectations about the future. Depression inhibits the energy needed to consider positive opportunities, and to facilitate change. Hope provides a buffer of resilience against hopelessness.

Isolation

Our feelings of hopefulness typically benefit from the emotional support and feedback provided by others. Their opinions help us make adjustments necessary in reaching our goals. Their experiences and support provide a protective factor against discouragement and keep hope alive during very challenging times. Social relationships reduce our loneliness and suffering and provide fuel for our hopefulness.

Lack of a Sound Plan

Hastily developed or unrealistic plans are not likely to be adequate for tackling problems and overcoming barriers in search of obtaining a goal. Hope contains a strategy that is based on realistic factors and allows for the possibility of substituting alternative ways to reach the desired goal.

Lack of Faith

Neither faith nor hope is tangible. You can't hold, measure, see, or taste them. But they are vital, and we need both of them. When our faith grows, we can find a sense of meaning, and our hope increases. Viktor Frankl, a Jewish psychiatrist who survived the Nazi concentration camps, witnessed many others die of starvation, disease, and in the gas chambers, including his mother, brother and pregnant wife. In his book, *Man's Search for Meaning*, Frankl wrote: "Man is not destroyed by suffering; he is destroyed by suffering without meaning." He observed that those in the concentration camps who found a sense of purpose and meaning in life, despite their extreme daily suffering, lived longer than those who were unable to find meaning, and hope.

Lack of Imagination

Sometimes minimized as belonging to the silliness of children, imagination plays a significant role in hopefulness. We should never grow up to the point where we lose connection with our ability to creatively consider alternative plans that help us face our struggles in fresh, creative ways.

Albert Einstein got it right when he said that imagination, "is the preview for life's coming attractions." When we have hope we are able to imagine a positive outcome. Our imagination guides us to the path we need to take to reach our goal and become more resilient.

Passive Waiting

Hope is about action, not waiting. To passively hope for something better is to only have a vague sense of what one wants, as opposed to having a plan. Passive waiting, sometimes done in the form of prayer, with no follow through on our part accomplishes nothing.

Perceptions of Hopelessness From Others

When important people in our lives, such as our support system, express negative thoughts or feelings about our situation, hopelessness can result. When emotional support is withheld, our sense of self-worth can diminish and our sense of loneliness can grow, adding to our difficulty in coping with existing stress. Furthermore, negativity from others may result in their choosing to not provide information and financial support, further impairing our ability to develop hopefulness.

Rigidity

Rigidity conflicts with hopefulness. When rigid, we don't roll with the punches, are not adaptable to changing ebbs and flows as we trod down the path towards change, and don't challenge ourselves to explore new skills or develop new competencies. And worst of all, rigidity narrows our vision, impairing our ability to look at the broader picture. If our goal is simply to play it safe and avoid risk, we will find ourselves remaining within the bubble of our known and familiar comfort zone. As a result, options for problem-solving will decrease, placing us at risk for making bad decisions and unable to meet our goals. Trust in our ability to control our situation will diminish, creating doubt that we can have positive impact on obtaining the future we want. Seeing no option, we risk becoming hopeless. We lose our resilience and quit trying.

Flexibility, on the other hand, enhances resilience. It makes us more inclined to be hopeful because we will not experience hopelessness when we hit an obstruction in our plans. Instead, we will consider numerous ideas, experience broader perspectives on problem solving, and feel confident in our ability to push through the blockage to reaching our goal.

Shame

Shame has a debilitating effect on everything in our lives, and nowhere does it create more havoc than on hopefulness. Shame causes people to feel worthless, causing them to isolate themselves from significant others in their social network out of embarrassment and a perception that they will be rejected by them. Feeling vulnerable and more likely to judge themselves negatively, they will have less confidence and little hope in moving forward.

Socioeconomic Status

Individuals who live in lower socioeconomic communities are more likely to have exposure to violence. Studies have found that people who had more personal experience with violence had a lower level of hope than those who had witnessed but not been personally affected by violence.

Traditionalism

Hope requires inspiration and the entertaining of fresh ideas in order to consider alternative paths to one's goal. Thinking that leads us away from our traditional comfort zone helps us create fresh ideas, which are valuable in moving us beyond the rough spots.

How to Use the Three Spheres of Support to Achieve Hope

We start developing the ability for hopeful thinking in early childhood. When we recognize as toddlers that one of our behaviors can create change, we begin to learn that we have the ability to make things happen. For example, we learn that when we have a goal, such as wanting our mother to remove us from our high chair, that we can develop plans for our goal to be met. We may reach out our arms to her, indicating we want to be held. If that attempt is unsuccessful, we may squirm around in our high chair, signaling her attention. Perhaps if that plan fails, the third effort to reach our goal will be to toss everything, including our spoon, dish, food, and cup, onto the floor. Having grabbed our mother's attention, she finally walks over and releases us from the high chair. Through this behavior, which is repeated by toddlers worldwide, we have successfully learned that if one plan is not successful in reaching our goal, then we can remain hopeful and engage in a second, or even a third plan, to bring about success.

These everyday types of experiences are important in the development of coping strategies that kindle hope. Learning how to develop our thinking helps us know we can find options when confronting difficult tasks. We will feel confident that there are people in our lives we can trust and who will help us focus on reaching our goals, and appreciate that we have skills needed to commit to solving problems. When facing a challenging situation in the future we will be able to reflect back on the experiences, insights and skills we used in pushing past it. We will be more empowered to successfully overcome new obstacles.

As toddlers, we learn to develop healthy, emotional bonds with our parents. This provides the foundation for learning trust not only in our parents but also enables us to generalize that trust to our broader existence. We have reason to hope that the world is a safe place to explore and prosper. After all, although it may have taken three approaches, our mother did eventually remove us from the high chair. Sadly, not everyone is raised in an environment in which hopefulness is fostered. Some caretakers are unresponsive, allowing the child's requests to go unheeded. Others may react negatively to the child, with punishment. Such negative experiences can result in a child developing a crippling "I-give-up" attitude about problem solving, and growing up passive and depressed.

However, Dr. Martin Seligman, renowned positive psychologist, and author of *Learned Optimism: How To Change Your Mind And Your Life*, emphasizes that despite our past experiences, hope can be learned. To become hopeful we have to understand that it is up to us to interrupt the harmful thought process we have developed when faced with adversity. Our challenge is to distance ourselves from those habitual negative beliefs that ruminate in our head, and which make us so miserable and hopeless. In a technique known as "disputing," we can challenge each and every one of those catastrophic beliefs until we have sufficiently ground them down and they no longer hold validity for us. By creating positive thoughts in place of the negative ones we have removed, we are changing our mindset, which in turn will help us feel more energized and hopeful.

By using our three spheres of support — Self, Society, and Spirituality — we also help ourselves maintain hope through adversity.

Self

Coping Mechanisms

Hope is essential when facing serious and prolonged experiences of adversity. Without it, our health is at risk, including an increased risk for depression and suicide.

We have within each of us a wide range of social, emotional, and psychological coping mechanisms that can influence our ability to experience hopefulness. Coping strategies can be constructive or maladaptive. Maladaptive coping strategies make things worse for us. They include escaping reality via illegal or prescription drugs, alcoholism, or other behaviors that inhibit our ability to develop hopefulness and move forward. Strategies that help us to successfully deal with the adversity are like grabbing that gold ring. They allow us to experience the wide range of emotions that result from it, are healthy and will increase the likelihood of developing hopefulness. The following examples describe some of these coping mechanisms.

Action Oriented Coping

Action-oriented people are doers. Being action oriented, as opposed to avoidant, is an empowering coping mechanism. Being engaged, seeking help, and taking action, rather than being avoidant means that we follow through on commitments and get things done.

Actively taking steps to resolve our problems reduces the buildup of negative emotions, such as hopelessness and self-blame. Even if we encounter obstacles and have to make adjustments, we are still engaged in the process of creating goals, and contributing to hopefulness.

Action-oriented behavior reduces the output of cortisol, a steroid hormone nicknamed the "stress hormone." Unabated stress that accompanies feelings of hopelessness, which can occur when we avoid dealing with adversity, can cause too much or too little cortisol to circulate. Over an extended period of time the cortisol can begin to tear down our body. High levels of cortisol sustained over an extended period of time can trigger high blood pressure, a lower immune function, depression, muscle weakness, and impair our ability to think straight. If our stress results in the adrenal glands becoming fatigued from too high a level of circulating cortisol, our cortisol level drops, and we can experience problems including sleep deprivation, impaired thinking, weight loss, and decreased thyroid and immune function. We can lose hope of being able to find a way out of our adversity, and our future will feel like doom and gloom. Being action-oriented gives our cortisol levels an opportunity to return to normal following a stressful event. When our cortisol levels are regulated, we are better able to have the clarity of thinking needed for hopefulness.

Critical Thinking

Critical thinking comes about by being able to evaluate or revisit a problem and think rationally about how to resolve it. We gather reliable information, ask questions, think open-mindedly, and incorporate input from others that will help us improve our plans and solve problems.

Focus on Strengths

Focusing on our personal strengths when life appears grim can be a motivating, positive coping mechanism. Assessing our previous successes and identifying what we did that was effective in helping us cope, can help us develop a course of action that will bring us closer to our current hoped-for goals.

Mindfulness

Attempting to overcome adversity can feel like being strapped into a speeding roller coaster. We have so many decisions to make, and our emotions can be all over the map, causing us extreme stress. In the early 1990s, medical school professor Jon Kabat-Zin found a way to help us decrease stress. Called "mindfulness," the practice helps us learn how, at any given moment, to be aware of how our thoughts are affecting our body.

Donald Altman, author of several books including *101 Mindful Ways To Build Resilience* and *Clearing Emotional Clutter*, refers to this improved relationship with our minds and bodies as regulating our brain. "When we are upset, triggered, or emotionally reactive, the inner core of the brain is lighting up like a Christmas tree. When we have reactive thoughts we can easily grab on to them, but they can pull us in a direction we don't want to go. The process of regulating the brain means being able to observe those thoughts from a safe distance. I call that 'constructively distancing' from your negative thoughts. When you're observing and noticing, you're using a different part of the brain that is behind the eyebrow ridge, which is called the prefrontal cortex. That is the most regulatory part of the brain," states Mr. Altman.

If an event triggers your anger, Mr. Altman suggests shifting "your perspective (from the event) and observing the anger by noticing your breathing, and rating the anger on a one to ten scale. The moment you start noticing the anger and start breathing, you're not grabbing on to that emotion any more. You have distance from it. And that is a skill that anyone can learn."

Mindfulness can be achieved in many ways other than observing every sensation of our breathing. A few examples include meditating, pausing between actions (such as between bites of food for mindful eating), connecting with our surroundings by walking mindfully (barefoot through the grass, walking slowly first landing on our heels, then soles, and then toes), or listening to someone without thinking about replying (while taking in their tone, expressions, awareness of our breathing, smells in the room, etc.)

"We also know from mindfulness research," continues Mr. Altman, "that when you observe your emotions in this way and just name or label them as anger, sadness, upset, disappointment, frustration, or whatever emotion it is, in that moment you are quieting down the emotional inner core of the brain. In other words, the Christmas tree lights are now dimming and not so bright. You're regulating the brain. You're integrating the more executive thinking center of the brain with the more emotional, reactive part of the brain and helping them connect in a more useful way."[9]

When practiced over time, mindfulness helps us understand and mobilize the natural and powerful resources we have within, contributing towards growing feelings of hopefulness. We learn that we can better deal with emotional crises resulting from adversity by connecting our emotions with the executive center of the brain. This allows us to develop a broader perspective at difficult times in our lives, feel more in control, and better able to make constructive decisions.

Solicitation of Social Support
Seeking support from others is a way to create an environment in which we can have both personal security as well as a safe place to sort out our feelings and thoughts. When we are isolated we can be overwhelmed and at increased risk of not being able to accurately assess a situation, take care of all our needs, or be aware of all the options available to us. This can impair our thinking, create feelings of anxiety and fear, prevent goals from being realized, and increase our risk of failing.

Acceptance of Reality
Hopefulness requires recognition of the seriousness of the situation. Reality is crucial in developing hope. We can't solve a problem without first recognizing that the problem exists. Many people shy away from examining the problem, thinking that paying too much attention to it will make them feel more hopeless, or that it will make the problem grow in size, or that ignoring it will make the problem go away. However, failure to recognize a problem and all of its complexities will almost always create more drastic problems, the longer they remain unaddressed.

Shane J. Lopez, Ph.D., one of the world's leading researchers on hope, points out that we can prepare for reality by thinking ahead of time of alternative plans should we encounter an unexpected obstacle. By acknowledging the problem we will be able to remain in the driver's seat. Planning ahead of time for the possibility of one path being blocked prevents us from feeling blindsided and at risk of abandoning hope. Knowing that we can redirect our energy onto another route helps us summon up the energy to remain hopeful, keeps us encouraged, and accelerates our resilience.

Emotional Intelligence

According to research, cognitive intelligence only accounts for 20 percent of the factors contributing to success in life. The remaining 80% consist of other factors, including emotional intelligence and hope. It was back in the 1980s that Israeli psychologist Dr. Reuven Bar-On discovered emotional intelligence. But it wasn't until the appearance of Daniel Goleman's book in 1995, *Emotional Intelligence: Why It Can Matter More Than IQ*, that emotional intelligence received international attention. Emotional intelligence differs from cognitive intelligence (intelligence quotient, or IQ), which is to a large degree, biologically based. Rather, emotional intelligence is about how well we understand others and ourselves, how well we understand the needs of others and express ourselves, and how well we cope with everyday pressures.

We've all heard of an exceptionally bright individual, perhaps an Ivy League college graduate, who experiences bitterness about being passed over for promotions at work despite his excellent contributions, and whose personal relationships are riddled with conflict. We also may know someone who does not come from privilege and works in an entry-level position, yet enjoys a strong and trusting group of friends, a devoted spouse, and the daily challenges of life. This person's success is probably due to his ability to be flexible to changing situations, and understanding the importance of his and other's feelings and emotions. He can "emotionally read" others, which leads to improved relationships, is highly regarded as a team player, and is respected for being able to prevent and successfully resolve conflict.

Much like people who rate high on emotional intelligence, people with high levels of hope use emotions to help in problem-solving and reasoning. They are in touch with their own feelings, are comfortable with expressing them, and care about the feelings of others. Understanding emotions provides a buffer against stressful events and creates an atmosphere in which feelings of hopefulness can grow.

This was validated in a study of pre-school teachers in Turkey, where the combination of hope and emotional intelligence resulted in a higher level of life satisfaction when responding to difficulties in their lives.[10] Their emotional intelligence impacted on their mood, which helped them feel empowered, which in turn helped energize them to keep going to achieve a chosen goal.

Finding Meaning

A lot is going on when something devastating occurs to us. We are filled with uncertainty and our view of the world is shaken. Our ability to move forward at such times is often diminished. We're left with questions such as "Why me?" and "How can I find meaning in life again, following this event?" Discovering meaning, even in this very difficult situation, will help in our ability to persevere.

Meaning is a subjective and complex experience. If we respond to adversity in a negative way, such as ruminating and feeling victimized, our mental and physical energy will be depleted and we may find ourselves engulfed in feelings of hopelessness. While it is fully understandable why we would find ourselves in this place, we can feel more in control and begin to heal our hurt by examining the significance the event has on us. In doing so, we can develop a new sense of meaning. From this new sense of meaning we can begin to recognize new goals. If the goals are realistic and lead us down a path that helps us heal, we can begin to establish hopefulness.

Hope will keep our momentum going forward in reaching our goals. The goals may be huge, such as establishing a charity or organization that serves to help others suffering from a similar situation, or they can be small. But regardless of size, all provide us with the sense that our needs matter. Knowing we are moving toward our ultimate goal increases our confidence, prevents us from getting overwhelmed and discouraged, and enhances the likelihood that we will persevere.

Humor

Humor is associated with coping well and moving towards hope. Ninety-four percent of the people in one survey identified "lightheartedness" as being "a necessary component in dealing with stressful life events."[11]

Humor enables us to detach ourselves from the painful situation and even reduce undesirable emotions such as anxiety and depression. Rather than narrowing our perspective, which is what we tend to do when upset, humor allows us to experience positive emotions and entertain new thoughts.

Smiling, laughing and enjoying a moment can not only be pleasurable but also help us bounce back to some degree because it reduces our stress and helps us feel more in control of our lives. This increase in self-efficacy can stimulate hopeful thinking, and result in our ability to develop new ways to overcome our adversity.

Maintaining Identity

It is possible to lose a sense of who we were before the adversity occurred. However, when we reflect on our beliefs, traditions, interests, and roles, we are reminded of what is important to us. This helps strengthen our hopefulness and helps us realize our potentialities, as opposed to our limitations, giving us more energy to keep moving toward our goal.

Personality Traits

Researchers believe that we each have individual characteristics that influence how we are motivated towards thinking, feeling, and behaving. They influence how we go about setting and achieving goals. These characteristics can be set into five major dimensions, known as the Big Five personality traits, which are genetic, fairly stable, and are reliable indicators of how an individual will react to adversity and experience hope. (Also see chapters one, three and four.)

Openness

This trait is about being present; engaged, intellectually curious, creative and flexible; all qualities found in hopefulness. Open to change, they will feel comfortable stepping away from the obvious into the more ambiguous. People low in this trait often are more traditional, and less comfortable examining their views and feelings. When faced with an obstacle that stands in the way of their achieving a goal, they may have more difficulty conceptualizing alternative strategies.

Conscientiousness

The conscientious are rock solid people. They are responsible and self-disciplined. While everyone has impulses, the conscientious person has good impulse control and will avoid acting on snap judgments. They tend to be goal directed, and are willing to work hard to achieve them. They experience success in reaching goals because they are organized and engage in purposeful planning. These organization, planning, and goal making qualities are important components of hope.

Extraversion

We all know the extravert: they are the warm and friendly outgoing people who appear to have been born for social settings so they can enjoy connecting and interacting with others. They have an intellectual curiosity that makes them interested not just in themselves but also in their environment. In addition to their social skills, they are capable of developing independent decisions and are open to accepting new ideas about their own lives and the goings-on in the outer world. Their openness and positivity allow them to make goals for themselves, which will increase the attainment of hopefulness.

Agreeableness

Of the five major factors of the personality, agreeableness is the strongest predictor of hope. Agreeable people are lovely to be around. They are kind, warm and optimistic. They work well with others because they are friendly, helpful, trusting, and flexible. These factors result in agreeable people relating to circumstances in a positive and hopeful manner.

People with low levels of agreeableness are more skeptical and competitive than those who are agreeable, which can result in cynicism. These negative emotions tend to drag them into future negativity, from suspicion to anger to apathy, making them less hopeful.

Neuroticism

People scoring high in neuroticism are more likely to experience negative feelings, which may inhibit their ability to feel hopeful. They tend to be emotionally reactive, demonstrating moodiness, anxiety, and mood swings. Their negative emotional reactions will persist and result in physical ailments such as stomach aches and headaches, which can spiral downward into anger, depression and even hopelessness. They won't be able to develop goals necessary for overcoming adversity because they interpret difficult situations as intimidating and tiring, and are less resilient to obstacles they encounter.

Physical Activity

Hope influences our physical well-being, and our physical condition influences our ability to feel hopeful about our outlook on life. It is well accepted in the medical field that even moderate physical activity offers significant benefits by altering the influence illness has on us, such as the likelihood of developing medical problems, the ability to recover from heart disease, diabetes, hypertension, osteoporosis, some cancers, and reducing the risk of premature mortality.

When we are physically active, we are engaged in activities similar to those we find in hopefulness, which includes setting goals and developing plans to pursue them. Creating goals helps us develop a sense of meaning and purpose in our lives, which is often lost when struggling with the day-to-day challenges resulting from adversity. In Turkey, the benefits of being physically active were observed in a study of female university students. It was discovered that regular physical exercise increased their self-esteem and decrease hopelessness. Feeling better about their physical appearance likely helped provide a buffer against stress, and helped them feel more confident in their ability to successfully reach a goal.

This physical activity impacts positively on our brain chemistry, which releases powerful neurochemicals called endorphins. As discussed in the previous section What Is Hope?, these natural painkillers work in a similar fashion to opiates but without any negative risks. They help to improve our well-being by quieting our fear, anger, and physical pain, creating emotional stability and hopefulness, and helping us feel more focused. Serotonin, another neurotransmitter, helps us by increasing our emotional level of happiness while also improving our sleep and mood.

Endorphins and serotonin not only reduce our anxiety and panic, they can stop it in its tracks before it gets triggered. As a result, our self-esteem is enhanced and concentration is improved. Feeling positive and rested, our problem solving skill capacity increases, our willpower is strengthened, and our ability to be more resilient in coping with adversity improves.

It is clear we must not ignore the relationship between hope and physical activity. Hope is tied in to our biological need to be active. The lack of physical activity can make us feel hopeless, even becoming a matter of life and death. Physical activity is one area we can control during times of adversity, in turn improving hopefulness, and making good life choices.

Reframing

Adjusting to arduous situations largely depends on our attitude. Hope is one of the factors that can help put a positive meaning in our life. This involves our ability to take a situation, often a disastrous situation, and view it differently. Psychologists call this process "reframing." It encompasses looking at a negative experience and seeing a different perspective or finding something positive in it. By changing our thoughts, we can change our emotional reaction to the stressful situation and identify new goals.

It isn't an easy task and can challenge us down to our core. But reframing how we view an event is beneficial because it enables us to shift from feeling victimized, overwhelmed, and experiencing solely negative emotions, to feeling that there is something positive we can do about our state of upset. It allows us to feel the power of hope rather than surrender.

We get to this point by examining our values and refocusing our vision to that which is important to us. We develop hopefulness by thinking about something positive rather than the negative emotions. This helps us look at the situation differently and create new pathways. An example of reframing might be a survivor of sexual assault who blames herself for submitting to, rather than attacking, her assailant. Under very traumatic circumstances, this sexual abuse survivor did what she felt she needed to do to stay alive. Looking at it in this way, she may be able to reduce the suffering she experiences from her critical self-judgmental thoughts. As a result, her view of herself can become more positive and she can feel more hopeful for her future.

Self-Compassion
Self-compassion is the process of being good to ourselves in all ways, emotionally, physically, and spiritually. Self-compassion helps us to reduce our sense of vulnerability because when we fail, we can pause, learn from it, and move forward. We avoid the self-blame and shame game that causes us to lose hope that we can change our destiny.

Instead, we evaluate ourselves, take responsibility for that which we need to do differently, and then develop new pathways to reach our goals. This kindness we extend to ourselves helps us create a buffer against feelings of powerlessness. When we make mistakes, we show ourselves compassion by recognizing that we are human and are not perfect.

When we are judgmental of ourselves, we are more likely to experience powerlessness. Powerlessness is the enemy of hopefulness. It causes us to withdraw both from opportunities and people that might help us develop plans and goals, the cornerstone of hopefulness that helps us through adversity.

Self-Control
Self-control influences how each of us will respond to stressful situations. It also impacts our ability to avoid making decisions we will later regret. If we exert our self-control and select healthy behaviors, we will find ourselves moving toward attainment of future goals.

With self-control, undesirable behavior can be contained or avoided altogether. Yet, curbing such behavior is challenging in times of adversity. The longer we are under stress the more at risk we will find ourselves to losing self-control. Also, the greater our stress is in relation to the strength of our coping skills, the higher our risk will be to losing self-control. We may be more likely to engage in unhealthy, impulsive, destructive behaviors (such as substance abuse or pathological gambling), or acting against our values; all which can undermine our ability to pursue desired goals.

Like a muscle, self-control can be strengthened. The more of a workout it gets, the stronger it becomes. But self-control is not an infinite resource. To prevent depletion of our self-control we need to take care of ourselves. Building skills in knowing how to manage behaviors are essential to finding success in staying on our path to resiliency. Acknowledging rather than repressing feelings is important. If feelings, including disappointment, fear, and anger are not recognized and dealt with, we may find they build up and trigger incidents of loss of self-control.

Self-Esteem

Self-esteem is about believing in ourselves. Self-confidence is vital when tackling problems because it helps us feel more hopeful that we can overcome severe obstacles and work towards our goals.

We are not born with a sturdy self-esteem; it develops as we grow. Unfortunately, some people hit bumps in the road along the way in life, develop a low self-esteem, and have a tendency to be more anxious, socially isolated, and depressed. Being able to control our emotions, accept criticism, relate to stress, and not be overly critical of ourselves contributes to a strong self-esteem, which is key to establishing resilience.

Society

Hope is complicated. It is an ever-changing and difficult process. When we are struggling with feelings of doubt and insecurity about how to overcome our adversity, and even struggling with feelings of hopelessness, our support system can be a safe and trusting resource.

Trust in others is critical. When we feel hopeful, we have the confidence that we can cope with the challenges facing us. Significant others in our lives, be they our family, friends, work colleagues, neighbors, or community/support/religious affiliated, have a major impact on our lives, offering us a pathway to hope. When our inner strength is depleted, being able to turn outward to our social network, and draw on the support from them helps us develop resilience and a sense of well-being, and even an opportunity to experience personal growth when coping with adversity.

Ways Our Social Networks Develop Hope

Helps us Feel Not so Alone

It has been shown over and over again that support from others who care about the person at risk has a huge bearing on developing resilience in difficult times. Being alone is isolating and lonely. Committed support from formal and informal connections in the community can help us create feelings of being closer to others and more distant from our pain. When we feel valued by others, our feeling of inner stability increases. Even the simple act of reminiscing about memories with someone else can help remind us of positive events in the past; of ways we have successfully moved past conflicts and areas in which we have meaning and value in life. Memories of shared challenges and goals provide a positive effect on our self-esteem and empower us to develop new objectives. This sense of belonging to something greater than us facilitates the development of hopefulness.

Helps Bring Out the Best in us

Our social network provides encouragement. This impacts on our ability to select healthy coping mechanisms when managing our challenges, can remind us of the positive qualities we had before the event, and can help us go back to feeling, thinking and behaving as the person we were prior to the event. This support from our social network helps us re-establish confidence with ourselves, trust in the world, and restores our ability to hope once again.

When he turned 45 years old, Mr. Steen's life was on a downward spiral. He realized he was probably going to spend the remainder of his adulthood in jail. Or he was going to die. His younger six sisters and brothers gave him the sense of purpose in life that motivated him to make changes about himself and his future.

His life had never been easy, and in many respects, he never had a childhood. "When I was in third grade, my father left because he caught my mother with another man. It wasn't long before she had us going from empty house to empty house and staying there until we had to leave," recalls Mr. Steen. They had become a family of squatters, breaking into and living in vacant homes. "We didn't even have a key to get in the houses. I remember my mother walking around the back of houses, trying to get in. We always went at nighttime. There was no electricity. Not one stick of furniture. I remember in one house just going to school for a month or two."

"When they remember our childhood, my sisters and brothers say, 'Ronnie always took care of us. He'd have us hold hands and tell us to go here and go there.' That is a blessing to me that they would say that," says Mr. Steen. "I kind of was the shepherd for them. They realized that, and it touches my heart."

Being the older brother, and knowing that his younger siblings relied on him, gave Mr. Steen a sense of purpose and ability to hope for a better life for all of them. "It upset me, but I'm the oldest of seven, and I had brothers and sisters I had to look after." He helped them escape their life of instability. After two years of living in this manner, Mr. Steen called his father, asked for his help, and all of the children went to live with their father.

Mr. Steen's struggles didn't stop there. "I had never been to jail until I was 45 years old. I never thought I'd have a felony or have a prison number and yet I kept going back to jail for drug-related charges for eight to ten months a year for 5 years."

Mr. Steen's siblings helped him resolve his problems by being his unwavering support network during this period. Where he had once been their protector, they were now his safety net, offering comfort and a feeling of purpose and connection.

"I realized how I let my family down," he reflects. "They were happy I was out of jail, but I kept messing up. I hurt them. Turning my life around was challenging because I had to become somebody new and understand where my mistakes were and how to not go back to those wrong choices."

His family's supportive caring and concern, and ability to remind Mr. Steen of his positive values and attributes, opened up his clogged faucet of hope, helping it flow again inside of him. "My life is changed now. I learned that by overcoming my obstacles, I have hope that I will be able to overcome the next venture. It's important for my family to see that I have a solid foundation now," says Mr. Steen.

Problems resulting from Mr. Steen's childhood, drug addiction, and legal matters, are a part of his history. But they no longer distort how he feels about himself or impair his ability to hope for his future. He has achieved stability in his community. He is now a happily married family man, owns a successful glass company in California that employs many family members, and is a preacher in his local church. Part of his growth following years of suffering includes wanting to help not only his siblings but also others in the community through his faith. Mr. Steen says, "Now I look at the community and think about how we are going to give them hope."

Mr. Steen is aware that it is the mutually reciprocated love he and his family have for each other that helped him find a safe, nontoxic environment in which he could think more clearly, make difficult changes, and plan for a better future. Paraphrasing from the Bible, Mr. Steen says, "Of love, faith, and hope, love is the strongest. With love, you'll have faith, and with faith, you'll have hope."[12]

Reduces Our Stress

Having hope reduces stress. Reduction in stress increases our self-esteem and ability to problem-solve because we feel less vulnerable and more hopeful in our ability to take care of ourselves. We are more confident that we can develop new goals, reduce barriers that get in our way, and develop steps for a better future.

An example of a social network reducing stress is found in a study of rural elementary school students in Korea. When students were able to develop consistent and enjoyable relationships with important individuals in their lives, including family, friends, teachers, and others in their surrounding environment, their stress was reduced and their self-esteem rose. With a higher level of self-esteem, their problem-solving skills increased.

Planning, a key component of problem-solving, is also a key component of hopefulness.[13]) This expanded ability to resolve problems resulted in the children experiencing fewer behavioral problems. The benefits of such stress reduction in can pay off in dividends throughout life, by enhancing problem-solving skills and hopefulness.

Helps Provide Information

Our social network is often our soft place in which we can land. When our anxiety is high, and our hope is low, they are the ones with whom we can allow ourselves to be vulnerable, reveal our insecurities and turn to for support. They can help us identify any of our thoughts, feelings, and behaviors that may be detrimental to creating new opportunities.

Empowering us by reminding us of our strengths while addressing our weaknesses, those close to us can teach us new skills, or provide new information, advice, or guidance that will enable us to generate better solutions, and how to move forward more successfully when we encounter barriers in our lives. Our support system can be there without judgment to teach us new skills that will help us develop different perspectives, insights, and lessons, helping us be hopeful for tomorrow.

Helps With Physical Resilience

Our social network provides health benefits that reach throughout our body. Social support makes us feel accepted and valued. The positive feelings created from these experiences lead us to making healthy lifestyle choices. We are more likely to eat nutritiously, engage in exercise, and less likely to indulge in unhealthy habits such as smoking, excessive alcohol or illegal drugs.

Less obvious to the naked eye but amazingly impressive are the health benefits our social network provides us. Decades of research have found direct relationships between social support, stress reduction, and illness.

The stress-buffering effect of feeling cared for not only helps us cope, but in doing so regulates our cortisol level, known as the stress hormone. (Also discussed above and in chapter four.) When our support is high, our cortisol levels will not remain chronically elevated, helping to reduce the prospect we will contribute to the risk of developing obesity, high blood pressure, osteoporosis, depression and coronary heart disease.

Influence of Socioeconomic Status

The ability to hope for a better future is closely linked to our socioeconomic status. People with financial resources are more likely to experience hopefulness about the future than those who experience economic hardship, family dysfunction, and unemployment. This is because the 'haves' are more likely to have fewer experiences with barriers to their success, and have more social connections to provide help. The 'have-nots,' on the other hand, may have a multigenerational history of discrimination and disappointment, affecting their ability to believe in feeling hopeful. Struggles with their day-to-day existence, such as substance abuse, crime, and violent behavior, keeps their focus on trying to meet immediate needs. Thus, the poor are less likely to be able to establish future goals, a central component of hope.

But it's not all hopeless. Sometimes the support of a single person is sufficient to puncture the profound hopelessness of an impoverished community and help them develop resilience.

Musician Lanny Cordola was on the path to rock and roll fame and fortune. A highly regarded hard rock guitarist, he toured with the Beach Boys, Nancy

Sinatra, Ozzy Osbourne, and Gilby Clark of Guns N' Roses, and appeared on the television sitcom, Full House.

The rest would have been rock and roll history had it not been for a newspaper article he read in 2012 about a 14-year-old suicide bomber near the NATO headquarters in Kabul, Afghanistan. Two of the victims were sisters Parwana and Khorshid, who were selling handkerchiefs and shawls to foreign soldiers. Moved by the story, Mr. Cordola traveled to Afghanistan to meet with the girls' parents and another child in the family, seven-year-old Mursal, who had survived the terrorist attack.

He was struck by what he saw. "It is one of the poorest areas in Kabul. They were living in a place with no running water, no bathroom, no kitchen. The father had left the family because of his drug addiction. In this family, the husband of one of the daughters had been killed so here she is, a 16-year-old widow with a little boy. Basically everything bad that has happened to Afghanistan has happened to this family; from the land mines to the drug addiction to suicide bombers to poverty to the war and other acts of violence."

Seeing other children, who Mr. Cordola recalled, "were so traumatized they weren't eating," he wanted to help. Believing music to be spiritually healing, he did what he knew best; he played his guitar. Pretty soon, the children were asking him to teach them how to play. He started giving lessons wherever he could safely go, including slums, orphanages, shantytowns, and even on the streets.

Singing and playing the guitar gave the children a creative outlet through which they could temporarily escape daily hardship and danger. Making up songs to express painful feelings reduced the girls' stress. Their self-esteem increased as they became proficient and developed dreams about a better future.

"Most girls in Afghanistan are married off between the ages of 13 and 15," recalls Mr. Cordola. "The cycle of misery and poverty continues. A portion of those girls are treated very badly and commit suicide."

Mr. Cordola has found change to be possible. Many of Mr. Cordola's original students are proficient enough to be able to teach other young girls how to play the guitar. His students are starting to set goals for themselves. Mursal, the younger sister of the two girls killed by the suicide bomber, now hopes for a future as a guitar teacher. He reflects, "The power of music to help them hope and help them heal has been remarkable. I went to Afghanistan because of tragedy and I stayed because of hope."[14]

Influence of Cultural Differences

Our cultural experiences influence how we move through life and influence our response to the concept of hope. Within our cultural setting, we tend to conform to social norms, which are the group's rules, regulations and expectations for our behavior. We also tend to conform to the group's values, such as what is good or bad, desirable, or worthy. The impact our cultural influences have on regulating our thoughts, feelings and behaviors is never more apparent than when we find ourselves teetering between hope and hopelessness.

Social norms and values differ between Western and Asian cultures. Western societies tend to value and promote individualism, competition, and uniqueness, whereas Asian cultures are collectivistic, emphasizing the importance of a group-oriented conformity, harmony, and sharing. These differences impact on an individual's perception and importance of hope.

Interpersonal relationships in Western cultures are less structured, with people more often living apart from their extended families than those in Asian societies. Without this structure, people have less influence or protection from the family and are more encouraged to express their own ideas.

Asian cultures, being more group oriented, focus less on personal happiness and expression of one's feelings and needs. Instead, the emphasis is more on the needs of others with whom they are associated. Social ties, such as those of the extended family found in collectivistic cultures, provide coping skills that can contribute to a reduction in hopelessness. For example, a study comparing the connection between substance abuse and hope in the Chinese and individualist cultures found hopelessness and substance abuse to be more prevalent in individualistic than in collective cultures.[15] With the focus being about the needs of the group, the Chinese cultures do not want to bring conflict or shame to the group, and adapt their behaviors and expectations of happiness from the group.

Whereas Americans view hope as being the seventh most useful emotion, and Germans rank it as second most important, the Japanese do not have a positive association of hope. Buddhism views hope as an emotion that is selfish and unfounded in bringing a desired change. So it is no surprise that their word for hope ("kibo") refers to a "wish" or a potential "trick" that lies waiting in the future.[16]

Even within a culture, differences will prevail. In the United States, minorities will likely respond to hope differently than the majority. Whites, who historically have been in a dominant social position, are more accustomed to successfully attaining goals. With feelings of satisfaction in the past, they will be likely to create hopeful thinking.

Native Americans were historically a collective society, connected to their social relationships, living close to each other on the original land of the maternal bloodline. For them, hope was found within their relationships with family and nature. Today, Native Americans have faced oppression, discrimination, and loss of their way of relating spiritually with their environment. As a result, many struggle with mental health problems, including depression, suicide, and alcoholism, all indicators of hopelessness.

Sampling of Influences Within Society Capable of Creating Hope
Sports Coaches
Coaches are in a unique position to help athletes learn hopefulness through the process of attaining the goal specific to their sport. The basketball player cannot just focus on dunking the ball in the basket. The steps required to dribble the ball up court, successfully deceive defenders with a crossover dribble, and then shoot for the basket while not getting fouled, is critical to success. It requires self-efficacy and contingency plans, skills similar to the concept of hope.

Athletes are hopeful people. In fact, we could even consider them to be high-hope people because they keep their goals in mind, are always thinking about ways to achieve them, and don't mind working hard to succeed. There may be multiple reasons for this. Growing up playing a sport and focused on goals may have taught young athletes the importance of visualizing what they want, identifying a goal, and planning a pathway to reach it. Perhaps it was years of repeated attempts to achieve a goal that taught them a level of concentration and focus not easily attainable to youth outside of sports. Or maybe they learned to successfully deal with adversity through sporting competitions.[17]

Educators
Schools are in the ideal position to provide programs geared to helping students learn how to be high in hopefulness. Research, discussed elsewhere in this chapter, points to hopefulness being a better indicator of academic success than grade point average or standardized college entry exams. Programs can help students learn skills necessary for creating goals resolving problems that arise along the way. These healthy coping skills will benefit students by providing them with techniques for overcoming conflicts at home, school, and peers,

and that also help them learn how to successfully cope with adversity throughout life.

Parents

Hope is learned, and what better place for children to learn it than from their parents? As a foundation for learning hope, children need to have a safe environment, in which parents are loving, predictable role models. This provides an atmosphere in which children feel safe to explore and create, which are central components of hope. Parents who model the ability to deal successfully with obstacles and challenges, and who are positive and enjoy learning, will convey to their children the importance of achieving new things and developing new goals. As Dr. C.R. Snyder, author of *The Psychology of Hope: You Can Get There From Here*, observes, the key to developing hopeful children is to help them learn how to seek goals, develop the willpower to pursue these goals, and be able to develop ways to reach the goals.[18]

Physicians

Physician–patient communication is often taken for granted, and yet it is central to the development of creating hope in patients. Patients who experience clear communication feel respected, and can express concerns with their physicians will be happier and more hopeful about their relationship, the accuracy of the information they are receiving, and their medical care. Studies find they will experience greater optimism, perceive themselves as having greater control over their lives, view themselves as being able to problem solve, and be less likely to get bogged down with negative emotions that will affect their mental as well as physical health.

Even with the recent changes in how medicine is practiced, which result in briefer appointments, shorter hospital stays and less choice of specialists, physicians can contribute to their patient's hopefulness by conveying that they are not alone. Making eye contact, listening for the concern behind the questions, answering difficult questions, and offering information in a way that conveys professional interest contributes to the patient's satisfaction, general confidence in the treatment plan, and sense of control.

Support Groups

Membership in support groups with others who are experiencing similar difficulties can enable healing by increasing hope, reducing psychological distress, and providing physical benefits as well. Often adversity creates feelings of powerlessness and disconnection from others. The group process provides connection, which in turn can validate and support us. Empathy and information from others kindles hope, as members develop goals and ways to achieve them. Studies have found a wide range of benefits from support groups. One study, in which women with metastatic breast cancer participated in a psychotherapy group, found the members lived longer than nonparticipants.[19] Another study involved a time limited, eight-week support group for people newly diagnosed with cancer. Each session lasted two hours, and included topics such as belief in oneself, relationships and spirituality. Ninety-five percent of the members of this group found it to be helpful. The beauty of this and similar groups is that they demonstrate that support can play a mighty role in tipping the balance between doing well and not doing well.[20]

Spirituality
Spirituality is comforting during challenging times, can help us see beyond our troubles, and be our beacon of light when the end of the tunnel appears dark and uncertain. To be spiritual is to believe in the existence of a transcendent (nonphysical) power. It is the belief that there is a power bigger and beyond us, although it may not be God, as defined by religions. In addition to finding spirituality in religion, it can be associated externally with ecology or nature, or internally with human achievement or potential.

Spirituality provides a buffer between the despair of today and the challenging days ahead by offering some stability. It helps us accept our current situation, gives us a sense of meaning in our discomfort and hope for the future. Without hope feelings of distrust, anger, or cynicism take its place. We may even find ourselves alienated from everything important to us, questioning the meaning and purpose of our lives.

Sometimes this faith is created vicariously, by simply observing the caring behavior of others and being inspired about the possibility of change. After years of feeling abandoned, punished by others, and believing she was worthless, Taletha Guinn of Oklahoma City found the ability to hope again by observing the benevolence of strangers.

Now 20 years old, Ms. Guinn recalls her childhood with pain. "I was bullied from having people talk about me, from people physically and emotionally hurting me, from elementary school on. School is where it mostly happened, where I felt completely alone. The teachers and students wouldn't do anything about it," she recollects. The bullying was unrelenting and unbearable, resulting in Ms. Guinn dropping out of school in 9th grade. She was depressed and had no hope for her future.

237

"When I had lost hope for there ever being a situation where somebody would be there for me, I witnessed this really tragic thing happen. We've had quite a few bad tornados in Oklahoma, and many of them are in Moore, which is where my family lives. When the tornados hit in the city of Moore in 2013, it was really terrible. There were lives lost, homes lost, and seven children died in a school that was torn to pieces," recalls Ms. Guinn.

In the aftermath of the destruction from the tornado, Ms. Guinn witnessed that, "when a tragedy happens, people in the community come together, rather than judging others based on how they look." She adds that, "People were helping others who lost their homes and even the people who lost their children from the school being hit. I saw people came together who didn't even know each other, donating money, building back the community, and giving back what they could."

Seeing that strangers were caring enough to respond to people who were in great need, both materially and emotionally, helped change her view of humanity in a positive way. "It made me think. I may have been alone (due to the unrelenting bullying), but maybe God has a better plan to make me a stronger person. It helped me open my eyes and realize that just because I went through something bad and there was no one there for me, and no one stood up for me, in another situation there will be someone there for me. So just when I started to lose hope and faith in who I was, that terrible situation in a sense gave me hope and faith back. I now believe that when times for me are hard, I will keep my head strong and high because in the end there's always going to be someone or something that is going to give me hope and faith for a better future. It's kind of like believing in myself, but faith is so much a better word for me. If you don't have faith, it's pointless," she notes.[21]

Ms. Guinn's experience is not unique. Adversity can be so disruptive and distressful to individuals that the world doesn't feel safe any longer. Instead of being able to see a future and know how to move forward, some may feel angry at, estranged from, or punished by God. Their feelings of alienation can generalize from their conflict with God to feeling disconnected from all supportive relationships. As their pain increases, they sometimes even become hopeless, questioning the purpose of life.

Research finds that losing one's faith following a severe adversity often contributes to poor mental health. One study of depressed adolescents found the loss of faith to be associated with more depression, and less remission of depressive symptoms over a six-month period. Another study of female sexual assault victims found that those who became less religious after a sexual assault experienced greater deterioration in their mental health than those who were similarly assaulted, but who did not lose faith. Fortunately for Ms. Guinn, she now has a desire, confidence, and hope. After years of hopelessness and subsequent poor mental health, she has rediscovered faith and believes in the possibility for a better future.

One can be spiritual without religion, but all religions view spirituality as essential. Religion is a commonly sought after place to find hope, and it is easy to see why. Hope is mentioned 142 times in the King James Version Bible and 182 times in the New International Version Bible, and almost 85 percent of the U.S. population identifies itself as being religious.[22]

In religion, spirituality is experienced in a specific setting, such as a synagogue, church, temple or mosque. Being religious typically means that members acknowledge that God or some other "higher power" governs the universe. Spirituality in religion is accompanied by a specific set of institutional beliefs and practices, such as membership, prayer study, and rituals. Congregants reflect, through prayers and sermons on what they believe God would want of them in these adverse situations. Feeling that a compassionate higher power is watching over them provides comfort and helps them develop better coping skills and hopefulness. Fellow congregants also provide compassion. Support groups help members find meaning in adversity, how to deal with grief and disappointment, and cope better in difficult times.

Pastor Michael Clark, of the Truth Community Church in Costa Mesa, California, has experience with individuals who find that certain aspects of their lives are beyond their experience and coping skills, and are feeling out of control and hopeless. He states, "I counsel people who are devastated, and try to give people hope. People can live about 30 days without food. They can go about three days without water, and only a few minutes without air. But people can't live 10 seconds without hope. If you don't have hope, it won't be hard to kill yourself at all."[23] Hope researcher Shane J. Lopez, Ph.D., shares a similar perspective, viewing hope as essential as oxygen. For many, religion offers the stability and predictability that enables them to be able to find hopefulness once again.

Formal religions often provide practical support, which helps people feel less isolated and more hopeful about their future. Victims of disasters, who lose all their worldly possessions, or the battered wife who has to leave home with her young children and no food, clothing or money, or political refugees who escape danger, may be able to have their basic needs met through the generosity of an organized religion. The emotional and concrete support gained from a stable faith and hope system has a wide impact on the lives of people undergoing adversity. Research shows they experience fewer hospitalization days, fewer days in jail or prison, more days in school, more days on the job, fewer suicides, and less spouse, child, and elder abuse.[24]

Conclusion

Life is challenging, and when faced with adversity we often experience profound losses. It takes strength to endure the suffering. The unrelenting emotional upset can make it almost unfathomable to believe that our future will ever improve.

Hope is essential when we are in this pain, and yet it all too often is overlooked and dismissed as being unimportant. What scientists, educators and coaches have recently discovered, and what religions have long recognized, is that the pathway to change is through hope.

To have hope is to have a bridge that allows us to cross over from despair to a place where we can once again find meaning and purpose in life. We take a risk in imagining that the future can be better than what we are experiencing today, and it isn't easy going down this path alone. We can create goals and activities that will help us reach our goals, but that alone may not be sufficient for us to find hopefulness. When we engage our social network we increase our chance of success. They may help us create strategies to reach the goals we set for ourselves. If our attempts fail, our support system can give us strength by motivating us, redirecting us towards new goals, or helping us learn new skills, thereby increasing our likelihood of success.

History has always closely associated hope and faith. When we put our trust in a higher power, we find the strength to hope that the future may hold something better for us. Feeling supported, and believing our goals and actions have a chance of experiencing success, we have confidence in taking necessary risks. Our resilience increases. We can keep going, despite our disappointments, because of hope. Hope pulls us through.

Suggested Exercises
for Using the Three Spheres of Support
to Enhance Your Hopefulness

Self

1. *Gratitude*

   Being grateful helps us to be hopeful. Focus on something positive, appreciate it and be grateful. Start a 'gratitude wall.' Each time you experience gratitude, write it down on a colorful sticky note. Select a wall (or closet door) and adhere it. Using different colored sticky notes, your wall will bring you joyous memories and reminders of what you appreciate in life.

2. *Meaning and Purpose*

   Find something to provide meaning and purpose. It will give you a sense of hope and will help you persevere. What matter, and what makes you happy? Look for opportunities in your everyday life. Look at the roles you currently have in life (parent, spouse, employee, etc.). Consider the importance of how you influence others in these roles.

3. *Writing Exercise*

   Start a writing exercise for hope-reminding. Write down your ultimate goal. Then write down the sub-goals that will get you to the larger goal.

4. *Examine Fears*

   Examine that which you fear. Sometimes we avoid thinking about it and by doing so give it more power than it deserves. Deciding to face the fear can result in it being lessened or fully removed.

5. *Read Books*

   Read books on hopefulness, such as:

   - *Authentic Happiness,* by Martin Seligman, Ph.D.
   - *Learned Optimism: How to Change Your Mind and Your Life,* by Martin Seligman, Ph.D.

- *The Happiness Advantage*, by Shawn Achor.
- *The Little Prince*, by Antoine de Saint-Exupery (for young readers).

6. *Restructure Your Sentences*

End your sentences with positives so that your mind is intentionally being tilted towards the optimistic rather than negative perspectives. This process will rewire your brain to becoming more hopeful.

7. *Re-Evaluate Your Beliefs*

Re-evaluate beliefs that block you from accomplishing what you would like. Sometimes these are beliefs that we have grown up with that no longer work for us and need to be discarded.

8. *Create New Reactions*

We hold onto our personal experiences for a long time. They end up shaping the choices we make in the future because we have now developed a way to respond emotionally, behaviorally and cognitively. As writer and novelist Aldous Leonard Huxley once said, "Experience is not what happens to a man. It is what a man does with what happens to him." Therefore our past teaches us to respond in a particular way.

You needn't be a victim of your memories and experiences. You can change by developing new opinions, understandings, and responses, and by creating new memories with those that are closest to you. These new experiences will change how you choose to react. If you succeed here, you will have more hope that you can make changes elsewhere.

9. *Relax by Stimulating Your Vagus Nerve*

Stimulating your longest cranial nerve, which acts as the mind-body connection, is a great way to reduce anxiety. The vagus nerve calms you down when you feel your fight-or-flight response being triggered. It slows your heart rate and blood pressure, releases anti-stress hormones and improves your memory. Deep and slow abdominal breathing, in which the belly goes up and down, can indirectly stimulate your vagus nerve and give you anxiety relief. So can singing or immersing your face in water. Try it!

10. *Recall Past Success*

Reflect back on previous times you have overcome adversity. What did you learn, how did it help you? This will help provide you with the tenacity to overcome the current challenges and embrace the belief that something positive will result from your efforts.

11. *Identify Hopeful Aspects of Your Life*

Focus not just on the part of your life that feels hopeless but the hopeful parts as well. It keeps your life in perspective. Identify past accomplishments. What were the areas of success, how were goals identified and pursued?

12. *Provide Self-Care*

Do something nice for yourself. Everything looks better, and more hopeful when you take care of yourself. It needn't be a huge or expensive project, just meaningful.

13. *Identify Self-Progress*

Learn how to identify and monitor self for signs of progress in experiencing optimism. In doing so you will be strengthening the muscle of hopefulness.

14. *Visualize Success*

Create a mental picture of going through the steps that will lead you to your goal. Develop great detail this picture in your mind. This will create more willpower that you will be able to draw on when encountering difficulties. Do this five minutes each day, adding another detail each day.

Society

1. *Ask for Help*

Identify someone who genuinely cares for you. Share with them how you struggle with asking for help. Ask them to help you with something for which you have felt was not fixable.

2. *Parents as Role Models*

   Parents can teach children how to hope by instilling the importance being able to create goals for overcoming obstacles. Discuss some examples of when you did this with your children.

3. *Create Sphere of Positivity*

   Surround yourself with hopeful people. You can learn from them. Their energy is positive.

4. *Interview Others*

   Talk with others and ask what they do that makes them hopeful. Listen to the words they use when discussing their struggles. It will help you expand your perspective.

5. *Join a Group*

   Become active in a group that holds meaning for you. It may be civic, faith-based, or activity oriented. Good relationships can be developed from group membership, out of which hope-reclaiming support is provided.

6. *Provide Hope to Others*

   Giving to others helps them feel cared for and respected. Giving to someone less fortunate can provide dignity that has been lost. Doing for others else may not only make a difference today, it may give them hope for tomorrow. They may even pay the gratitude forward, bringing hope to still another person's life.

Spirituality

1. *Reminisce About Positive People*

   Start a dinner conversation about someone who has brought hope into your life in the past. Share how you felt before they came into your life, and how it changed your life. Thank your higher power for this experience.

2. *Grace*

   Say grace at the dinner table, and reflect on all that you have.

3. *Affirmations*

   Use affirmations to express your wishes for a better world. For example, the Dalai Lama said, "With realization of one's own potential and self-confidence in one's ability, one can build a better world." Louise Hay said, "The past is over and done and cannot be changed. This is the only moment we can experience." Norman Vincent Peale stated, "Change your thoughts and you change your world."

Try one of these hope wishes once a week. Repeat it often, such as when you are sitting in your car at a signal, waiting in line at the grocery store, or waking up in the morning. See how these affirmations inspire you to feel more hopeful. Discover additional affirmations, or create ones that express your feelings for hope.

4. *Establish Goals*

    Identify a short-term and a long-term goal. Be clear that the goal you set is one you really want. Develop recognizable and specific ways to know when you have reached both short and long-term important goals.

5. *Gratitude About Blessings*

    Recognizing how much you have to be thankful for is to have gratitude. Taking the time to recognize, with gratitude, how much your higher power helps you feel more hopeful. Create a new habit of scheduling in ten to fifteen minutes each morning or evening to reflect on the blessings in your life.

Afterword

I wrote this book so anyone undergoing adversity will have the opportunity to find new meaning in life, a sense of purpose, and be able to set goals to overcome adversity. This book recognizes that there is no quick fix when coping with adversity. Nor is there a magic pill that will make it all go away and make us feel better again. Our lives may be irrevocably changed, and yesterday's normal may seem like a distant memory. In many circumstances, we feel that we have lost a part of who we were prior to the event.

I hope in reading this book you have gained an understanding of the paradox in rebuilding our lives; that getting to the other side of adversity isn't about closing the loop, locking the door behind us, or being done with the difficulty. Rather, it is about realizing that even though life as we know it may never be the same again, we can, and must, move forward.

Regardless of how the adversity occurred, or how tragic and psychologically devastating the loss was, I have attempted to explain that there are patterns in the recovery process that apply to all of us.

Throughout the book you have read of the three supportive resources — the three spheres of support: Self, Society, and Spirituality — that are available to all of us, and how they supply us with the strength to face these undertakings. The more we surround ourselves with these three supportive resources, the more empowered and successful we will be at dealing with stress. We will find ourselves able to create a deeper spirituality, more meaningful relationships, feel better about ourselves, and able to make plans for our future. We will develop greater resilience and be more capable of finding an inner peace again.

Without this support we are at risk of experiencing stress of such magnitude that it will cause us to pull away and isolate ourselves. Although we innately do so in an attempt to stop the emotional pain, unfortunately, it makes our recovery less achievable. This is because withdrawal from our support system prevents us from having the strength to deal with what I have identified as the five components in recovery: forgiveness, courage, perspective, perseverance, and hopefulness. There is no shortcut. We must work through each of these issues, and support is the means to guide us through the process.

Overcoming adversity can be a long and challenging journey, filled with struggle. It is a personal and unique experience for each of us. It cannot occur in a predetermined number of steps or amount of time. Yet as I have conveyed in this book, how we develop resilience is no mystery, and following a pathway to recovery, along with practice exercises, as detailed in these chapters, provides direction and purpose to that journey.

I hope a take-away from this book is that adversity needn't be perceived exclusively as a negative. Benefits can be drawn from our hurt. Through shifts in our thinking, and changing how we view the world, we can grow and find ways to thrive in spite of our suffering. With determination, we can seize this experience as an opportunity to push the reset button on our life, to reevaluate what path we are taking and explore what we want to do differently as we proceed to rebuild our life.

Many individuals interviewed for this book shared their stories of finding such opportunities, and the benefits they gained despite the powerful losses and disruption to their lives. They were able to overcome adversity by using it as a stimulus for evaluating and clarifying their values and finding new meaning. In doing so, all became not only more resilient, but thrived.

Ideally, this book has provided you with both the information as well as specific tools to help reduce the painful impact of the adversity that has confronted you. Going forward, I hope you will have some comfort knowing that when you can't return to your life as it previously was, you always have the opportunity and ability to reestablish your goals, and discover a new sense of purpose in life.

Eileen S. Lenson

Chapter 1

1. Bruce Wexler, *The Hatfields and The McCoys* (New York: Skyhorse Publishing, 2013), 8–9.

2. Major Edward Pulido, oral communication, June 4, 2015.

3. tFrederic Luskin, introduction to *Forgive for Good, A Proven Prescription for Health and Happiness* (New York: HarperCollins, 2002), vii– viii.

4. Sonja Lyubomirsky, *The How of Happiness: A Scientific Approach to Getting the Life You Want* (New York: Penguin Books, 2008), 170–171.

5. Julie H. Hall and Frank D. Fincham, "Self–Forgiveness: The Stepchild of Forgiveness Research," *Journal of Social and Clinical Psychology,* Vol. 24, No. 5 (2005), 621–637.

6. Melissa Coleman, oral communication, August 8, 2015.

7. "List of school shootings in the United States," Wikipedia, accessed April 2, 2017.
   https://en.wikipedia.org/wiki/List_of_school_shootings_in_the_United_States

8. H. Clutton-Brockas, and G.A. Parker, "Punishment in Animal Societies," *Nature,* January, Vol. 373 (January 19, 1995), 209–216. doi:10.1038/373209a0, accessed April 6, 2017. http://altruism.i3ci.hampshire.edu/files/2009/10/punishment-in-animal-societies.pdf

9. "Elephants Take Revenge: Angry Herd Storms Indian Villages, Smashes Homes After Train Kills One Of Their Own," Philip Ross, *International Science Times,* available at www.isciencetimes (August 9, 2013), accessed April 6, 2017.

10. Dalai Lama, XIV, *Ethics for the New Millennium* (New York: Riverhead Books, 1999), 62.

11. Amy Banks and Leigh Ann Hirschman, *Four Ways To Click: Rewire Your Brain For Stronger, More Rewarding Relationships* (New York: Penguin Group, 2015), 3.

12. Johan C. Karremans, Paul A.M. Van Lange, and Rob W. Holland, "Forgiveness and its associations with prosocial thinking, feeling, and doing beyond the relationship with the offender." *Personality and Social Psychology Bulletin,* October , Vol. 31, No. 10 (2005), 1315–1326, accessed April 6, 2017, https://www.ncbi.nlm.nih.gov/pubmed/16143664. doi:10.1177/0146167205274892

13. Everett L. Worthington, edited by, *Dimensions of Forgiveness: Psychological Research & Theological Perspectives* (Philadelphia & London, Templeton Foundation Press, 1998), 129–130; and Julie J. Exline, Everett L.Worthington, Jr., Peter Hill, & Michael E. McCullough. "Forgiveness and Justice: A Research Agenda for Social and Personality Psychology," *Personality and Social Psychology Review,* Vol. 7, No. 4 (2003), 337–348.

14. Dr. Fred Luskin, *Forgive For Good,* Harper, San Francisco, 2002.

15. Adam B. Cohen, Ariel Malka, Paul Roin, and Cherfas, Lina. "Religion and Unforgivable Offenses," *Journal of Personality,* Vol. 74, No. 1 (February. 2006), 85–118.

16. B. Pfefferbaum and P. B. Wood, "Self-Report Study of Impulsive and Delinquent Behavior in College Students," *Journal of Adolescent Health,* Vol. 15 (1994), 295–302.

17. Michael E. McCullough, C. Garth Bellah, Shelley Dean Kilpatrick, Judith L. Johnson, "Vengefulness: Relationships with Forgiveness, Rumination, Well-Being, and the Big Five," *Personality and Social Psychology Bulletin, Inc.,* Vol. 27, No. 5 (May 2001), 601–610.

18. Leonard Berkowitz, "On The Formation and Regulation of Anger and Aggression: A Cognitive-Neoassociationistic Analysis," *American Psychologist* Vol. 45, (April, 1990), 494-503; and G. V. Caprara, J. Manzi, and M. Perugini. "Investigating Guilt In Relation To Emotionality And Aggression," *Personality and Individual Differences,* Vol. 13, (1992), 519–532; and W. G. Graziano, L. A. Jensen-Campbell, & E. C. Hair, "Perceiving Interpersonal Conflict and Reacting To It: The Case For Agreeableness," *Journal of Personality and Social Psychology,* Vol. 70 (1996), 820–835; and Michael E. McCullough, C. Garth Bellah, Shelley Dean Kilpatrick and Judith L. Johnson, "Vengefulness: Relationships With Forgiveness, Rumination, Well-Being, and the Big Five," *Personality and Social Psychology Bulletin, Inc.,* Vol. 27, No. 5 (May 2001), 601–610.

19. Carol S. Dweck, *Mindset: The New Psychology of Success.* (New York: Random House, 2006), 46.

20. Richard O'Connor, *Happy at Last: The Thinking Person's Guide to Finding Joy* (New York: St. Martin's Press, 2008), 11.

21. Briana Root and Julie Exline, "Gender Differences in Response to Experimental Forgiveness prompts: Do Men Show Stronger Responses Than Women?" *Basic and Applied Social Psychology*, Vol. 33 (2011), 182–193.

22. Shelley E. Taylor, Laura C. Klein, Brian P. Lewis, Tara L. Gruenewald, Regan A.R. Gurung, and John A. Updegraff, "Biobehavioral Responses To Stress In Females: Tend–And–Befriend, Not Fight–Or–Flight," *Psychological Review*, Vol. 107, No. 3 (2000), 411–429.

23 Loren L. Toussaint, David R. Williams, Mark A. Musick, and S.A. Everson. "Forgiveness and Health: Age Differences in a U.S. Probability Sample," *Journal of Adult Development*, Vol. 8, (2001), 249–257; and Michele Girard, Etienne Mullet, "Forgiveness In Adolescents, Young, Middle-Aged, And Older Adults," *Journal of Adult Development*, Vol. 4 (1997), 209–220.

24. Richard O'Connor, *Happy at Last: The Thinking Person's Guide to Finding Joy* (New York: St. Martin's Press, 2008), 218–219.

25. R. L. Gorsuch and J.Y. Hao, "Forgiveness: An exploratory factor analysis and its relationships to religious variables," *Review of Religious Research*, Vol. 34 (1993), 333–347.

26. Buddha Quotes. (n.d.). BrainyQuote.com. Retrieved March 3, 2016, from https://www.brainyquote.com/quotes/quotes/b/buddha384547.html

27. Eknath Easwaran, editor, *God Makes the Rivers to Flow: An Anthology of the World's Sacred Poetry & Prose*, (Canada, Nilgiri Press, 2009), 86.

Chapter 2

1. Marc Medina, "Everyday Courage, Living Courageously Without Being A Hero, Existential Analysis," *Journal of the Society for Existential Analysis* Vol. 19, No. 2 (2008), 280–298.

2. S. J. Rachman, F*ear and Courage* (2nd ed.). (New York: W.H. Freeman and Company, 1990), 293–317.

3. Michael Beschloss, *Presidential Courage: Brave Leaders and How They Changed America, 1789–1989* (New York: Simon and Shuster, 2007), 96–126.

4. Max Defoe, oral communication, October 14, 2014.

5. Rollo May, *The Courage To Create* (New York: W.W. Norton & Co., 1994), 12.

6. Preeity Verma, *Small Changes, Big Differences* (Partridge, India: Partridge Publishing Co, 2014), 84.

7. Editors of the Official John Wayne Magazine and Ethan Wayne, *Duke In His Own Words*. (New York: Topix Media Lab Books, 2015), 181.

8. Uri Nili, Hagar Goldberg, Abraham Weizman, and Yadub Dudai. "Fear Thou Not: Activity of Frontal and Temporal Circuits in Moments of Real-Life Courage." *Neuron*, Vol. 66, No. 6 (June 24, 2010), 949–962, http://doi.org/10.1016/j.neuron.2010.06.009, accessed February 15, 2016.

9. Garrett Thomson and Marshall Missner, *On Aristotle* (Australia: Wadsworth/Thomson Learning, 2000), 78.

10. Maxwell Peters, oral communication, October 21, 2014.

11. Joshua Sias. Buddhism, Confucianism, and Western Conceptions of Personal Autonomy. *The Downtown Review.* Vol. 1. No. 1, Article 5 (2015), 1–22, available at http://engagedscholarship.csuohio.edu/tdr/vol1/iss1/5

12. Salvatore Maddi, Ph.D, The personality construct of hardiness: I. Effects on experiencing, coping, and strain. *Consulting Psychology Journal,* Vol. 51 (1999), 83–94.

13. Charles A. Nelson, III, Ph.D. The Effects of Early Life Adversity on Brain and Behavioral Development, Dana Alliance, October 22, 2012, available at http://www.dana.org/Publications/ReportOnProgress/The_effects_of_early_life_adversity_on_brain_and_behavioral_development/

14. Seth Goldin, *Tribes: We Need You to Lead Us* (New York: Penguin Group, 2008), 55.

15. Peter Fuda,Ph.D. *Leadership Transformed*, (New York: Houghton Mifflin Harcourt Publishing Company, 2013), 23–48; and Peter Fuda, Ph.D, and Richard Badham, Ph.D, "Fire, Snowball, Mask, Movie: How Leaders Spark and Sustain Change," *Harvard Business Review* Vol. 89, No. 11 (2011), 145–148, 167.

16. Dacher Keltner, Ph.D., *Born To Be Good: The Science of a Meaningful Life,* (New York: W.W. Norton & Company, 2009), 249.

17. Stephan Madelon, oral communication, March 7, 2015.

18. Donald Altman, oral communication, February 15, 2017.

19. Alain Basto, oral communication, June 15, 2015.

20. Thinkexist.com at http://www.thinkexist.com/quotes/charles_darwin/

21. Silvio Scaglia, oral communication, April 02, 2015.

22. Ron Lum Shue Chan, oral communication, October,22, 2014.

23. Available at https://quotesthoughtsrandom.wordpress.com/2015/12/20/do-you-want-more-courage/

24. Stephanie Parker, oral communication, October 10, 2014.

25. Rabbi Richard Steinberg, oral communication, July 24, 2015.

26. Daisaku Ikeda, *Courage Buddhism For You*, (Santa Monica, CA: Middleway Press, 2006), 1–2.

27. David Klein and Bert Klein, oral communications, October 27, 2015.

Chapter 3

1. Joyce Stromberg, oral communication, September 12, 2014.

2. Erin Runnion, oral communication April 29, 2015.

3. Shali Wu and Boaz Keysar, "The Effect of Culture on Perspective Taking," *Association for Psychological Science* Vol. 18, No. 7 (2007), 600–606.

4. Jeffrey A. Gray, "Brain systems that Mediate Both Emotion And Cognition," *Cognition & Emotion* Vol. 4, No. 3, (1990), 269–288.

5. C. M. Aldwin, "Does age affect the stress and coping process? Implications of age differences in perceived control.". *Journal of Gerontology: Psychological Sciences* Vol. 46, (1991), 174–180.

6. Viktor E. Frankl, *Man's Search For Meaning: An Introduction to Logotherapy*, (Boston, MA: Beacon Press, 1962), 135.

7. Azadeh Tabazadeh, oral communication, January 18, 2016.

8. Dwight Stones, oral communication, June 9, 2015.

9. Sarah Gilchriese, oral communication, February 18, 2015.

10. Vann Henderson, oral communication, October 29, 2014.

Chapter 4

1. Alan Levy, oral communication, February 25, 2017.

2. Camile Farrington, Melissa Roderick, E. Allensworth, J. Nagaoka, T.S. Keyes, D.W. Johnson, & N.O. Beechum, *Teaching adolescents to become learners. The role of noncognitive factors in shaping school performance: A critical literature review* (Chicago University of Chicago Consortium on Chicago School Research, 2012), 26.

3. Angela Duckworth, *Grit: The Power of Passion and Perseverance* (New York, NY, Scribner, 2016), 3, 12.

4. Daniel Goleman, *Social Intelligence: The New Science of Human Relationships* (New York, NY, Bantam Book, 2006), 56.

5. Roy F. Baumeister, and John Tierney, *Willpower: Rediscovering the Greatest Human Strength* (New York: Penguin Books, 2011), 2.

6. Christopher Bergland, Psychology Today, 'The Neuroscience of Perseverance," www.psychologytoday.com/blog/the-athletes-way/20111, Blog posted 12/26/2011.

7. Todd Kashdan, Ryne Sherman, Jessica Yarbro & David C. Funder, "How are Curious People Viewed and How Do they Behave in Social Situations? From the Perspectives of Self, Friends, Parents, and Unacquainted Observers," *Journal of Personality*, Vol. 81, No. 2,(April, 2013), 142–154.

8. H. J. Eysenck, (1967) The biological basis of personality. Springfield, IL: Charles C. Thomas. in Laura Matias, *The Effects of Music Complexity on Memory in Introverts and Extroverts*, The Huron University College Journal of Learning and Motivation, Vol. 52, No. 1, Article 10 (2014), 131–151.

9. Jerry Bame, oral communication, December 16, 2016.

10. Nicholas A. Turiano , Benjamin P. Chapman, Stefan Agrigoroaei, Frank J. Infuma, and Margie Lachman. "Perceived Control Reduces Mortality Risk at Low, Not High, Education Levels," *Health Psychology*, Vol. 33, No. 8 (2014), 883–890.

11. J. Smyth, & S.J. Lepore, S.J. *"The writing cure: How expressive writing promotes health and emotional well-being,"* Washington, D.C.: American Psychological Association, (2002); and J.W. Pennebaker, "Writing about emotional experiences as a therapeutic process," *Psychological Science,* Vol. 8, No. 3 (1997) 162–166.

12. Laura Ratchave, oral communication November 07, 2016.

13. Lisa Marie Warnera, Benicio Gutiérrez-Doña, Maricela Villegas Angulo and Ralf Schwarzere, "Resource loss, self-efficacy, and family support predict posttraumatic stress symptoms: a 3-year study of earthquake survivors," *Anxiety, Stress, & Coping*, Vol. 28, No. 3 (2015), 239–253; and F.K. Arnberg, C.M. Hultman, P.O. Michel, & T. Lundin, "Social support moderates posttraumatic stress and general distress after disaster," *Journal of Traumatic Stress*, Vol. 25, No. 6 (2012), 721–727.

14. Jasmin K. Riad, Fran H. Norris, R. Barry Ruback, "Predicting Evacuation in Two Major Disasters: Risk Perception, Social Influence, and Access to Resources," *Journal of Applied Social Psychology* Volume 29, Issue 5, May (1999), 918–934.

15. James R. Elliott & Jeremy Pais, "Race, class, and Hurricane Katrina: Social differences in human responses to disaster," *Social Science Research* (Vol. 35, Issue 2, June 2006) 295–321.

16. Jill Yanke, oral communication, November 9, 2016.

17. M.A. Schuster, B.D. Stein, L.H. Jaycox, R.I. Collins, G.N. Marshall, M.N. Elliott, A.J. Zhou, D.E. Kanouse, J.L. Morrison, & S.H. Berry, "A national survey of stress reactions after the September 11, 2001, terrorist attacks," *The New England*

Journal of Medicine, Vol. 345, No. 20 (2001), 1507–1512. doi: 10.1056/NEJM200111153452024

18. H. G.Koenig, "Use of religion by patients with severe medical illness," *Mind/Body Medicine,* Vol. 2, No. 1 (1997), 31–36.

19. L.Verdelle Clark, "Effect of mental practice on the development of a certain motor skill," *Research Quarterly* Vol. 34, No. 4 (December (1960), 560–569.

20. Blog entry, "Lincoln Never Quits," available at http://www.rogerknapp.com/inspire/lincoln.htm

Chapter 5

1. C.R. Snyder, "Hope Theory: Rainbows of the Mind" *Psychological Inquiry,* Vol. 13, No. 4, (2002) 249–275.

2. One Scholar's Take On The Power Of The Placebo. *NPR, Talk of the Nation* (January 6, 2012), audio transcript, available at http://www.npr.org/2012/01/06/144794035/one-scholars-take-on-the-power-of-the-placebo

3. E.D. Raleigh, Sources of hope in chronic illness, *Oncology Nursing Forum,* Vol. 19, No. 3 (1992), 443–448.

4. C.R. Snyder, J. Cheavens, & S.C. Sympson, "Hope: an individual motive for social commerce," *Group Dynamics,* Vol. 1, No. 2 (1997) 107–118; and D. McDermott and C. R. Snyder, *The Great Big Book of Hope: Help Your Children Achieve Their Dreams,* (Oakland, CA: New Harbinger Publications, 2000); and C.R. Snyder, Hal S. Shorey, Jennifer Cheavens, Kimberley Mann Pulvers, Virgil H. Adams III, and Cynthia Wiklund, "Hope and Academic Success in College," *Journal of Educational Psychology,* Vol. 94, No. 4 (2002), 820–826.

5. C.R. Snyder, Hal S. Shorey, Jennifer Cheavens, Kimberley Mann Pulvers, Virgil H. Adams III, and Cynthia Wiklund, "Hope and Academic Success in College," *Journal of Educational Psychology* (Vol. 94, No. 4, 2002) 820–826; and Allison D. Martin & Kevin L. Rand, "The Future's So Bright, I Gotta Wear Shades: Law School Through the Lens of Hope, retrieved from www.mckinneylaw.iu.edu/insructors/martin/shades_martin-rand.pdf

6. Shelley Jones, oral communication, March 24, 2017.

7. Lewis A. Curry, C. R. Snyder, David L. Cook, Brent C. Ruby & Michael Rehm, "Role of Hope in Academic and Sport Achievement," *Journal of Personality and Social Psychology,* Vol.73, No. 6 (1997), 1257–1267.

8. Misty Wilson, oral communication, November 11, 2016.

9. Donald Altman, oral communication, February 25, 2017.

10. Hakan Saricam, Ismail Celik, Lütfiye Coskun, "The Relationship Between Emotional Intelligence, Hope and Life Satisfaction in Preschool Preserves Teacher," *The International Journal of Research in Teacher Education*, Vol. 6, No. 1, (2015), 1–9.

11. Kay Hearth, 1993 study in *Why Good Things Happen To Good People: The Exciting New Research That Proves The Link Between Doing Good And Living A Longer, Healthier, Happier Life*, by Stephen Post, Ph.D., Jill Neimar, Broadway Books, NY), 143.

12. Ronnie Steen, oral communication, October 26, 2016.

13. Chang Seek Lee1 and Yeoun Kyung Hwang, "The Effects of Hope, Emotional Intelligence, and Stress on the Self-esteem of Rural Elementary School Students in Korea: The Mediating Effect of Social Support," *Indian Journal of Science and Technology*, Vol. 9, No. 26). doi 10.17485/ijst/2016/v9i26/97278, July 2016 ISSN (Print): 0974-6846 ISSN (Online), 0974-5645, accessed 15 March, 2017.

14. Lanny Cordola, oral communication, November 17, 2016.

15. Hongfei Du, Xiaoming Li Dnhua Lin, and Cheuk Chi Tam, "Hopelessness, individualism, collectivism, and substance use among young rural-to-urban migrants in China," *Health Psychology Behavioral Medicine*, Vol. 1, No. 2 (2014), 211–220.

16. Anthony Scioli, Ph.D., Henry Biller Ph.D. *Hope in the Age of Anxiety*, Oxford University Press, (2009), 71.

17. Lewis A. Curry, C.R. Snyder, David L. Cook, Brent C Ruby, and Michael Rehm, "Role of Hope in Academic and Sport Achievement," *Journal of Personality and Social Psychology*, Vol. 73, No. 6 (December 1997), 1257–1267.

18. C.R. Snyder, *The Psychology of Hope: You Can Get There From Here* (New York: Free Press, 1994), 30–31.

19. David Spiegel, Helena Kraemer, Joan Bloom, & Ellen Gottheil. "Effect of psychosocial treatment on survival of patients with metastatic breast cancer". *The Lancet*, Vol. 334, No. 8668 (1989), 888–891.

20. Tone Rustøen, Bruce Cooper, Christine Miaskowski "A longitudinal study of the effects of a hope intervention on levels of hope and psychological distress in a community-based sample of oncology patients". *European Journal of Oncology, Nursing*, Vol. 15, No. 4 (2011), 351–357.

21. Taletha Guinn, oral communication, 09/24/15.

22. "Percentage of Christians in U.S. Drifting Down, but Still High," Frank Newport, available at www.gallup.com, accessed December 24, 2015, http://www.gallup.com/poll/187955/percentage-christians-driftingdownhigh.aspx?g_source=religion%20affiliation&g_mediuM = search&g_campaign = tiles

23. Rev. Michael Clark, oral communication, February 29, 2016.

24. Rabbi Moshe ben Asher, Ph.D., "Spirituality and Religion in Social Work Practice," *Social Work Today*, Vol. 1, No. 7 (2001), 15–18.

CPSIA information can be obtained
at www.ICGtesting.com
Printed in the USA
JSHW022037021220
9949JS00004B/87